Working with DB2, SQL/DS, SQL, and QMF

Working with DB2, SQL/DS, SQL, and QMF

Tony Fabbri
A. Robert Schwab, Jr.

TAB Professional and Reference Books

Division of TAB BOOKS
Blue Ridge Summit, PA

TPR books are published by TAB Professional and Reference Books, an imprint of TAB BOOKS. The TPR logo, consisting of the letters "TPR" within a large "T," is a registered trademark of TAB BOOKS.

Published by **TAB BOOKS**
FIRST EDITION/FIRST PRINTING

Library of Congress Cataloging-in-Publication Data

Fabbri, Tony.
Working with DB2, SQL/DS, SQL, and QMF / by Tony Fabbri, A. Robert Schwab, Jr.
p. cm.
ISBN 0-8306-9508-7 ISBN 0-8306-3508-4 (pbk.)
1. Data base management. 2. IBM Database 2 (Computer system) 3. SQL (Computer program language) 4. SQL/DS (Computer program)
I. Schwab, A. Robert. II. Title.
QA76.9.D3F23 1990
005.75′65—dc20 89-20506
CIP

TAB BOOKS offers software for sale. For information and a catalog, please contact TAB Software Department, Blue Ridge Summit, PA 17294-0850.

Questions regarding the content of this book should be addressed to:
Reader Inquiry Branch
TAB BOOKS
Blue Ridge Summit, PA 17294-0850

Acquisitions Editor: Jerry Papke
Technical Editor: Sandra L. Johnson
Production: Katherine Brown
Book Design: Jaclyn J. Boone

Contents at a Glance

Contents

Appendices

Introduction

We personally believe that relational databases, and in particular IBM's DB2, will be the dominant database structure and database product within that structure in the near future. The use of fourth-generation languages in an industrial environment (such as Pansophic's TELON product) in conjunction with DB2 permit relatively easy and fast development of application software. End-users are demanding more and more information. Their inability to get it in a timely manner leaves data processing installations no other choice but to use relational databases in conjunction with nth generation languages to accommodate their needs. By using relational databases, and in particular DB2, the end-users can generate their own reports using a query facility—most probably IBM's QMF.

Having both taught and used relational databases for many years, we have found a need for a text on the construction of relational tables and the use of Database 2 on them. This is particularly true since most books on DB2 are steeped in theoretical issues, and programmers need a more "hands-on" approach. After you fight battles with the troops, you gain new insight into what is really needed in a text and what is just fluff. This book has little or no fluff to it. It covers DB2 from both the applications programmer's and the end-user's point of view.

This book does not contain everything there is to know about relational databases and DB2, but rather it contains the information you need to get an application up and running fast. We save all the idiosyncrasies of DB2 and relational databases for the manuals.

We make two assumptions. The first is that the reader wants the meat of DB2 and SQL with little or no fat. The second is that although you don't have to have programming experience to understand SQL and DB2, it helps to have it in the overall understanding of the products involved.

If the reader is an experienced programmer in a mainframe environment, this text will provide valuable information to get an application up and going fast. If the reader is a student taking a relational database or similar type course, all the drudgery of searching through manuals and other texts is done for you. Here is a text you can easily read and understand on the subject of relational databases. This text covers "hands-on knowledge;" complex theory is left to other source materials. Note that this is not a theory text. It is a "doing" text. You will see all the commands you need to create and access DB2 using SQL.

Because DB2 operates only on MVS systems, IBM has developed another relational database product for the other operating systems in its family of systems. This database product is SQL/DS for SQL Data Systems. It is essentially the same product as DB2 but with a name change and a different operating system executing the product. Therefore, you can substitute the word SQL/DS for the word DB2 everywhere in this book if you are using SQL/DS instead of DB2. Except for a few minor exceptions, SQL/DS has the same features, commands, and statements as DB2. One exception is that you use the SQL/DS catalog rather than the DB2 catalog. Also, the number of possible databases in DB2 is slightly higher than the number you can create in SQL/DS (you can create over 100,000 different databases in DB2, and only 64,000 different databases in SQL/DS).

You don't have to be an expert on systems to use this text. DB2 is easy to understand and use, and there is no reason to make it difficult. Also, we don't see any reason to cloud up the issue by introducing topics and concepts you won't ever use or use once in a lifetime. However, some mainframe terms are scattered through the text. Such systems problems as installing the product, repairing databases, assigning passwords to VSAM datasets, and other systems software interactions are absent from the text. Although one of us is a systems programmer, we assume that you are not.

You should read the first chapter on the overview of DB2 to get an overall understanding of what is involved in creating and using a DB2 object. The language of SQL is then covered in detail in Chapters 2 through 6. For those interested in accessing DB2 via code, we have included several chapters on program preparation and the use of COBOL in accessing the database. Finally, we have included problem exercises after several chapters so that you can test your understanding of the topics and commands of that chapter.

1

Overview of DB2

We can describe DB2 as a relational database management system capable of handling a large number of transactions at a high rate of speed (i.e., 40–70 transactions per second) and which includes a fourth-generation language, Structured Query Language (SQL), which in turn is used by both end-users and programmers to define, manipulate, and control access to data. This description emphasizes the relational nature of DB2, the high-volume data processing capacity of DB2, and the fourth-generation nature of DB2. A *relational* database is a database that consists of several interrelated files (*tables*) that can be made to appear to end-users and programmers as one file. A *fourth-generation language* (4GL) is a *nonprocedural* language, i.e., the user of the language simply tells the computer what to do, not how to do it. Note that these are not formal definitions, but they are instead intended to give a practical understanding of the terms.

The relational and fourth-generation aspects of DB2 mean that most databases within DB2 are relatively easy to design and create, enabling most applications to be developed and implemented quickly. The relational and fourth-generation aspects of DB2 also permit end-users to generate *queries* (where output is formatted by DB2) against data in the database or to use it in the development of *reports* (where output is formatted by the user).

Typically, a DB2 database is designed and created by programmers or systems analysts using the DB2 Interactive (DB2I) facility. Frequently, the programmer also uses various utilities to load, or INSERT, the initial data. Once the database is created and data INSERTed into it, the end-user can access the data via the Query Management Facility (QMF). QMF allows the user to retrieve information, generate reports, and INSERT, DELETE, and UPDATE data in the database. With QMF, the end-user has the power to monitor and use the data without interaction with the programming staff.

DB2 Administration

The person responsible for maintaining the DB2 software package is the *Systems Administrator* (SYSADM). Some of the duties of SYSADM include:

- Assigning of DASD space for DB2 databases.
- Generating database names in that storage space.
- Assigning rights to use the database to individuals.
- Creating Database Administrators (DBADMs) for each database.
- Maintaining system support for DB2.
- Interfacing DB2 to the operating system and other software products.
- Updating and maintaining the menus within DB2.

In fact, the SYSADM has total control over the DB2 software package and the databases within it.

The persons responsible for specific databases within the DB2 framework are called *Database Administrators* (DBADMs). One SYSADM can create numerous DBADMs, each responsible for a selected database. Generally, a DBADM will be a systems analyst, lead programmer, or other developer responsible for a specific application development.

Each DBADM subdivides the storage space assigned to his or her database into units called *tablespaces*. Each tablespace can contain one or more tables as shown in FIG. 1-1. DB2 uses tables to store data in the database and a table consists of *rows* (records) and *columns* (fields). Note that most end-users are already familiar with rows and columns in the reports they receive and quickly pick up on most DB2 concepts.

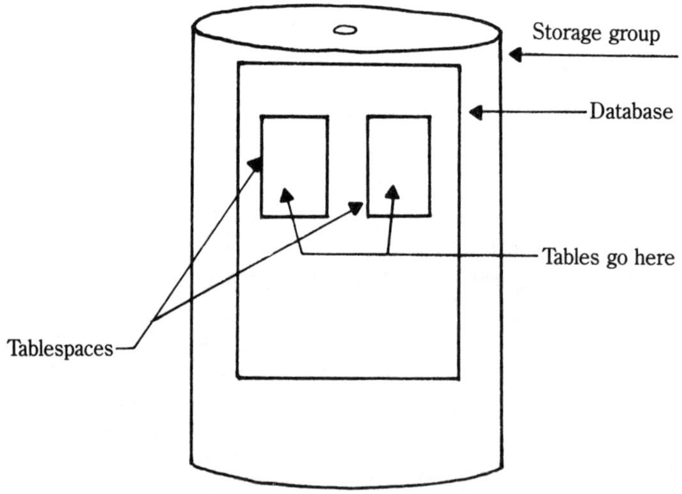

Fig. 1-1. Storage groups, databases, tablespaces, and tables.

DB2 Database Creation

Generally, the steps to create and use a DB2 database are:

- Duties of SYSADM:
  1. Create a storage group for the database:

```
CREATE STOGROUP EU8001 VOLUMES (ASW1, ASW2)
```

  2. Create a database name with parameters using the storage group:

```
CREATE DATABASE EDUCBASE
       STOGROUP EU8001
       BUFFERPOOL BP1
```

  3. Assign rights to the database to a DBADM:

```
GRANT DBADM ON DATABASE EDUCBASE TO $EPTF
```

- Duties of a DBADM who is $EPTF in this case:
  4. Create tablespaces in the database, for example:

```
CREATE TABLESPACE EPTFS1 IN EDUCBASE
         USING STOGROUP EU8001
         PRIQTY 30 SECQTY 20
         LOCKSIZE ANY
         BUFFERPOOL BP2
         CLOSE NO
         ERASE NO
```

  5. Create a table in the tablespace, e.g:

```
CREATE TABLE EMPLOYEE
        (EMPLNUMB  CHAR (5) NOT NULL,
         LASTNAME  CHAR (20) NOT NULL,
         FIRSTNAME CHAR (20) NOT NULL,
         ZIP       CHAR (5),
         AMOUNT    DECIMAL (8,2))
IN EDUCBASE.EPTFS1
```

  6. Assign rights on the table and tablespace to the development team and/or end-users such as:

```
GRANT USE OF TABLESPACE EPTFS1
        TO $JOHN, $MARY

GRANT CREATETAB ON DATABASE EDUCBASE
        TO $JOHN, $MARY
```

- Duties of the development team or end-user:
  7. Load the data into tables.
  8. Make queries on tables using SQL (interactively or embedded in program code) or QMF (interactively).

Here, $EPTF is DBADM for the database EDUCBASE, and $JOHN and $MARY have the capabilities of creating their own tables within the tablespace EPTFTS1. Also, $EPTF has created a table called EMPLOYEE within tablespace EPTFTS1, but $EPTF has not assigned anyone (but himself or herself) the power to access the table.

One of the responsibilities of the development team is to design tables for the tablespaces so that data in one table can easily cross-reference data in another table. In other words, you want to create a *relational* database. The first step in designing tables is to interview end-users to determine their needs. After each end-user inputs into the development cycle, you can then plan the structure of the tables. That is, you determine which columns (or fields) belong in which table and what columns, if any, have an index. The establishing of a unique index on a column guarantees a unique key within the table. After you complete the design phase by determining the structure of the tables, you must actually CREATE the tables within the allocated tablespace and then CREATE indexes, if any.

For example, the table EMPLOYEE containing employees' numbers, last names, first names, zip codes, and amount paid might look like:

EMPLNUMB	LASTNAME	FIRSTNAME	ZIP	AMOUNT
15	BIRD	LAWRENCE	11233	1433.22
16	BROWN	ELSIE	12211	1343.76
21	LION	FREDDY	44501	3487.55
34	WHITE	SUSAN	63022	8322.44
54	JOHNSON	HORACE	01017	3943.37
43	JONES	STANLEY	43276	5442.67
41	BLACK	SHIRLEY	98222	234.49
90	KONG	KING	00012	4567.71

while the table OFFICE containing the employees' office locations, phone numbers, and sizes of offices might look like:

EMPLNUMB	LOCATION	PHONENUMB	SIZE
15	1241	555-1234	12x20
16	1321	555-4321	20x20
21	3276	555-5499	16x20
34	5465	555-4300	12x12
54	4019	555-6537	12x16
43	3098	555-9222	16x20
41	2332	555-0900	14x16
90	8211	555-2201	16x20

Note that we separated the data into two tables. If an employee resigns or is fired, we do not want to destroy office data when we delete the employee from our list. By using two tables, we can delete the employee by DELETEing the row containing the employee number in table EMPLOYEE and UPDATE the employee number in table OFFICE to blanks, nulls, or some other coded number so that we can later assign that row to the replacement employee.

After creating the tables and indexes within the tablespace, you can create a VIEW for each user. A *view* lets each user access only selected rows and columns within a table and provides a security mechanism within DB2. A view can also restrict a user's ability to change data in the table by restricting his or her access to the commands of UPDATE, DELETE, INSERT, and SELECT.

For example, to create a view on the table EMPLOYEE above, we could use

```
CREATE VIEW EMPLVIEW AS
        SELECT LASTNAME, FIRSTNAME, AMOUNT
        FROM EMPLOYEE
```

Here, the view EMPLVIEW has access to only columns LASTNAME, FIRSTNAME, and AMOUNT. You could then give $MARY the power to only look at these columns by using

```
GRANT SELECT ON TABLE $EPTF.EMPLVIEW TO $MARY
```

Because EMPLOYEE and EMPLVIEW were created by $EPTF, only $EPTF can access the information in the table and view. The only way other users can access data in $EPTF's tables or views is for $EPTF to explicitly GRANT someone else access to it. Note that views are logical representations. That is, by creating a view, DB2 keeps track of the view parameters in the DB2 catalog, but does not duplicate the data from the original table. All data comes from the original base table, and the view is only a window for viewing selected data in the base table.

Now $MARY can extract data from table $EPTF.EMPLVIEW using

```
SELECT FIRSTNAME, LASTNAME, AMOUNT
        FROM $EPTF.EMPLVIEW
```

A view can also be used to make several tables appear to the user as one table, i.e., to JOIN several tables. For example, you could create a view consisting of employee names from table EMPLOYEE and employee phone numbers from table OFFICE by using:

```
CREATE VIEW PHONLIST AS
        SELECT LASTNAME, FIRSTNAME, PHONENUMB
        FROM EMPLOYEE, OFFICE
        WHERE EMPLOYEE.EMPLNUMB = OFFICE.EMPLNUMB
```

To the user, it now appears that you have a new table, $EPTF.PHONLIST, which looks like:

LASTNAME	FIRSTNAME	PHONENUMB
BIRD	LAWRENCE	555-1234
BROWN	ELSIE	555-4321
LION	FREDDY	555-5499
WHITE	SUSAN	555-4300
JOHNSON	HORACE	555-6537
JONES	STANLEY	555-9222
BLACK	SHIRLEY	555-0900
KONG	KING	555-2201

You can now GRANT others the authority to access the view, just as you did with $EPTF.EMPLVIEW.

Note that whoever created the original table owns the table, and all other noncreators must use the fully qualified name (in this case, $EPTF.EMPLVIEW) of the table. Note also, as far as $MARY is concerned, EMPLVIEW is a table. That is, the fact that she has only a view of the original table is not apparent to her. She treats the view as a table and all actions on her view happen on the original table.

The creation of tables and views via the CREATE command does not put data into tables. The CREATE command simply updates the DB2 catalog with the description of the table. That is, CREATE only defines the structure of the table, not the data that goes into it. There are several ways you can place data in tables:

- Use the INSERT command interactively via DB2I or QMF.
- Use the INSERT command in a load program via COBOL, Fortran, etc.
- Use the LOAD utility (which is an option in the DB2I menu) to load a sequential file into a table. If the file is not a sequential file, use IBM's data extractor product to convert certain nonsequential files into sequential files.
- Use vendor software to load the data (e.g., IBM's DBEDIT product or Easytrieve Plus from Pansophic, Inc.).

DB2I

After you create the structure of the table and load data into it, you can make queries on the data using either DB2I or QMF. The DB2I menu is one of the menus available in DB2 and generally has the following options:

```
1 SPUFI               (Process SQL statements)
2 DCLGEN              (Generate SQL & source language
                      declaration)
3 PROGRAM PREP        (Prepare a DB2 application pro-
                      gram to run)
4 PRECOMPILE          (Invoke DB2 precompiler)
5 BIND/REBIND/FREE    (BIND, REBIND, or FREE applica-
                      tion plans)
6 RUN                 (RUN an SQL program)
7 DB2 COMMANDS        (Issue DB2 commands)
8 UTILITIES           (Invoke DB2 utilities)
D DB2I DEFAULTS       (Set global parameters)
X EXIT                (Leave DB2I)
```

Because the DB2 menus are installation-site dependent and can be modified by SYSADM, the actual menus the users see might vary from one installation to the next.

The first option is the *SQL Processor Using File Input* (SPUFI). This option is typically used by SYSADM, DBADM, or programmers to create tables and views, grant authorization to use them, and to test SQL statements before embedding them in a program. SPUFI allows you to use an editor such as the ISPF/PDF editor to create a file consisting of SQL statements and then execute them.

The second option is the *declarations generator* (DCLGEN). When creating a program which accesses DB2 tables, it is advisable to include declarations of those tables in the source code. Declarations describe the tables that the program accesses and allow DB2 to do more extensive error checking at compile time. DCLGEN is a utility which generates declarations for you.

The third option allows you to precompile, compile, BIND, link-edit, and execute a DB2 program from one menu option. Of the previous terms, only *precompile* and *BIND* are specific to DB2. These terms are defined later.

The fourth option allows you to use the DB2 precompiler. Before compiling a program that contains SQL, you must *precompile* it. Precompiling translates the SQL into compiler-compatible subprogram calls.

The fifth option allows you to create (BIND), update (REBIND), or delete (FREE) an application plan. After a DB2 program is compiled, an application plan is created and is used by DB2 at run time to determine how to access the data in the tables.

The sixth option allows you to execute certain programs containing SQL.

The seventh option allows you to issue certain DB2 commands. The commands can make a database unavailable to applications (STOP), make the database available again to applications (START), and display certain information about a database (DISPLAY). These commands would most likely be issued by the SYSADM.

The eighth option allows you to execute certain utilities, such as inserting initial data into a database (LOAD), updating information about a database used by BIND (RUNSTATS), or making unused space in a database available for use (REORG).

The last two options allow you to set certain personal defaults for DB2I parameters and to exit DB2I.

QMF

Query Management Facility (QMF) is a user-friendly querying facility and report generator and contains the two primary options QUERY and FORMS. You use SQL statements within QMF's QUERY screen to extract data from the database. The SQL statement and the data it extracts are stored in buffers which you can later use or save. QMF maintains the following three buffer areas shown in FIG. 1-2:

- A query buffer contains the SQL query instruction.
- A data buffer contains the data retrieved from the database using the query.
- A forms buffer contains a user-changeable form for formatting and viewing the data.

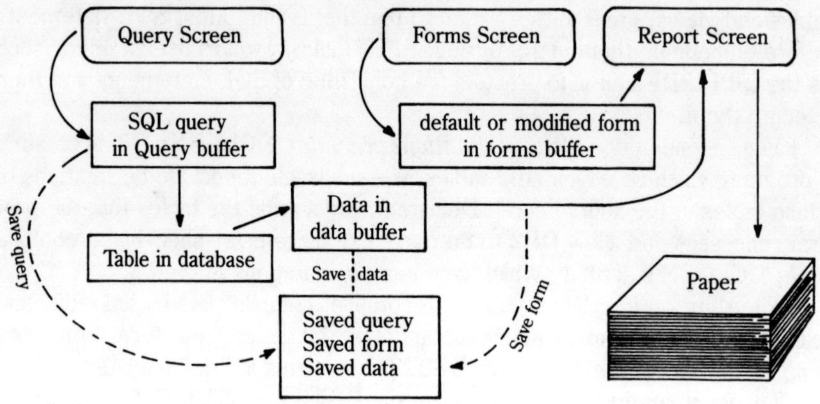

Fig. 1-2. Diagram of QMF buffers and screens.

You can save the information in the three buffers using

```
SAVE QUERY AS savename
SAVE DATA AS savename
SAVE FORM AS formname
```

on a command line in QMF.

When you display data, QMF uses a default form in the FORMS screen. The default form uses the DB2 catalog's definition of the table. You can modify this predefined form using options available in the FORMS screen and save the results using

```
SAVE FORM AS savename
```

as a command in QMF.

The end-user will need to know how to write SQL statements in the QUERY screen and modify the printout using options in the FORMS screen in order to generate the reports. This can result in additional training needs for the end-user staff or for the programming staff who support the end-user departments. For those end-users who are reluctant to learn SQL and FORMS screen options, the programming staff can produce procedures or PROCs within QMF containing programmer-generated SQL and FORMS screen commands which the end-user can easily execute.

SQL

All the DB2 commands we have been using so far are part of Structure Query Language (SQL). SQL contains the following three general types of instructions:

- *Data Definition Language* (DDL) with the commands of CREATE, ALTER, and DROP.
- *Data Manipulation Language* (DML) with the commands of INSERT, DELETE, UPDATE, and SELECT.
- *Control Language* (CL) with the commands of GRANT and REVOKE.

You can enter SQL commands interactively by using either the DB2 Interactive (DB2I) menu or the QMF menu, or you can hardcode them in COBOL, Fortran, assembler, PLI, or other languages supporting DB2.

DDL Commands

DDL commands interact with the DB2 Catalog and CREATE, ALTER, or DROP (or delete) database entities. These entities include

Storage group
Database name
Tablespace
Table
Index
View
Synonym

Some examples of DDL commands are:

```
CREATE TABLE EMPLOYEE
       (EMPLNUMB CHAR(5)           NOT NULL,
        LASTNAME CHAR(20)          NOT NULL,
        FIRSTNAME CHAR(20)         NOT NULL,
        ZIP CHAR(5),
        AMOUNT DECIMAL(8,2))
IN EDUCBASE.EPTFTS1

ALTER TABLE EMPLOYEE
        ADD YEAR CHAR(6)

DROP TABLESPACE EPTFTS1
```

Commands dealing with storage group, database name, and tablespaces are generally issued by SYSADM while commands dealing with tables, indexes, views, and synonyms are issued by DBADM. Note that each installation sets its own standards and procedures for granting authorization to create, change, or delete DB2 entities. DDL commands affect the DB2 Catalog and establish the structure of the entities in DB2.

DML Commands

The four DML commands of SELECT, DELETE, INSERT, and UPDATE access data in tables. Some examples are:

```
SELECT EMPLNUMB, LASTNAME, AMOUNT
        FROM EMPLOYEE

DELETE FROM EMPLOYEE
        WHERE EMPLNUMB = '16'
```

```
INSERT INTO EMPLOYEE
        VALUES ('15', 'BIRD', 'LAWRENCE', '11233', 1433.22)

UPDATE EMPLOYEE
        SET FIRSTNAME = 'LARRY',
            ZIP = '99099'
        WHERE EMPLNUMB = '15'
```

The programming staff and end-users are the main individuals who issue these commands. The four DML commands provide a vehicle for them to add, erase, change, or access data in databases.

CL Commands

CL commands limit access to DB2 items and form the nucleus for security within the DB2 software structure. Because access to DB2 is from Information Management System (IMS), Customer Information Control System (CICS), or Time Sharing Option (TSO), the user might have been already screened by the system and have a valid account on it. In addition, all users of DB2 must be GRANTed access to DB2 by either SYSADM, DBADM, or other DB2 administrator. Some examples of DB2's Control Commands include:

```
GRANT USE OF TABLESPACE EPTFTS1
      TO $JOHN, $MARY

REVOKE DELETE ON TABLE OFFICE
      FROM $JOHN

GRANT USE OF TABLESPACE EPTFTS1
      TO PUBLIC
```

The last example above makes use of a predefined user, PUBLIC. The user PUBLIC is automatically defined by DB2 as all DB2 users, so the last example GRANTs access to EPTFTS1 to all DB2 users.

Note that once you define the table structure and load data into it, you must create any views you want and grant each user authorization to use them before they can begin writing queries on the data. If an individual has not been explicitly granted authorization to use an entity within DB2, that person cannot access it until such authorization has been given. Unlike most vendor products, anyone wanting to use DB2 must already have a predefined database, tablespace, and other entities and must have been granted authorization to use them before he or she can effectively use DB2.

Data Security

Before someone can use any DB2 resource that person must be given authorization (or privilege) to use that resource. These authorizations are given by the administrators of DB2 entities (i.e., SYSADM, DBADM, or others), by the owners of the entities (or the creator of a table), or by other persons who have power to pass on a privilege to other users (such as persons with GRANT OPTION authority).

Some of the resources a user needs authorization for include the following:

- Using the DB2 menus.
- Creating and using databases, tablespaces, tables.
- Using the SQL commands (SELECT, INSERT, GRANT, etc.).
- Using the utilities.
- Using the commands.
- Generating a PLAN and doing a BIND.
- Executing load modules needing a PLAN.

SYSADM, DBADM, or the owner of an entity gives explicit authorization to another user by issuing a GRANT to that user. This user also receives implicit authorization by the DB2 system when he or she creates certain entities or performs certain tasks in DB2 (i.e., creating a table or performing a BIND). For example, when you create a table, you own that table, and DB2 assigns you certain inherent privileges while using it. Some of these privileges include the right to:

- SELECT, UPDATE, DELETE, INSERT on the table.
- GRANT and REVOKE the use of these four commands on the table to other users.
- CREATE views and indexes on the table.

These rights and privileges are independent of SYSADM or DBADM and require no intervention by them other than the initial GRANT of CREATE authority.

The DB2 catalog keeps track of all authorizations in SYSIBM.SYSxxx-AUTH tables found in the DB2 catalog. Note that you need authorization from SYSADM to access these or any DB2 catalog tables. You can access these tables in the same way you can access any table within DB2—by using SQL. Note also that you can only use SQL to retrieve data from these tables; you cannot update them.

Program Preparation

You can embed SQL statements in COBOL, Fortran, assembler, PL/I, and other languages. You can do this by first testing the SQL statement interactively in the DB2I menu. You then embed it in the code with a delimiter before and after the tested statement as shown in FIG. 1-3. Note that each SQL statement must be separated by a delimiter even though you code multiple SQL statements one after another as shown in FIG. 1-4. Using a delimiter is similar to making a hamburger: place a bun on the bottom, then add meat in the middle, and finally put a bun on the top, with no double-meat hamburgers permitted.

In COBOL

```
EXEC SQL
DELETE FROM CUSTOMER
END-EXEC.
```

In Fortran

```
 EXEC SQL
XDELETE FROM CUSTOMER
^
└── column 6
```

In PLI

```
EXEC SQL
DELETE FROM CUSTOMER;
```

In assembler

```
EXEC SQL               X
DELETE FROM CUSTOMER
                       ^
                       column 72
```

Fig. 1-3. COBOL, Fortran, PLI, and assembler versions of embedded SQL statements.

```
EXEC SQL
DELETE FROM CUSTOMER
END-EXEC.
EXEC SQL
DELETE FROM BUILDING
END-EXEC.
```

Fig. 1-4. Multiple SQL statements in a COBOL program.

Because the compiler (or assembler) will flag SQL statements as unidentifiable code, you must first pass the code through a precompiler. The precompiler "massages" the embedded SQL instructions within the source code by:

1. Making them comments within the source code.
2. Converting them to CALLs or language instructions.
3. Writing each SQL statement to a sequential file (called a Database Request Module or DBRM).
4. Placing either a time tag or a version tag on the results of the precompile (the modified source code and the DBRM).

You can now perform a normal compile on the precompiled source code and link it to produce a load module. However, since DB2's security requirements demand that you have authorization for using the DB2 entities (tables, views, etc.) and statements, (SELECT, DELETE, etc.), you must perform an additional step called a BIND. The BIND validates the authorizations for using DB2's entities and statements, designs the navigation of the database, and compares the table definitions in the DB2 catalog with SQL statements in the code.

After you resolve all BINDer errors (and redo the BIND if needed), the BIND creates a PLAN and stores it in the DB2 catalog for referencing by the load module. When the load module accesses SQL statements, DB2 accesses the PLAN to validate security, finds the navigation of the database and locking strategy for it, and verifies that the DB2 items accessed in the code still exist in the DB2 catalog. Note that the DB2 catalog is an active catalog because the PLAN must access it each and every time a SQL statement is processed.

2

Database Design

Virtually all successful projects are planned in some way. Many organizations use a prescribed methodology to guide the analyst-developer in planning the overall project. Other organizations simply rely on the ability of the systems analyst or systems designer to "get the job done," not worrying about the method he or she uses to accomplish the task. Regardless of whether the analyst uses a formal methodology or simply "wings it," some planning must take place. Such planning is easiest to accomplish with fewest errors when a formal methodology is used.

Overview of Systems Development

Many methodologies for systems development have been published and taught, but most of them include the following phases:

Feasibility study
Preliminary plan
System analysis
System design
System implementation

Each phase has its inputs, and each phase produces outputs that are inputs for the next phase. This chapter is mainly concerned with the system design phase as it relates to database design; however, the other phases are briefly described below so that you can consider database design in context.

Feasibility Study

The first task of the application development team is to perform a feasibility study. Here, you define what the user needs and capture sufficient information to evaluate the proposed system. You must match the function of the current system with the user requirements and identify all currently unsupported requirements.

If possible, you should specify several approaches to meet the user's requirements. As part of the feasibility study, you can estimate the cost of the system in terms of personnel, equipment, and materials. For most systems, this gross cost estimate is not intended to estimate the actual cost for the completed system but rather is an attempt by the developer to give the user some idea as to the enormity of the project (i.e., 100, 5,000, or 100,000 man hours and its financial cost).

The main outputs of the feasibility study are a grocery list of what the user wants, a rough estimate of the resources needed for the project, and an agreed solution. It is at this stage that you identify the type of database structure you intend to use: hierarchial, network, or relational.

Preliminary Plan

In the preliminary plan phase, you define the scope of the project, including identifying its business purpose, boundaries, limits, and overall objectives. In this phase, you identify the system components and divide the system into subunits and list their characteristics. You will also finally design an overall plan for the implementation of each component and the overall project.

You should produce several outputs in the preliminary plan. First, create a list of characteristics for each component and their identifiable limitations. Second, produce a schedule for implementation of each component including general time and resource estimates. Third, produce a *data flow diagram* (DFD) which defines the scope of the project. You typically use data flow diagrams (DFDs) to graphically represent the physical flow of data and the processes involved in converting or manipulating data.

System Analysis

It isn't until the analysis phase that you begin a full-scale study of both the existing physical and logical systems. When you study the existing physical system you take a detailed look at the existing system, diagramming the physical flow of information. Next, study the existing logical system. Here, concentrate on the inputs and outputs of the information flow. The two main products of the analysis phase are a graphical representation of the current physical and logical systems (the Analysis DFD) and a logical model of the new system (the Model DFD).

The ability of an analyst to convert these two studies into a new systems model and eventually into the final design of the database is the key to a successful project.

System Design

In the design phase, you are concerned with both data and process design. Each of these design activities generates its own outputs. *Data* design consists of creating the database; while *process* design consists of creating the system structure chart and the program specifications.

It is impossible, at least in the latter stages of system design, to separate database and process design. The way you physically arrange the data will ultimately determine the methods you must use to process it in order to achieve the overall goals of the system. Also, the way you must process the data will impose restrictions on how you can arrange it. For these reasons, database design and process design usually take place concurrently in a series of iterations. You will reach a point in your process design which will cause you to redo a portion of your database design; this in turn might cause you to redo a portion of your process design. This procedure continues until you have a tight, integrated design of both data and processes.

Here you must remember that one of the major goals of using a methodology is to correct design errors in the most cost-effective manner possible. Errors are corrected most cheaply during the design phase when most of the system exists only on paper. Design errors are more expensive to correct after coding has begun, are still more expensive to correct after testing has begun, and are most expensive to correct after production installation. For this reason, you should never be reluctant to go back and redo some portion of your design. If it becomes necessary to do this during the design phase, you have corrected the error in the least expensive manner; even if it becomes necessary to do this during or after the implementation phase, going back to the design phase to redesign and correct the error helps insure against compounding the error with more errors.

System Implementation

The implementation phase consists of coding, testing, installing, and documenting the system. Coding, testing, and installing should be done in a structured manner. Structured code improves readability and allows the testing process to overlap the coding process. Structured testing, or testing each routine by itself before testing lower-level routines (each by itself), simplifies debugging. Structured installation allows phasing the system into production one part at a time, which simplifies parallel testing (testing the new system's output against that of the old system), simplifies user training, and allows early implementation of the most critically needed parts of the system.

The effort required for system documentation is considerably lessened when a methodology is followed. Documentation becomes less a matter of creating output than of collecting and organizing existing outputs from the previous phases such as the context DFD, the model DFD, the physical database design, the system structure chart, and the program specifications.

Database Design

Before we discuss database design, we need to define a few key terms. When you define a database to DB2, you simply request specific space on a Direct Access Storage Device (DASD) pack. This space is assigned a name, called a *database name*. You subdivide that space into one or more tablespaces to hold your tables. A *table* is a series of rows and columns related in some way. In classical file jargon, *rows* are records and *columns* are fields. You define the column names to DB2 using Data Definition Language which places the description of the table in the DB2 Catalog. You insert data into tables using Data Manipulation Language. DML places the data in a page within the tablespace. Each page is 4K long. If we create an index or key for a table, that key is one or more columns in the table and is said to be a *primary* key. Primary keys can be either unique or non-unique. If the table contains data in a column that is a key to another table, that column is said to be a *foreign* key. Foreign keys are used to logically connect or join multiple tables together as shown in FIG. 2-1.

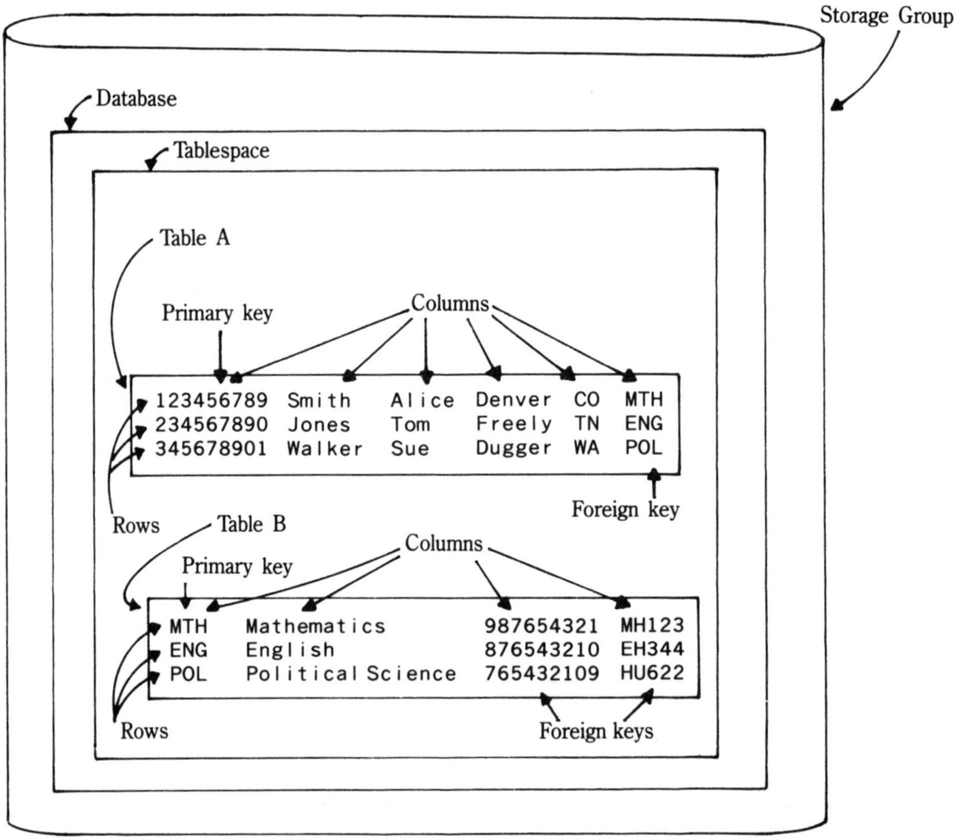

Fig. 2-1. The relationship between rows, columns, primary keys, foreign keys, tables, tablespaces, and databases.

Database design takes place during the design phase and has three parts:

- Defining the data you want to store in the database.
- Defining the relationships between the data.
- Designing the database.

Defining the Data

There are several methods of defining the data you want to store. If you use a methodology similar to the one described above, you would start with the data stores shown on the DFDs. One way of using this information is to begin with the outputs from each data store. You then work your way backwards from the outputs to determine the processes that are necessary for those outputs to be produced and the inputs that are necessary for the processes to take place.

Different users obviously have different needs and uses for data. It is the analyst's job to interview the user and identify the data requirements for each user. After you capture the data requirements of the users, you can create a contents list for each data store. That is, you must list each user's data requirements by identifying that user's data needs. This involves first itemizing the variable fields in each of their teleprocessing screens, if such screens exist. Next, itemize the data in other user documents that are critical to your project.

As an example, look at a simple billing system for an attorney's office and assume that your feasibility study led you to choose a relational database form. The main output from this system is a bill such as the one in FIG. 2-2.

```
                         10/09/89

Joe Client
222 Any Street
Anytown, XX 99999

For Services Rendered:

Preparation of wills for Joe Client and spouse:
     Consultation, Legal research, Drafting will    600.00
Representation of Joe Client in Smith v. Client:
     Facts investigation, Legal research,
     Deposition, Court appearance,                1,232.97

Total                                            12,208.29
Representation of Joe Client in Client v. Jones:
     Facts investigation, Legal research, Court
     appearance, settlement negotiation          10,975.32
```

Fig. 2-2. A sample bill.

An analysis of the bill allows you to determine some of the data items necessary to create it. The bill begins with the client's name and address. It then lists various legal services categorized under legal "matters." (The difference between a legal matter and a legal service is that a legal matter is the basic reason a client contacted the attorney, e.g., to draft a will, to represent the client in court, or to give legal advice (consultation). A legal service is what the attorney does on the client's behalf in a given legal matter. For example, to represent a client in court, an attorney might do legal research, make court appearances, and give consultation on whether to accept a settlement offer.)

Following each list of services is the total amount the attorney charges for each service for a particular matter. This attorney charges three different types of fee. Certain types of work, such as consultation and legal research, are charged on an hourly basis. Other types of work, such as drafting a simple will, are charged at a set fee, such as $300 per will. Finally, certain types of work, such as court representation, are charged on a contingent basis; in other words for example, the attorney gets a certain percentage of whatever he collects for the client.

You now know some of the data items necessary to create the bill:

```
CLIENT NAME
BILLING ADDRESS
LEGAL MATTER
LEGAL SERVICE
HOURLY FEE
SET FEE
CONTINGENT FEE
```

From conversations with your user (the attorney), you learn that three additional data items will be required. The attorney wants to be able to keep track of a client's balance, how much the client was charged and how much has been paid. This means that you must add two data items, BILL and PAYMENT, to the list of data items. In this case, BILL is an item that will allow you to keep track of the total amount that has been billed to the client as of a certain date, because, regardless of what charges have accrued, the attorney cannot expect the client to pay until he has been billed for them. Also, the attorney wants to be able to query the billing system to find the file folder for any given matter; the file folder will have copies of agreements between the attorney and clients, notes on legal research, copies of court documents, etc. Thus, you must add FILE FOLDER to the list of data items. The list of data items so far is:

```
CLIENT NAME
BILLING ADDRESS
LEGAL MATTER
LEGAL SERVICE
HOURLY FEE
SET FEE
CONTINGENT FEE
BILL
PAYMENT
FILE FOLDER
```

Note that some of the data items are elementary data items (data *elements*) and that they cannot be further broken down into other data elements. Other data items are not data elements. For example, LEGAL MATTER is just a descriptive phrase; there is no meaningful way to subdivide it. On the other hand,

BILLING ADDRESS can be broken down into street address, city, state, etc. For a full understanding of the data requirements of your system you must create a contents list which contains all of the elementary data items:

```
CLIENT NAME
        LAST NAME
        FIRST NAME
        MIDDLE NAMES
BILLING ADDRESS
        STREET ADDRESS FIRST LINE
        STREET ADDRESS SECOND LINE
        STREET ADDRESS THIRD LINE
        CITY
        STATE
        ZIP
LEGAL MATTER
LEGAL SERVICE
HOURLY FEE
        HOURS WORKED
        HOURLY RATE
SET FEE
CONTINGENT FEE
        BASE AMOUNT
        PERCENTAGE
BILL
        DATE
        TOTAL BILLED
PAYMENT
        DATE
        AMOUNT PAID
FILE FOLDER
```

Eventually, each of these data items will be represented by tables in our database. Where a data item is subdivided into data elements, the data elements will become columns in the database.

Defining Relationships Between Data

The next step in defining a database is to define the relationships between the data you want to store. The three possible kinds of relationships between data items are one-to-one, one-to-many, and many-to many. An example of a one-to-one-relationship is the relationship between LEGAL MATTER and FILE FOLDER because the attorney keeps a separate physical file folder for each legal matter; thus, each legal matter has one file folder, and each file folder has one legal matter. An example of a one-to-many relationship is the relationship between LEGAL MATTER and LEGAL SERVICE because each legal matter can have many legal services associated with it, but each legal service is performed for one legal matter. An example of a many-to-many relationship is the relationship between BILL and PAYMENT. A payment could cover many bills, and a bill might result in many payments by a client.

Note that you can determine the relationship between data items by asking a "has" question: How many file folders can a legal matter have? The answer is one. How many legal matters are contained in each file folder? Again, the answer is one, so you have a one-to-one relationship between LEGAL MATTER and FILE FOLDER. Similarly, how many legal services can a legal matter require? The answer is many. How many legal matters can a legal service relate to? The answer is one, so you have a one-to-many relationship between LEGAL MATTER and LEGAL SERVICE. Finally, how many payments can a bill have? The answer is many. How many bills can a payment cover? Again, the answer is many, so you have a many-to-many relationship between BILL and PAYMENT.

Defining the relationships between the data you want to store consists of creating an Entity-Relationship diagram and simplifying the diagram.

Creating an Entity-Relationship Diagram

Figure 2-3 is an Entity-Relationship diagram for the billing system.

To create an Entity-Relationship diagram, list each data item (*entity*) and use lines with arrows to show one-to-one, one-to many, or many-to-many relationships between each entity and the other entities. For example, FOLDER and LEGAL MATTER is a one-to-one relationship, so we use a line with one arrow pointing to each box. BILLING ADDRESS and BILL is a one-to-many relationship, so we use a line with one arrow pointing to BILLING ADDRESS and two arrows pointing to BILL (signifying "many"), to show that each bill is sent to one address, but each address can have many bills. Finally, for the many-to-many relationship between PAYMENT and BILL, we use a line with two arrows pointing to both boxes, i.e., each payment can cover many bills, and each bill can generate many payments.

Note that you might still need to consider outputs and the processing which create them to fully understand the relationships between the data elements. For CLIENT NAME, we show the following relationships in FIG. 2-3:

- Each client is billed at one address, though many clients can live at one address.
- Each client can make many payments, though each payment is considered to come from one client, even if it is made by someone other than the client on the client's behalf.
- Each client can receive many bills, but each bill is billed to one client.
- Each client can have many legal matters, but each matter has only one client. (In this sense, the client is simply the person who has agreed to be billed on a given matter.)
- Each client can have many legal services performed for him, but each service is performed for one client.
- For each of the three types of fee, the client can have several fees billed to him, but each fee is billed to only one client.

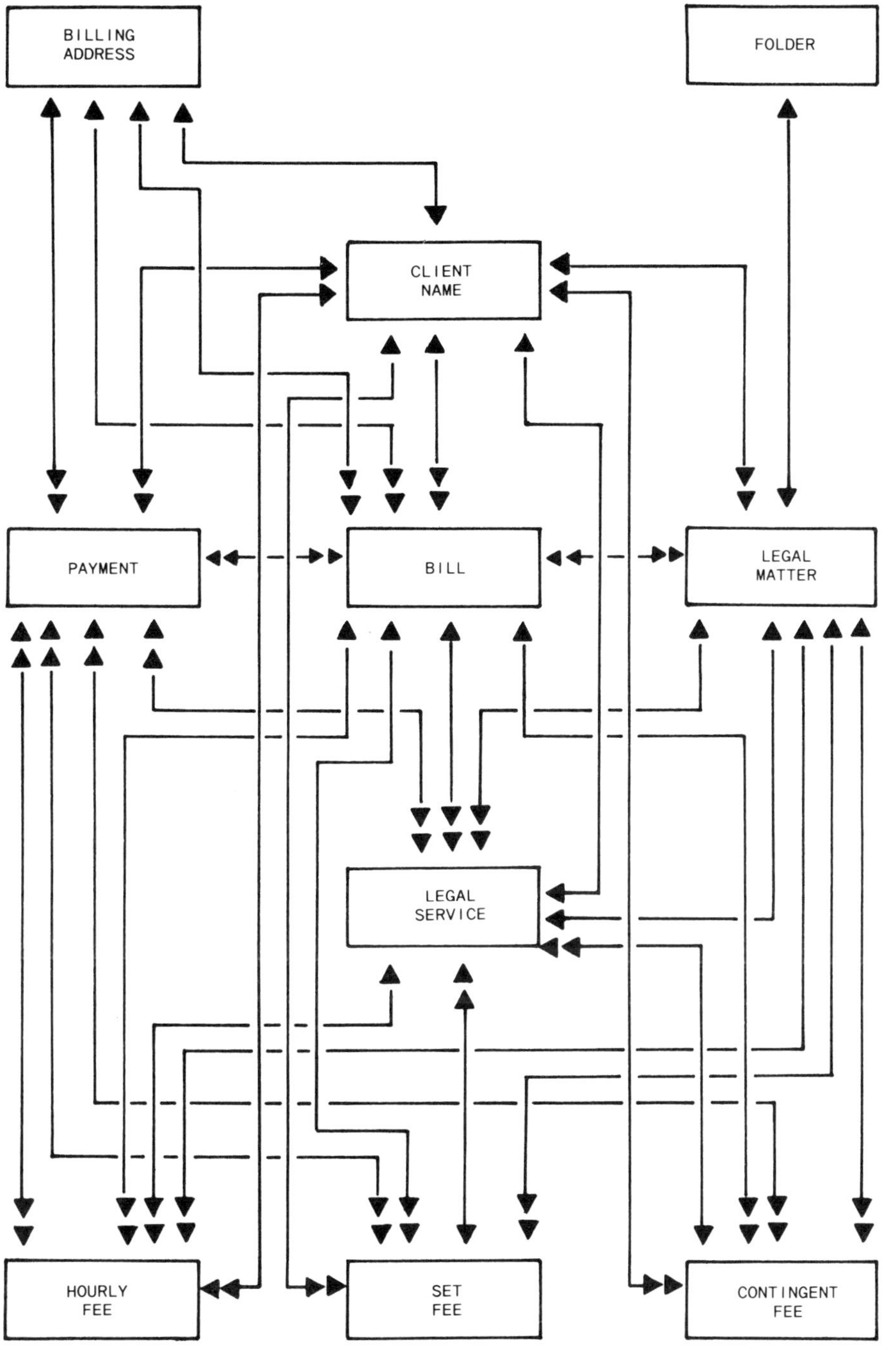

Fig. 2-3. Entity-relationship diagram for billing system.

The above process of relating an entity to each of the other entities is repeated until you have diagrammed all of the relationships between the entities. Note that each type of fee will only be billed to the client once, though many payments might be made on any fee.

Simplifying the Diagram

The next step in defining the relationships between the data elements consists of simplifying the Entity-Relationship diagram. There are four methods of accomplishing this:

- Consider combining entities with one-to-one relationships.
- Eliminate redundant relationships.
- Eliminate unneeded relationships.
- Combine entities where one is logically a subset of another.

Note that none of these methods involves a hard-and-fast rule. You must use good judgment to determine where the diagram can be simplified and where it cannot.

Figure 2-3 has one one-to-one relationship, the relationship between LEGAL MATTER and FILE FOLDER. These entities should be combined. FILE FOLDER has no meaningful relationships to any other entities and can be easily combined with LEGAL MATTER.

The relationships between BILL and LEGAL MATTER and between BILL and LEGAL SERVICE are redundant given the relationship between LEGAL MATTER and LEGAL SERVICE. If you have one of the relationships, you can derive the other through a JOIN. To decide which relationship to keep, look ahead to processing. The primary processing of the database will be to produce a bill each month. This will entail summarizing unbilled services under legal matters. If there is a relationship between BILL and LEGAL SERVICE, this can easily be done by utilizing a JOIN on those two tables with a GROUP BY clause specifying the matter. Thus, you will remove the relationship between BILL and LEGAL MATTER in your diagram.

Several unneeded relationships are in FIG. 2-3. For example, since you simply want to know a client's balance, the relationship between BILL and PAYMENT is not needed; you are not interested in which bills have been paid.

When combining entities that are logical subsets of another, it is useful to look for entities that have the same relationships to all other entities. An example is SET FEE and CONTINGENT FEE. Conversations with your user would indicate that a contingent fee is just a type of set fee. For billing purposes, it is unnecessary to differentiate between them, since a service covered by a contingent fee agreement will not be billed until the matter is settled by a court judgment or out-of-court settlement, at which time the amount of the fee is known.

The simplified Entity-Relationship diagram is shown in FIG. 2-4.

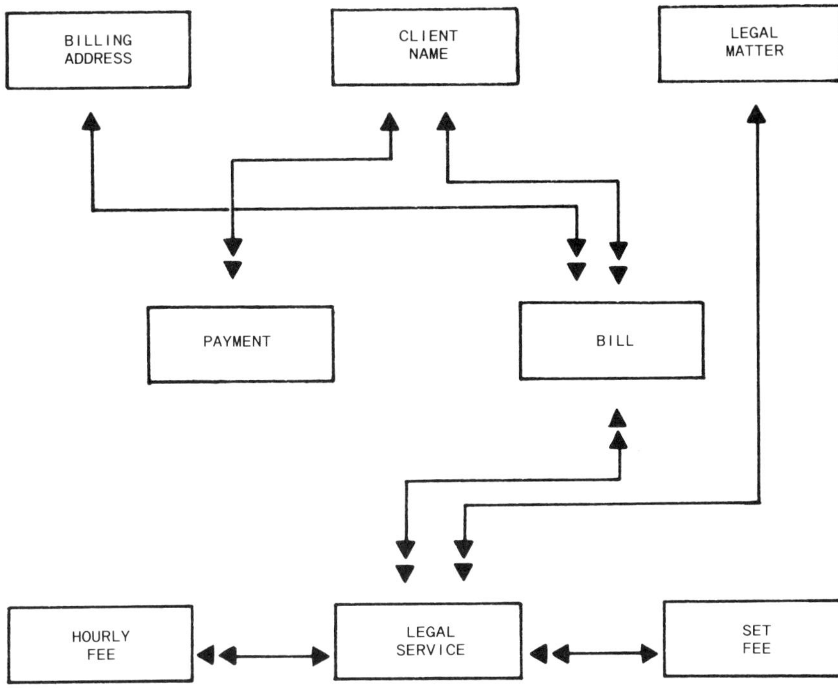

Fig. 2-4. A simplified entity-relationship diagram.

Designing the Database

You are now ready to design the database. The purpose of this is to translate your Entity-Relationship diagram into a set of interrelated tables, or a relational database. Each entity on your diagram will eventually become a table. This translation process consists of:

- Defining keys for each entity.
- Expressing relationships as foreign keys.
- Normalizing the database.
- Determining referential integrity needs.

Defining Keys for Each Entity

The two types of keys in a table are *primary* keys and *foreign* keys. A primary key (or simply *key*) is an identifier for the data elements in the row; the data elements can be viewed as facts about the key. A foreign key is a primary key to another table to which the table containing the foreign key is related.

In formal relational theory, a primary key is always unique; no two primary keys in a given table are identical. DB2 does not require that primary keys be unique, but it does give you a way to make a key unique by creating a unique index on the key. In practice, performance usually is enhanced if unique keys are used. Also, in most logical designs, the primary data entities that a table stores information about are in fact unique; they should logically have unique identifiers. For example, the main output of your billing system, the bill, showed you that the client name is necessary, and names are certainly not unique, because there might be several John R. Smiths in a city. Some analysis, however, indicates that CLIENT is logically more than just part of a mailing address; the client is the one who accepts responsibility for paying one or more bills and is logically a unique entity. Thus, CLIENT should have a unique key in your logical database design.

There are several ways to design a unique key. One way is to make a non-unique key unique by adding a suffix to it. For example, the keys for different clients could be:

```
John R. Smith      01
John R. Smith      02
George A. Smith    01
George A. Smith    02
```

When this method is used, it is best to use separate columns for the name and the suffix, so that the key consists of both columns (a *composite* key). Otherwise, you would need to separate the name from the suffix for most uses of the name.

Another method of designing a unique key is to use date- and time-stamping as the key or as a suffix to a non-unique key. In this method, system date and time are accessed when a key is added and are used to form the key.

A final method of designing a unique key is simply to generate a unique number each time a record is added. These numbers can simply be in sequential order, starting with 00001 and incrementing by one each time a new record is added. Note that you must make your key field large enough to hold all the records you anticipate adding until you purge and reorganize the database.

This last method has several advantages over the other two. Such a key is shorter than the suffix method, which results in less space needed when storing this key as a foreign key in other tables. This type of key can also be made more meaningful in certain situations than the date- and time-stamping method. For example, your billing key can take form of YYMMNN, where YY is the year, MM is the month, and NN is the number of the bill sent during the month; thus, your key for BILL could be:

```
880501
880502
880601
```

Note that NN is not the same as the day of the month the bill is sent, because multiple bills can (and probably will) be sent on a given day. However, your key gives you a simple and efficient way to select all bills sent in a given month or a given year.

Note also that a key can be maintained in any system in a manner that is transparent to the user. In this case, your attorney does not wish to use a client number or billing number in correspondence with the client (including monthly bills); he feels that this downgrades a "personal touch" and certainly wishes to avoid the practice of telling his clients, "Please include your client number in any written correspondence." In a properly-designed system, you can accommodate your user's need: Teleprocessing screens can allow users to input last, first, or middle names and present a screen which allows users to select from all matches found; the client number can be maintained internally, without requiring the user's knowledge of the value, or even the existence, of any given key.

With the above points in mind, we will use the method of generating a unique number each time a key is added for each of our tables except BILL and PAYMENT; with these tables, we will use the YYMMNN method.

Expressing Relationships as Foreign Keys

After simplifying the Entity-Relationship diagram, you have only two types of relationships in your design: one-to-many and many-to-many. One-to-many relationships are expressed by placing the key of the table on the "one" side of the relationship into the table on the "many" side of the relationship. Thus, you can add two columns to BILL: CLIENT_KEY and ADDRESS_KEY. Similarly, you can add foreign keys to CLIENT, LEGAL_MATTER, PAYMENT, LEGAL_SERVICE, HOURLY_FEE, and SET_FEE.

A many-to-many relationship between two tables is expressed by creating a third table to relate the first two. In this system, you have one many-to-many relationship, the relationship between BILL and LEGAL_SERVICE. Thus, you can create a third table, BILL_LEGAL_SERVICE, which contains nothing but the keys of BILL and LEGAL_SERVICE. From a practical standpoint, it might seem that BILL_LEGAL_SERVICE has no primary key of its own; however, from the standpoint of relational database theory, the composite key consisting of the two foreign keys is the primary key. Logically, this is a valid concept, because the data entity represented by this table is a relationship between two other tables which is uniquely identified by the unique keys of the other tables.

After you have expressed all relationships as foreign keys, your database consists of the tables and columns shown in FIG. 2-5.

Normalizing the Database

Normalizing a database consists of following a set of formal rules from relational database theory that are designed to minimize data redundancy to organize the data into tables. Some methods of relational database design rely almost exclusively on normalization. Here, however, normalization is used more as a method of verifying the effectiveness of your previous design activities; the methodology described above tends to produce designs that are already normalized.

ADDRESS	CLIENT	LEGAL_MATTER
ADDRESS_KEY	CLIENT_KEY	LEGAL_MATTER_KEY
STREET_LINE_1	LAST_NAME	DESCRIPTION
STREET_LINE_2	FIRST_NAME	FILE_FOLDER
STREET_LINE_3	MIDDLE_NAMES	CLIENT_KEY
CITY	ADDRESS_KEY	
STATE		
ZIP		
PAYMENT	**BILL**	**LEGAL_SERVICE**
PAYMENT_KEY	BILL_KEY	LEGAL_SERVICE_KEY
AMOUNT	TOTAL	DESCRIPTION
DATE	DATE	BILL_KEY
CLIENT_KEY	CLIENT_KEY	LEGAL_MATTER_KEY
	ADDRESS_KEY	SET_FEE_KEY
HOURLY_FEE	**SET_FEE**	**BILL_LEGAL_SERVICE**
HOURLY_FEE_KEY	SET_FEE_KEY	BILL_KEY
HOURS	SET_FEE	LEGAL_SERVICE_KEY
HOURLY_RATE		
LEGAL_SERVICE_KEY		

Fig. 2-5. Database definition using tables and their column names.

Determining Whether to Normalize

Note also that the rules of normalization are highly theoretical; practically no database is ever completely normalized according to all of the normalization rules. Here, the rules of normalization are to be only guidelines. The reason is that minimizing data redundancy, the goal of normalization, might involve tradeoffs with processing efficiency that are unacceptable in a given situation.

An example of some of the tradeoffs involved in a decision to normalize or not to normalize is the following hypothetical EMPLOYEE table:

```
EMPLOYEE
————
SOC_SEC_NUMBER
NAME
DEPARTMENT_NAME
LOCATION
```

Note that LOCATION is carried in every row; if each department is located in one place, then you have data redundancy in this table. This can lead to data integrity problems if a given department moves to a different location. All rows of EMPLOYEE that refer to an employee in the moving department would have to be updated with the new location. If this updating is done by use of a teleprocessing system, one record at a time, errors are almost certain to occur. Normalization rules would dictate that the information in EMPLOYEE be broken out into two tables:

EMPLOYEE	DEPARTMENT
SOC_SEC_NUMBER	DEPARTMENT_KEY
NAME	DEPARTMENT_NAME
DEPARTMENT_KEY	LOCATION

Now, when a department moves, only one row in DEPARTMENT needs to be changed.

Note that a tradeoff occurs between data integrity on updates and processing overhead on retrieval because two tables must now be accessed to determine a given employee's location. Note also that the data integrity problem will not necessarily occur if updates to the first version of the EMPLOYEE table (which includes DEPARTMENT_NAME and LOCATION) are done in batch, where you can design and test a program specifically for processing department moves. On the other hand, if the tables involved are such that updates are made often and retrievals will be made rarely (for example, if you are storing data for archival purposes), processing efficiency might well be less important than data integrity. Thus, a decision on whether to normalize in a given situation depends on balancing the need for data integrity versus the need for processing efficiency while keeping in mind the dynamics of processing, such as the method of processing, frequency of updates, frequency of retrieval, etc.

Normalization Terminology

Normalization rules are expressed in terms of "normal forms," each of which is a description of how the data will be arranged when a given rule of normalization has been satisfied. For example, a database is said to be in "first normal form" (1NF) when it conforms to the first rule of normalization.

First normal form. The *first normal form* (1NF) requires tables to have the same number of columns in each row, with no variable-length rows or records. The first normal form is the selection and identification of the tables needed for the application from the universal set of all existing tables. Although 1NF identifies the user's preliminary data needs, it generally contains many undesirable elements: redundant data, repeating data, and dependent data. To eliminate these faults, normalize the table one step further.

Second and third normal form. The *second normal form* (2NF) requires a table where nonkey fields are not dependent on subkey fields. In other words, the data in a record is dependent on (or is a fact about) the entire primary key and not on some part of the key. Any data in a record that is dependent only on part of the key is stripped out of that record and placed in a record containing the foreign key as primary key.

The **third normal form** (3NF) requires tables where no nonkey field is functionally dependent on (is a fact about) another nonkey field. Here you list all the fields in a record which are not keys. The fields in this list must not be functionally dependent on any other field in the list. If you find a field in this list that is dependent on another field in the list, remove that field from that record and place it in another table.

Additional normal forms go beyond the scope of this discussion. In fact, many textbooks are devoted entirely to the topic of normalization. For now, we will restrict the design to satisfying these first three normal forms; the remaining normal forms are primarily theoretical and are rarely used in practice.

Normalization Methodology

To create a design satisfying the first three normal forms, we establish the following criteria:

1. *Eliminate redundant data.* Place data that appears in multiple tables into one table and identify it with a primary key. Put a foreign key in each of the multiple tables in place of the extracted data.
2. *Eliminate repeating or variable length records.* Place data that appears multiple times in the same record into another table and access it using foreign keys.
3. *Eliminate dependent data.* List all the fields in a record that are not keys. Place all the fields that are dependent on a foreign key in that record or on a subset of the primary key into another table. In addition, place all the remaining fields in the list that are dependent on each other into another table.
4. *Override normalization if needed.* If the results of normalization do not produce a better design, override normalization.

Applying the above criteria to the database, you will find that the first criterion is already satisfied: No data appears in more than one table.

The second criterion might be violated, however, in ADDRESS: STREET_LINE_1, STREET_LINE_2, and STREET_LINE_3 appear to be a repeating group. Certainly not all addresses will use all three lines, so it appears that the database is not in 1NF, because it is a variable-length record. However, it is by no means certain 1NF has been violated for two reasons. First, street address can be viewed as one entity that is subdivided for ease of processing (i.e., printing on bills); if, instead of the three street address variables, we simply had one variable, STREET, we probably wouldn't question the design. Thus, while it appears to be a repeating group, to a certain extent we have simply artificially created it. From a logical standpoint, the design is still good. Second, from a practical standpoint, there is no harm in having the data arranged this way. We do not expect to ever have to add another line for street address, because we have arbitrarily decided we will handle a maximum of three lines. Also, update integrity is not an issue, because we do not expect to have to change street names (i.e., the probability of this happening is low enough to be ignored). The second reason carries more weight than the first, because it implies that you do not get a better design from normalizing; thus, we will override normalization rules (if we have really violated them) in this case.

There are no violations of the second criterion in any of the other tables, so we now apply the third criterion. Again, ADDRESS might be a violation of 3NF, because ZIP could be considered to be a fact about street, city, and state, because it is dependant on them as well as the key. Again, we will override normalization, because creating a table with only ZIP and ADDRESS_KEY would further complicate the design without producing any practical results.

Note that any time normalization produces a table with a small amount of data, such as a zip code table, you should suspect that you have a situation where normalization should be overridden. However, a table with a small amount of data in and of itself is not necessarily reason for suspicion. Two other tables, SET_FEE and BILL_LEGAL_SERVICE, have small amounts of data. However, SET_FEE is necessary to contain fee information that really doesn't fit anywhere else, and BILL_LEGAL_SERVICE is necessary to express the many-to-many relationship between bills and legal services. The fact that these tables were created as a result of translating the entity-relationship diagram instead of as a result of normalizing is a clue that they are a necessary part of our design.

Note also that we have chosen to override normalization with regard to ZIP because of the specific requirements of our system: We are restricting our focus to only a billing system—nothing more. If this were part of a large system which might include, for example, a client-information database with multiple addresses per client (home, work, etc.), ZIP might very well be broken out into its own table which would contain several foreign keys. In addition, if we foresee a need to expand this system to contain such information in the future, we might want to go ahead and break ZIP out now, along with other fields from various tables. Only the user can tell us if there might be a need to expand the system later; as programmers and analysts, however, it is our job to foresee the possibility and raise the question.

There are no violations of the third criterion in any of the other tables, so we have finished normalizing our design. In this case, the normalization process has served mainly to verify that we have a good logical design.

Determining Referential Integrity Requirements

Determining referential integrity requirements consists of determining the parent-dependent relationships between the tables you will create and then considering the logical relationships between parents and dependents in order to determine the DELETE rule that we wish to enforce for parent tables—CASCADE, SET NULL, or RESTRICT.

Figure 2-6 shows the parent-dependent relationships between the tables in our database; each dependent table is shown under its parent tables with a line connecting it to them. Note that FIG. 2-6 also shows, when read from top to bottom, the order in which the tables must be defined if you wish DB2 to enforce referential integrity requirements. Tables which are shown on the same level can be defined in any order with respect to each other; that is because it makes no difference whether we define SET_FEE or ADDRESS first.

Each of the parent tables (SET_FEE, ADDRESS, CLIENT, LEGAL_MATTER, BILL, and LEGAL_SERVICE) will be created with the PRIMARY KEY clause. A unique index will also be created on each table. For dependent tables (CLIENT, PAYMENT, LEGAL_MATTER, BILL, LEGAL_SERVICE, HOURLY_FEE, and BILL_LEGAL_SERVICE), we must consider the logical relationships between them.

CLIENT will have a foreign key to ADDRESS with an ON DELETE RESTRICT clause. Logically, we do not want to delete an address as long

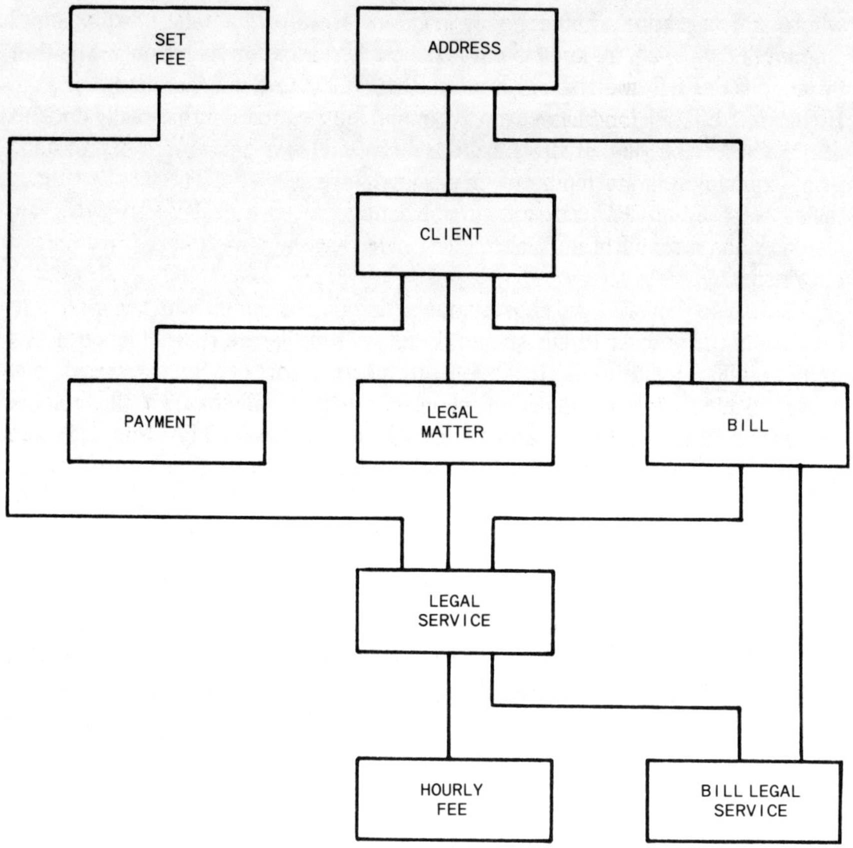

Fig. 2-6. Parent-dependent relationships between tables.

as any client lives there; instead, we require that CLIENT first be properly updated such that there are no references to the ADDRESS row we want to delete.

PAYMENT will have a foreign key to CLIENT with an ON DELETE CASCADE clause. The only reason we would normally want to delete a client record would be to purge the database of clients who no longer do business with the user. In this case, there is no reason not to go ahead and purge payment records as well.

LEGAL_MATTER will have a foreign key to CLIENT with an ON DELETE CASCADE clause. Again, this is to support purging the database periodically.

BILL will have a foreign key to ADDRESS with an ON DELETE SET NULL clause. If we delete an address because, for example, one client moves in with another, we still need to keep that client's bill records in order to calculate a balance, but we do not need address information in order to do this. BILL will also have a foreign key to CLIENT, but with an ON DELETE CASCADE clause. If we are purging the client table, it is acceptable to delete old bill records for a client.

The example of purging the client table brings up another referential integrity requirement. Before deleting a client who no longer does business with the user, we would want to run a balance on the client to ensure that the account has been settled and has a zero balance. However, there is no way you can have DB2 automatically enforce this. You must remember that some referential integrity needs you must enforce through your program code.

LEGAL_SERVICE will have a foreign key on SET_FEE with an ON DELETE RESTRICT clause. There is really no reason why a set fee record should ever be deleted unless the legal service is deleted or updated first. LEGAL_SERVICE will also have a foreign key to LEGAL_MATTER with an ON DELETE CASCADE clause. When purging the database, there is no reason not to delete legal services when a given legal matter is deleted. Finally, LEGAL_SERVICE will have a foreign key on BILL with an ON DELETE CASCADE clause. Note that we must do this in order to be consistent with our ON DELETE CASCADE clause in BILL's foreign key to CLIENT. If we coded ON DELETE RESTRICT, for example, this would in effect nullify the cascading effect on BILL when we delete a client row; the dependent rows of BILL could not be deleted if they had dependent rows in LEGAL_SERVICE.

HOURLY_FEE will have a foreign key on LEGAL_SERVICE with an ON DELETE CASCADE clause. Again, this is to facilitate purging the database.

BILL_LEGAL_SERVICE will have a foreign key on LEGAL_SERVICE with an ON DELETE CASCADE clause. BILL_LEGAL_SERVICE will also have a foreign key on BILL with an ON DELETE CASCADE clause. In both cases, the reason is again to facilitate purging the database.

Exercise

2-1. Convert the following COBOL definitions for a nonrelational database to the appropriate normalized tables.

```
01 EMPLOYEE-PAYROLL-RECORD
   05 EMPL-ID                             PIC X(9).
   05 EMPL-LAST-NAME                      PIC X(25).
   05 EMPL-FIRST NAME                     PIC X(25).
   05 EMPL-M-I                            PIC X(1).
   05 EMPL-STREET                         PIC X(25).
   05 EMPL-STATE                          PIC X(2).
   05 EMPL-ZIP                            PIC X(5).
   05 EMPL-PHONE                          PIC X(10).
   05 DATE-HIRED                          PIC X(6).
   05 SEX                                 PIC X.
   05 BIRTHDAY                            PIC 9(6).
   05 RACE                                PIC X.
   05 SALARY-INFO.
      10 WEEK-WORKED                      PIC X(6).
      10 RATE-OF-PAY                      PIC 999V99.
      10 HOURS-WORKED                     PIC 999V9.
   05 TAXES.
      10 FEDERAL-INCOME                   PIC 9(5)V99.
```

```
        10 SOC-SEC-TAX                         PIC 9(4)V99.
        10 STATE-TAX                           PIC 9(4)V99.
        10 CITY-TAX                            PIC 9(4)V99.
    05 OTHER-DEDUCTIONS.
        10 TYPE-DEDUCTION OCCURS 10 TIMES              PIC X(10).
        10 AMOUNT-DEDUCTED OCCURS 10 TIMES             PIC 9(5)V99.
    05 NUMBER-DEPENDENTS                               PIC 99.
    05 DEPARTMENT-EMPLOYEED                            PIC X(15).
    05 JOB-TITLE                                       PIC X(16).
    05 DEPARTMENT-SUPERVISORS-NAME                     PIC X(40).
    05 UNION-MEMBERSHIP-CODE                           PIC X.
    05 EMERGENCY-CONTACT-NAME                          PIC X(40).
    05 EMERGENCY-CONTACT-INSTRUCTIONS                  PIC X(40).
```

3

Data Definition Language

We use the techniques of Chapter 2 to generate a logical design for the database. This logical design consists of tables containing rows and columns and identifies the structure of the database. When we define a database to DB2, we simply request specific space on a DASD pack. This space is assigned a name, called a *database name*. We subdivide that space into one or more *tablespaces* that will hold our tables. A *table* is a series of rows (records) and columns (fields) related in some way. Each tablespace can contain one or more tables.

We define the column names to DB2 using Data Definition Language (DDL) which places the description of the table in the DB2 Catalog. We insert data into tables using Data Manipulation Language (DML). DML places the data in a page within the tablespace. Each page is 4K long and contains rows from one or more tables.

If we create an index or key for a table, that key is one or more columns in the table and can be either primary or foreign. Figure 3-1 illustrates these terms.

Using Data Definition Language

The Data Definition Language (DDL) commands include CREATE, which defines a new object; ALTER, which modifies an existing object; and DROP, which deletes or expunges the existing object. CREATE defines the structure of an entity and stores it in tables found in the DB2 catalog. ALTER modifies the structure of DB2 entities in the catalog, and DROP removes entities from the catalog. Because the DB2 catalog is composed of tables, the CREATE, ALTER, and DROP commands are converted by DB2 into INSERT, UPDATE, and DELETE commands that affect one or more DB2 catalog table rows. The

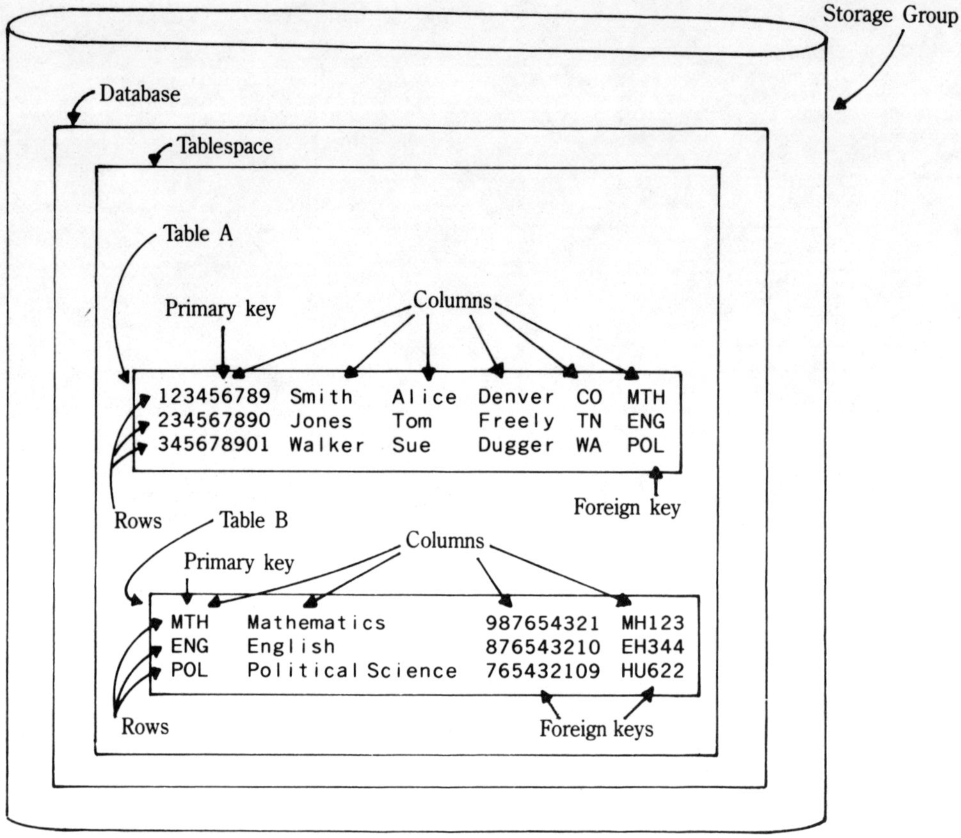

Fig. 3-1. Relationships between storage groups, tablespaces, and tables.

entities affected are storage groups, databases, tablespaces, tables, views, synonyms, and indexes. You can only ALTER storage groups, tablespaces, tables, and indexes. Any change to already existing structures of databases, views, or synonyms requires DROPing that entity and recreating it with the modification included in the rewritten CREATE statement.

Obviously, you must create entities in a certain sequence. You cannot create a table unless a tablespace exists, and you cannot create a view on a nonexistent table. Therefore, you can create an object only after its supporting entity exists. The sequence for creating objects is:

1. Create the storage group.
2. Create the database name on the storage group.
3. Create tablespaces in the database.
4. Create tables in the tablespaces.
5. Create indexes, views, and synonyms on the tables as needed.

Note that you can create a view of a table without first creating an index, and you can create a synonym (of a table) without creating either an index or a view.

When you drop an entity, you lose the objects that are dependent on that entity. For example, if you drop a table, you lose all indexes, views, and synonyms associated with that table including synonyms of the views and views of the views. In other words, when you drop an entity, a cascading effect occurs whereby the DB2 catalog DELETEs from its tables all the created and altered entities dependent on the drop item.

Obviously, dropping a database has serious ramifications on all structures created under that database name. For example, if you must change the storage group of the database, you would have to drop the database because you cannot ALTER any database. DB2 would then delete from the DB2 catalog tables all references to tablespaces, tables, views, indexes, and synonyms defined under that database. Note that the data in the database is not destroyed—DB2 only deletes the structure of the database from the DB2 catalog. However, without the structure, you cannot access the data. To place the structures back into the DB2 catalog, you would simply reenter all the CREATE and ALTER commands that you used initially. Here, saving all CREATE, DROP, and ALTER statements in a file (within the DB2I menu) will greatly facilitate this recreation of the database and its supporting entities.

Storage Groups

To create a storage group named EU8001 on volumes DOC1 and DOC2 you would use:

```
CREATE STOGROUP EU8001
    VOLUMES (DOC1 , DOC2)
```

You must have CREATESG privilege or be a SYSADM to create a storage group. The name of the storage group cannot be longer than eight characters and must be unique to DB2.

Volumes DOC1 and DOC2 are DASD volumes used for assigning space for tables and indexes. On these volumes, DB2 defines the necessary VSAM (Virtual Storage Access Method) data sets it needs and maintains them by extending and deleting them when necessary.

If you need to modify the storage group by either removing a volume or adding additional volumes, you would use:

```
ALTER STOGROUP EU8001
   ADD VOLUMES (DOC3)
   REMOVE VOLUMES (DOC2)
```

Here, DB2 does not actually remove the volume from the connection to DB2 but rather prohibits any new storage allocation to be made on the removed volume. Again, you must have SYSADM authority or be the creator of the storage group before you ALTER it.

Databases

After you create the storage group, you need to create the database on that storage group using:

```
CREATE DATABASE EPTFEDUC
    STOGROUP EU8001
    BUFFERPOOL BP1
```

You must have CREATEDBA or CREATEDBC privilege or be a SYSADM to create a database. The name of the database cannot be longer than eight characters and must be unique to DB2. Here database EPTFEDUC is assigned to volumes DOC1 and DOC2 on storage group EU8001. In this example, we are using buffer pool BP1 for tables and indexes within the database. The buffer pools available are BP0, BP1, and BP2 of size 4K and BP32K of size 32K. If we do not use the BUFFERPOOL option, BP0 becomes the default buffer pool.

You must be careful in selecting the storage group for your database. Because you cannot alter the database once you create it, the storage group you select will be dedicated to your database for some period of time. If other user departments have access to the same storage group, their future demands and needs might conflict with your demands and needs forcing you to vacate the group. Therefore, you should check with the system programmers and other users of the storage group for possible future conflicts on it. Generally, the creation of the storage group and database is performed by the SYSADM. After the SYSADM creates the storage group and database, he or she then uses Control Language commands and issues authorizations (to developers and users) to use the database and create entities on it.

Tablespaces

A *tablespace* is physical space on an external storage device defined by the database and holds tables. You can create one or more tables within a tablespace, and you can have multiple tablespaces within the database. For example, the statement:

```
CREATE TABLESPACE EPTFTS1
       IN EPTFEDUC
       USING STOGROUP EU8001
       PRIQTY 30
       SECQTY 20
       LOCKSIZE TABLESPACE
       BUFFERPOOL BP0
       CLOSE NO
       ERASE YES
```

creates the tablespace EPTFTS1 in database EPTFEDUC on storage group EU8001. The primary space allocation is for 30K with secondary allocations of 20K to handle overflows. The tablespace uses the 4K bufferpool BP0 as the buffer area when it accesses a table. Also, DB2 locks the entire tablespace when it accesses a table and does not close the VSAM datasets after each access. When you drop the tablespace, DB2 ERASEs all data in it by overwriting the data with zeros as a security measure. Note that if you remove the BUFFERPOOL option, DB2 defaults to the bufferpool defined by the CREATE DATABASE statement.

You must have CREATETS privilege, be the SYSADM or a DBADM, or have other administrative authorization to create tablespaces. The name of the tablespace cannot be longer than eight characters and must be unique to the database.

You can modify the tablespace using the ALTER command and change certain characteristics of it. For example, the statement:

```
ALTER TABLESPACE EPTFEDUC.EPTFTS1
        BUFFERPOOL BP2
        CLOSE YES
        LOCKSIZE PAGE
        ERASE NO
```

modifies the definition of the tablespace in the catalog. Here, BP2 becomes the bufferpool, all VSAM datasets close after they are accessed, DB2 performs page locks (instead of tablespace locks) as the locking strategy, and DB2 does not overwrite the data with zeros when you drop the tablespace. To use the ALTER command, you must be the creator of the tablespace or have SYSADM or DBADM authority.

Exercises

3-1. Write the DDL statements to create the storage group PR3200, the database PAYFILE, and tablespaces PRSPACE1 and PRSPACE2 in them.

3-2. Write the DDL statements to create the tablespaces EPTFTS3 in database EPTFPROD on storage group EP8001 using bufferpool BP2 and with page locking. What installation standards are necessary to use ERASE NO as an option? To use CLOSE NO as an option?

3-3. Write an ALTER statement to change the statement in Exercise 3-2 to allow for tablespace locking and using BP1 as the bufferpool.

3-4. Why would you establish a storage group on multiple volumes for the same database instead of defining a different database name for each volume?

Tables

After you set up the criteria for space allocations within DB2, you must then create the structure of the table in a tablespace within the database. The general form of the CREATE TABLE statement is:

```
CREATE TABLE tablename1
        (C1 S1 N1,
         C2 S2 N2,
         C3 S3 N3,
         C4 S4 N4
```

```
        .
        .
        .
        PRIMARY KEY (C1, C2...)
        FOREIGN KEY relationship (C3, C4...)
             REFERENCES tsname2.tablename2
             ON DELETE action)
   IN dbname.tsname1
```

In this segment of code, the terms are as follows:

tablename1—the name of the table you are creating.
C1, C2, C3, C4—the column names.
S1, S2, S3, S4—the columns' types.
N1, N2, N3, N4—either "NOT NULL" or blank.
C1, C2—primary keys for the table you are creating.
relationship—the name of the relationship between the table you are creating and the table you are referencing through foreign keys.
C3, C4—foreign key references to a parent table.
tsname2—the tablespace name of the parent table.
tablename2—the name of the parent table.
action—CASCADE, SET NULL, or RESTRICT.
dbname—the database name for the table you are creating.
tsname1—the tablespace name for the table you are creating.

The table names can be simple names or fully qualified names. Simple names must begin with an alphabetic character and can be no more than 18 characters long. Except for the first character, the name can contain any alphanumeric character including the special characters of _(underscore), @, #, and $.

A fully qualified table name is a simple name preceded by the owner's ID. If user $QWER created the table HISTORY, its fully qualified name is $QWER.HISTORY. The owner accesses the table using its simple name while all non-owners access it using its fully qualified name. However, the table name cannot be a reserved word (such as INSERT or CREATE) nor can it contain certain special characters (+, /, *).

Column names can also be simple or fully qualified. Simple column names follow the same criteria as that of simple table names. Fully qualified column names have the table name preceding the column name (as in HISTORY. EVENT).

The relationship name is not required. If you do not code it, DB2 will create one from the first foreign key column coded, which would be C3 in the example above. The relationship name will be used by DB2 in certain error messages and in the DB2 catalog. You would use the relationship name in queries to the catalog and in ALTERing a table to DROP the foreign key. You would probably never code an explicit relationship name unless you had more than one FOREIGN KEY clause beginning with the same column name.

Alphanumeric Data

Data in a column can be either alphanumeric or numeric. For alphanumeric data, the column type is either

```
CHAR(n)
```

or

```
VARCHAR(n)
```

where n is the number of characters in the column (with a maximum of 254 characters for CHAR and 4056 characters for VARCHAR). Use CHAR for columns containing alphanumeric data of the same length. Columns containing social security numbers, zip codes, middle initials, phone numbers, and two-character state abbreviations all are in this category.

Use VARCHAR for columns containing data of variable length. Columns containing last names, first names, and city names all contain data of variable length, and hence, should be VARCHARed. When you use VARCHAR for variable length data, DB2 removes nonessential blanks, thereby condensing the data and saving storage space.

Numeric Data

For numeric data, you can define the column as:

SMALLINT—for integer values from -32768 to $+32767$ (i.e., a halfword)
INTEGER—for integer values from $-2^{32}-1$ to $+2^{32}-1$ (i.e., a fullword or $-2{,}147{,}483{,}648$ to $+2{,}147{,}483{,}647$)
DECIMAL (L, D)—for fractional values up to a maximum of 15 digits where L is the total number of digits and D is the number of digits to the right of the decimal.
FLOAT—for double precision numbers.

Assume a user department wants to store the data as shown here in tablespace USERTS1 in database USERBASE:

Column	COBOL PIC clause	Required field
Customer ID	X(10)	Y
Amount owed	99999V99	Y
Amount paid	99999V99	Y
Highest balance	9(8)V99	N
# items ordered	999	N
Name of item	X(15)	N

You can define the table to DB2 using the following CREATE statement:

```
CREATE TABLE  CUSTITEMS
    (CUSTID   CHAR(10)          NOT NULL,
```

```
      AMTOWED   DECIMAL(7,2)     NOT NULL,
      AMTPAID   DECIMAL(7,2)     NOT NULL,
      HIGHBAL   DECIMAL(10,2)            ,
      NUMBORD   SMALLINT                 ,
      ITEMNAME  VARCHAR(15)              )
  IN USERBASE.USERTS1
```

Here, you create the table with three columns set as NOT NULL and three set with implied nulls. When you insert data into the table, the NOT NULL columns must contain data (or be set to spaces). If a user has a view of a table which excludes a NOT NULL column, that user cannot insert rows into the table. Therefore, when developing the table configurations and the views given the various users, you must make sure that if the user wants to insert rows into the table, that user must be given access to all NOT NULL columns in that table.

Once the table exists in the DB2 catalog, additional columns can be added to the table using the ALTER command. Its general form is:

```
ALTER TABLE tablename
ADD columnname type
```

where

`tablename` is the already existing table name.
`columnname` is the new column to be added to the table.
`type` is either CHAR, VARCHAR, SMALLINT, INTEGER, DECIMAL, or FLOAT.

You must have SYSADM or DBADM authority or have ALTER privilege to ALTER a table. A typical ALTER command would look like

```
ALTER TABLE BUILDING
ADD CLASSSIZE INTEGER
```

Here we add the column CLASSSIZE to table BUILDING and set it to contain integer values. The ALTER statement must contain only one column per statement. The new column becomes the right-most column and is set to NULLs automatically. If data already exists in the table, the value in all the rows for that column is set as null.

We used the ALTER command to add a new column to the table. However, to change the size or name of an existing column or to change a column from NOT NULL to NULL (or vice versa), we must drop the table and recreate it with the changes made in the new CREATE statement. That is, if we wanted to change the column CUSTID in the CUSTITEMS table mentioned above from CHAR(10) to INTEGER and ITEMNAME to NOT NULL, we would use the following series of commands:

```
DROP TABLE CUSTITEMS;
CREATE TABLE CUSTITEMS
    (CUSTID          INTEGER                  NOT NULL,
     AMTOWED         DECIMAL (7,2)            NOT NULL,
     AMTPAID         DECIMAL (7,2)            NOT NULL,
     HIGHBAL         DECIMAL (10,2)                   ,
```

```
      NUMBORD           SMALLINT                          ,
      ITEMNAME          CHAR(15)                   NOT NULL)
   IN USERBASE.USERTS1
```

When DB2 physically deletes a table's structure from the catalog it also deletes from the catalog all other entities based on that table. Views, views on views, and synonyms based on the dropped table are deleted from the catalog. To regenerate these lost items, we would have to recreate them using their appropriate CREATE statements. Hence, it is wise to save all CREATE, ALTER, and DROP statements in a file within DB2I so entities deleted can easily be salvaged.

Exercises

3-5. Convert the following COBOL description to a table:

```
01 PAYROLL.
        05 EMPLOYEE-ID                     PIC X(8).
        05 EMPLOYEE-NAME.
              10 EMPLOYEE-LAST-NAME        PIC X(20).
              10 EMPLOYEE-FIRST-NAME       PIC X(20).
        05 WEEKLY-GROSS-SALARY             PIC 9(4)V99.
        05 YTD-GROSS-SALARY                PIC 9(6)V99.
        05 YTD-VACATION-PAY                PIC 9(5)V99.
        05 WEEKS-ON-PAYROLL                PIC 9(4).
        05 DATE-FIRST-EMPLOYED.
              10 YEAR-EMPLOYED             PIC 99.
              10 MONTH-EMPLOYED            PIC 99.
              10 DAY-EMPLOYED              PIC 99.
```

where only EMPLOYEE-NAME and EMPLOYEE-ID are required fields. Place the table in tablespace PAYTS3 on database PAYPROD.

3-6. Given the following tables with their COBOL picture clause:

EQUIPMENT TABLE

PRODUCT ID	PRODUCT NAME	PRODUCT TYPE	INITIAL COST	WHERE PURCHASED	NUMBER BOUGHT
X(4)	X(15)	X(2)	9(6).99	X(20)	9(3)
4211	WRENCH	ST	4.23	KMART	6
5318	TRUCK	HM	15983.22	GM	2
3402	DRILL	LM	4532.99	ARGON	5
7321	PRESS	LT	165.66	DARGO	1
0900	CHAIR	FU	230.00	LITTLES	4
0901	TABLE	FU	500.00	LITTLES	2
0790	PRINTER	CE	650.00	IBM	2
2100	FAN	ET	125.00	KMART	2

SALVAGE TABLE

PRODUCT TYPE	NUMB. YEARS DEPRECIATE	PERCENT SALVAGE	TYPE NAME
X(2)	99	99	X(20)
LM	10	10	LIGHT MACHINERY
HM	15	20	HEAVY MACHINERY
ST	1	0	SMALL TOOL
LT	1	0	LARGE TOOL
ET	3	25	SMALL ELECTRIC TOOL
FU	5	30	FURNITURE
CE	10	10	COMPUTER EQUIPMENT

Write the DDL statement to create the tables in tablespace COEQUIP on database BUDGET.

3-7. Write the DDL command to add column EMPLOYEE-SEX with PIC X to the PAYROLL table in Exercise 3-5.

3-8. Write the DDL commands to change:

a. The field "NUMBER BOUGHT" in the EQUIPMENT table to PIC 9(4).

b. The field "PRODUCT ID" in the EQUIPMENT table to PIC X(5).

Edit and Validation Routines

You can write an edit routine called an EDITPROC or a validation routine called a VALIDPROC and link it to a table using the CREATE TABLE statement. Edit routines encode and decode data either by compressing and then expanding or by encrypting and then decrypting data. That is, an EDITPROC encodes the data as it stores it on the external storage device and then decodes it when it is brought back into memory for use. On the other hand, a VALIDPROC verifies that data is within certain parameters, has certain required characters, or is in a certain format. You create an EDITPROC and VALIDPROC on a table when you create the table. The statement:

```
CREATE TABLE CUSTITEMS
    (CUSTID CHAR(10)            NOT NULL,
     AMTOWED DECIMAL(7,2)       NOT NULL,
     AMTPAID DECIMAL(7,2)       NOT NULL,
     HIGHBAL DECIMAL(10,2)              ,
     NUMBORD SMALLINT                   ,
     ITEMNAME CHAR(15)                  )
 IN USERBASE.ESERTS1
 EDITPROC CODE01
 VALIDPROC ROUTINE2
```

assigns the programs CODE01 and ROUTINE2 as an EDITPROC and VALIDPROC respectively. Once you create an edit routine on a table, you must drop the table to unlink it from the table. However, you can unlink a validation routine or change to another validation routine by using a variation of the ALTER TABLE command. The statement:

```
ALTER TABLE CUSTITEMS
  VALIDPROC NULL
```

unlinks the validation routing from table CUSTITEMS while the statement:

```
ALTER TABLE CUSTITEMS
   VALIDPROC ROUTINE1
```

changes the validation routine to ROUTINE1. Note that neither an EDITPROC or VALIDPROC edits or validates data already existing in the table. After you establish the linkage, all data passes through the procs when you use the commands SELECT, UPDATE, and INSERT.

Synonyms

It might not be convenient to use the fully qualified name of a table, especially if the table is assigned a particularly long name or if the name of the table is not meaningful to the user. The user of a table can create a *synonym* for the table by assigning another name to it using the CREATE SYNONYM statement. For example, if the development team with I.D. $DEVELOP creates the table BUILDING_MAINTAIN, a user could create the synonym UPKEEP by entering the following statement:

```
CREATE SYNONYM UPKEEP
   FOR $DEVELOP.BUILDING_MAINTAIN
```

Now the user can use the name UPKEEP to access the table rather than the fully qualified name $DEVELOP.BUILDING_MAINTAIN. The user enters the CREATE SYNONYM statement in his or her DB2 account. Although the user can generate a synonym without authorization from anyone, the user must be given authorization to access a table from its owner because only the table owner and authorized users can access a table. Note that you cannot ALTER a synonym, but instead you must drop it and recreate it.

Views

After the development team designs the tables and creates them in the DB2 catalog, their next step is to create views of the tables for the users. Obviously, you would not want data in payroll or medical history tables to be accessed by just anyone. By creating views, the development team can restrict access to certain columns and rows within tables. The CREATE VIEW statement combines elements of both DDL (i.e., CREATE) and DML (i.e.,

SELECT) commands. For example, to restrict the user $USER1 to accessing only the columns LASTNAME, FIRSTNAME, and SEX of table CUSTOMER, you use:

```
CREATE VIEW PARTCUST AS
        SELECT LASTNAME, FIRSTNAME, SEX
        FROM CUSTOMER
```

To further restrict the user to accessing only females, you would use:

```
CREATE VIEW PARTCUST AS
        SELECT LASTNAME, FIRSTNAME, SEX
        FROM CUSTOMER
        WHERE SEX = 'F'
```

Note that as far as the user is concerned, the table name can be a base table name, a view name, or a synonym name. In fact, the user might not even know that the table name they are using is just a synonym or a view. DB2 handles the data based on what is defined in theDB2 catalog and accesses it through various buffer mechanisms. The fact that the data came from a base table directly, through a window called a view, or through a synonym is transparent to whoever is accessing that data.

There are several restrictions on using DDL commands (INSERT, UPDATE, and DELETE) on views. You can INSERT through a view only if you have a view of all the NOT NULL columns. Remember, NOT NULL columns require some value to be entered for the column at load time and if the user does not have authorization for that column, the user cannot INSERT anything into the table. If the column in the view is an expression such as SCORE + GOALS or SALARY/26, or if the view contains GROUP BY, DISTINCT, a join, or a summary function (SUM, AVG, MAX, MIN, COUNT, etc.), DB2 cannot INSERT, UPDATE, or DELETE through that view. A DELETE on a view deletes from the base table even though the view does not include all columns in the table.

Like synonyms, you cannot alter a view but must first drop it and then recreate it. To drop the view PARTCUST created above, you would use:

```
DROP VIEW PARTCUST
```

If the user has authorization to use a table, synonym, or view with GRANT OPTION (see Chapter 5), that user can create views of his or her view. That is, a user with the view PARTCUST and with GRANT OPTION authorization could create a subview for another user by using:

```
CREATE VIEW CUSTNAMES AS
        SELECT LASTNAME, FIRSTNAME,
        FROM CUSTOMER
        WHERE SEX = 'F'
```

Exercises

3-9. Two users $KAREN and $MARK want views of the table in Exercise 3-5.

User $KAREN needs only YTD information while user $MARK needs only nonfinancial information. Write the DDL commands to create their views.

3-10. Write the DDL command to give user $MARY a view of the EQUIPMENT table in Exercise 3-6 for columns product id, product name, and product type.

3-11. User $BETTY created the table EQUIPMENT_LIST. User $STEVE wants to create the synonym MYEQUIP for the table. Write the DDL command user $STEVE must enter to create this synonym.

3-12. User $SUSAN wants a partial view of $MARK's view in Exercise 3-9. She wants her view to be named GENINFO. Unlike $MARK's view, she does not need or want the column WEEKS ON PAYROLL included in her view. Write the DDL command to create a view based on the original table. Write the DDL command to create the view based on $MARK's view name. What are the advantages and disadvantages of creating each of these views?

Indexes

The last step in designing the structure of tables is the creation of the various indexes on them. An *index* is a list of values from the table and their page and row location within the tablespace. You can create indexes on any column in the table, including columns containing unique, non-unique, and foreign keys. Next (if you can anticipate what type of queries are likely to be made) you create indexes on all the columns used in:

- Search arguments (such as WHERE SEX = 'F', WHERE STATE = 'TX').
- Joining tables (for example, WHERE ITEMID=PRODUCTID).
- GROUP BY clauses (such as GROUP BY BUILDTYPE).
- ORDER BY clauses (such as ORDER BY CUSTNAME).
- Foreign key clauses (e.g. FOREIGN KEY (EMPLOYEE, DATE))

Use the CREATE INDEX statement to both create the index and the indexspace to hold them. Note that DB2 does not have an explicit create indexspace command. To create the index CUSTINDEX on the columns CUSTID and ITEMNAME for table CUSTITEMS using storage group EU8001 and destroy the data in the indexspace when you drop it, you use:

```
CREATE INDEX CUSTINDEX
ON CUSTITEMS
(CUSTID, ITEMNAME)
USING STOGROUP EU8001
PRIQTY 10
SECQTY 5
ERASE YES
```

If you did not create CUSTITEMS, you must have SYSADM, DBADM, or INDEX authority to create indexes on other owners' tables. You automatically have authority to create indexes on your own tables.

DB2 creates the indexspace on the assigned storage group, maintains the index in tables within the indexspace, and uses the page and row references in them to physically locate rows in tablespaces. Note that a page is a 4K section of memory the system uses to store rows of a table. Because DB2 references the index (if one exists) to locate rows for queries, it does not have to scan the tablespace to find the data. Not only does this save time, it also enables DB2 to access and lock only a page at a time rather than lock the entire tablespace and start a systematic search of all pages in the tablespace. Note that DB2 does not physically have a table stored as a unit within the tablespace. Everything is stored on 4K pages somewhere within the tablespace and DB2 extracts pages from it. If no index exists on the table, DB2 reads every page containing data in the tablespace looking for the search argument criteria. For large tablespaces, this can be both time consuming and frustrating to other users as entire tablespaces, perhaps containing multiple tables, are locked for long periods of time. As a general rule, if in doubt about creating an index, go ahead and create it.

If you want a unique index or multiple unique indexes on the same table, you would use:

```
CREATE UNIQUE INDEX...
```

For columns with unique indexes, all duplicate values are rejected either at load time or when you INSERT or UPDATE a row. For any index, if data already exists in the table, DB2 performs a tablespace scan and creates the index immediately. If data does not already exist in the table, DB2 creates the index as rows are inserted into the table.

To create a unique index on table CUSTITEMS with CUSTID indexed in descending order and ITEMNAME in ascending order (column defaults to ascending order), you would use:

```
CREATE UNIQUE INDEX CUSTINDEX1
ON CUSTITEMS
(CUSTID DESC, ITEMNAME)
USING STOGROUP EU8001
PRIQTY 10
SECQTY 5
ERASE YES
CLOSE NO
BUFFERPOOL BP2
```

You can alter an index to change the bufferpool name, the CLOSE option, or the password for the VSAM dataset. You can alter its description using:

```
ALTER CUSTINDEX1
        BUFFERPOOL BP1
        CLOSE YES
        DSETPASS YNOT11
```

Here you change the bufferpool to BP1, close the VSAM datasets after usage, and change the VSAM dataset password to YNOT11.

You can drop the index using

```
DROP INDEX CUSTINDEX1
```

Dropping an index invalidates all plans based on the index and the plans must consequently be rebound. In Chapter 1, we briefly discussed the concept of a plan and how to create them with a BIND. We will further discuss the concept of a plan and bind in Chapter 8. For now, you need only to be aware of the fact that dropping indexes could dynamically affect other entities you have created.

If you enter SQL statements through DB2I, DB2 performs a dynamic BIND and creates a PLAN. If you imbed SQL within code, you must perform a BIND using options in DB2I to generate the PLAN. Even if you create an index, DB2 software algorithms at BIND time might countermand the use of the index and force a tablespace lock and scan. These preestablished algorithms within DB2 calculate the number of disk I/Os needed to access the data in the tablespace in determining index usage. Too many disk I/Os result in tablespace locks and scans. Note that even if we try to force DB2 to lock on PAGE in options in the CREATE TABLESPACE command, the BINDer might countermand it and generate tablespace locks and scans.

Exercises

3-13. What columns in Exercise 3-5 should be indexed? Why?

3-14. Write the DDL statement to create a unique index on columns EMPLOYEE-ID for the table in Exercise 3-5.

3-15. Write the DDL statement to create an index on the COBOL columns in Exercise 3-5 for YTD-GROSS-SALARY, YTD-VACATION-PAY, and a descending index on WEEKS-ON-PAYROLL.

3-16. For the tables in Exercise 3-6, write the DDL statement to create a unique index on PRODID. Create an index on PRODNAME, VENDOR, and PRODTYPE. Create a decending index on YRSDEPREC.

Referential Integrity

Referential integrity describes a set of requirements for maintaining the reliability of data in a relational database. The need for referential integrity is inherent in the fact that a relational database stores data in a set of related tables which express the relationships between them by containing references to each other. For example, suppose you want to maintain the following data concerning students and dormitory assignments:

```
STUDENT_NUMBER
STUDENT_NAME
DORMITORY_NUMBER
DORMITORY_LOCATION
```

Note that you are actually storing data about two different ''entities''—students and dormitories. In a relational database, this information might be stored in two tables, STUDENTS and DORMITORIES, with the following columns in each table:

STUDENTS	DORMITORIES
STUDENT_NUMBER	DORMITORY_NUMBER
STUDENT_NAME	DORMITORY_LOCATION
DORMITORY_NUMBER	

Note the reference (DORMITORY_NUMBER) to the DORMITORIES table in the STUDENTS table, which expresses the relationship between them. Each student will be assigned to one dormitory, and each dormitory may have several students assigned to it. In this case, DORMITORIES is known as a *parent* table; STUDENTS is known as a *dependent* table.

Referential integrity requires that each row in the STUDENTS table should either reference a valid row in the DORMITORIES table or, possibly, be null. (Whether a reference can be null depends on whether it logically makes sense in a given application; in this case, a student who lives off-campus could logically have a null dormitory number.) Referential integrity requirements can be expressed as a set of rules governing INSERTs, DELETEs, and UPDATEs of rows of both parent and dependent tables.

SQL allows you to automatically enforce most of these rules when you CREATE tables; other rules must be enforced through the logic of your programs which modify DB2 databases.

Parent Table Rules

You can always insert a parent table row regardless of dependent references. Logically, this makes sense. A new dormitory could be built, for example, before students are assigned to it. DB2 automatically enforces this rule.

When you delete a parent table row, you maintain referential integrity for those dependent table rows which reference it only when the DELETE does one of the following:

- *cascades,* or all rows in STUDENT which reference the deleted row in DORMITORY are also deleted.
- *sets null,* or all rows in STUDENT which reference the deleted row in DORMITORY have their reference set to null.
- *is restricted,* or DELETE is not allowed for a row in DORMITORY which has one or more rows in STUDENT which reference it.

Recall that the ''sets null'' rule might not be an option if it does not logically make sense in a given application. DB2 allows you to automatically enforce the rule i.e., (CASCADE, SET NULL, or RESTRICT) you select. Which rule you select depends on the logical requirements of your application.

When you update a parent row, referential integrity requirements might be violated if you change that row's key. You maintain referential integrity for those dependent rows which reference it only when the UPDATE does one of the following:

- *cascades,* or all rows in STUDENT which reference the updated row in DORMITORY are also updated to reference the new key.
- *sets null,* or all rows in STUDENT which reference the updated row in DORMITORY have their reference set to null.
- *is restricted,* or UPDATE is not allowed for a row in DORMITORY which has one or more rows in STUDENT which reference it.

Again, the "sets null" rule might not be an option in certain applications. DB2 automatically enforces only the RESTRICT rule.

Dependent Table Rules

You can always delete a dependent table row regardless of which parents it references, and DB2 automatically allows this. However, you can insert a dependent table row only if it either references a parent table row which actually exists or if the reference is null. In other words, you cannot add a student to your database who is assigned to a nonexistent dormitory, but you can add a student who lives off-campus. DB2 automatically enforces whichever rule you select, so either the row references an existing parent or the reference is null. Similarly, you can only update a reference to a parent table row in a dependent table row if the parent table row exists or if the reference is null; therefore, you cannot assign an existing student to a nonexistent dormitory, but you can set the dormitory assignment to null for a student who moves off-campus. In either case, i.e., inserting or updating, setting the reference to null is an option only if it makes sense in the application.

Enforcing Referential Integrity Rules

You can always enforce referential integrity requirements by coding your program logic in such a way as to prevent undesirable table updates, deletes, or inserts. You can also let DB2 enforce most referential integrity requirements; we do this by identifying parent and dependent tables and their relationships when we define them. For example, the STUDENTS and DORMITORIES tables might be defined with the following SQL:

```
CREATE TABLE DORMITORIES
      (DORMITORY_NUMBER        SMALLINT       NOT NULL,
       DORMITORY_LOCATION      CHAR(40)       NOT NULL,
       PRIMARY KEY (DORMITORY_NUMBER))
IN EDUCBASE.EPTFTS1
```

```
CREATE TABLE STUDENTS
      (STUDENT_NUMBER          CHAR(5)       NOT NULL,
       STUDENT_NAME            CHAR(40)      NOT NULL,
       DORMITORY_NUMBER        SMALLINT,
       FOREIGN KEY (DORMITORY_NUMBER) REFERENCES
             DORMITORIES ON DELETE RESTRICT)
 IN EDUCBASE.EPTFTS1
```

Note that you need to identify a parent table with the PRIMARY KEY clause, and that you identify a dependent table with the FOREIGN KEY clause that gives an ON DELETE clause to specify which rule you want to enforce—ON DELETE RESTRICT, ON DELETE CASCADE, or ON DELETE SET NULL. Recall that for DB2 to enforce referential integrity requirements, PRIMARY KEYs in parent tables must have unique indexes.

You can also use the ALTER command to add or delete primary keys. For example, if you wish to make the CUSTITEMS table a parent table with CUSTID as a primary key, you can issue the following SQL statement:

```
ALTER TABLE CUSTITEMS
PRIMARY KEY (CUSTID)
```

Unlike the CREATE command, the ALTER command requires the primary index to exist when you use the PRIMARY KEY clause.

To delete a primary key, you can use the DROP clause:

```
ALTER TABLE CUSTITEMS
DROP PRIMARY KEY
```

This will cause the relationship between CUSTITEMS and any dependent table to be deleted, and DB2 will no longer enforce referential integrity requirements.

When you drop a table the parent-dependent relationships for that table are deleted from the catalog. However, an ON DELETE clause does not take effect upon dropping a table.

You can also use the ALTER command to add or delete foreign key references:

```
ALTER TABLE CUSTITEMS
FOREIGN KEY (ITEMNAME) REFERENCES ITEMTABLE
      ON DELETE RESTRICT
```

You must use some caution in ALTERing a table to create a foreign key. If data already exists that would violate the referential integrity requirements you specify, the table will be put in what is known as "check pending status." This means, in effect, that you will be unable to use the table until a utility is run (CHECK) which purges the offending data.

To delete a foreign key reference, you must use the DROP clause:

```
ALTER TABLE CUSTITEMS
DROP FOREIGN KEY ITEMNAME
```

Note that you need only to use the first (or only) column name in the FOREIGN KEY clause which CREATEd or ALTERed the table as the relationship name in the DROP clause. If you had specified an explicit relationship name when you CREATEd or ALTERed the table, you would have used the explicit name instead.

This DROP clause causes the relationship between CUSTITEMS and the parent table referenced by ITEMNAME to be deleted. Note that you must have ALTER authority on both CUSTITEMS and its parent table to issue this command.

ALTERing a table to create or drop a primary key or a foreign key marks all plans which reference that table as invalid and you must then rebind those plans.

4

Data Manipulation Language

The second type of language in SQL is the Data Manipulation Language (DML) which contains the commands of SELECT, INSERT, UPDATE, and DELETE. While the DDL commands of the last chapter dealt with the structure of the DB2 entities, DML commands deal with the data that goes into DB2 tables. Using DML, you can retrieve data using SELECT, add data using INSERT, change data using UPDATE, and destroy data using DELETE.

The SELECT Statement

SELECT serves as a read command accessing data in the database, placing it in a buffer area, and displaying it on the screen. The general form of SELECT is:

```
SELECT list
 FROM  table name
  WHERE selection criteria
   GROUP BY  column name(s)
    HAVING argument
     UNION
      ORDER BY column name(s)
```

A simple SELECT to read all the rows and columns of the table BUILDING is:

```
SELECT *
    FROM BUILDING
```

Here, the symbol * serves as a wildcard listing all the columns and displaying them in the order they exist in the DB2 catalog. Because you did not restrict the number of rows (with a WHERE clause), all rows in table BUILDING display on the screen. Note that the table name is not a fully qualified name. By not using the fully qualified name, you either created the table yourself, or you have a view of another table where BUILDING is the view name and you were given authorization to access it. If BUILDING is a view name, SELECT only accesses the columns and rows authorized by the view.

To access $ETRT's table DEPRECIATE, you use:

```
SELECT *
       FROM $ETRT.DEPRECIATE
```

or you could create a synonym for the table with:

```
CREATE SYNONYM MYDEPRECIATE
       FOR $ETRT.DEPRECIATE
```

and then use:

```
SELECT *
       FROM MYDEPRECIATE
```

You might not want to display all the columns from the table, and you probably do not want them in the order in which they were originally created or later altered. You can selectively choose what columns and the order in which they are listed by placing the column names in SELECT. The order in which you list the column names in SELECT determines the order in which they display. For example, to display data in columns LASTNAME, FIRSTNAME, CITY, STATE, and ZIP from table ADDRESSES you would use:

```
SELECT LASTNAME, FIRSTNAME, CITY, STATE, ZIP
       FROM ADDRESSES
```

This query produces the following results in the SPUFI option:

LASTNAME	FIRSTNAME	CITY	STATE	ZIP
WASHINGTON	GEORGE	COLUMBUS	OH	13211
JEFFERSON	TOM	CHICAGO	IL	20001
ADAMS	SAMUEL	CINCINATTI	OH	43000
FRANKLIN	BEN	CHICAGO	IL	20011
LINCOLN	ABE	COLUMBUS	OH	13212
KENNEDY	JOHN	SPRINGFIELD	IL	22010
WASHINGTON	MARTHA	CINCINATTI	OH	43211

In SELECT, use commas to separate the items in the list and use one or more spaces between words. Here, DB2 extracts the data from the tablespace in the order in which it was stored, places it in a buffer, and displays the results on the screen. You enter the query in the SPUFI screen of DB2I or in the QUERY screen of QMF. In SPUFI, you cannot access the buffer area nor can you format the data in it. However, in QMF, you can format the data, save it, and generate reports as needed.

The WHERE and ORDER BY Clauses

Use WHERE to restrict the number of rows which DB2 accesses in the table. If you only want to display data in the LASTNAME and CITY columns of table ADDRESSES for all the cities in Ohio, you would use:

```
SELECT LASTNAME, CITY
       FROM ADDRESSES
       WHERE STATE = 'OH'
```

producing the following:

```
LASTNAME        CITY

WASHINGTON      COLUMBUS
ADAMS           CINCINATTI
LINCOLN         COLUMBUS
WASHINGTON      CINCINATTI
```

Note that you do not have to display the column STATE. When you want to rearrange the columns in the display, you simply rearrange the columns in SELECT.

Sort the results of the query by modifying the query to include ORDER BY. ORDER BY sorts the results in a buffer and displays it either in ascending order (the default), or in descending order if you add DESC to the statement. The query:

```
SELECT LASTNAME, CITY
       FROM ADDRESSES
          WHERE STATE = 'OH'
          ORDER BY CITY
```

sorts the data in column CITY and produces the following results:

```
LASTNAME              CITY

ADAMS                 CINCINATTI
WASHINGTON            CINCINATTI
WASHINGTON            COLUMBUS
LINCOLN               COLUMBUS
```

To sort CITY in descending order, change ORDER BY CITY to:

```
ORDER BY CITY DESC
```

Note that unlike WHERE, the columns appearing in ORDER BY must also appear in the list of columns SELECTed. That is, the statement:

```
SELECT LASTNAME, CITY
      FROM ADDRESSES
         WHERE STATE = 'OH'
         ORDER BY STATE
```

generates an error message and the query fails.

The columns you use in WHERE and ORDER BY should have indexes. Without an index on the columns, DB2 locks the tablespace containing the table and scans the entire tablespace systematically searching for the rows. By creating an index beforehand, DB2 uses the index to locate the page containing the data, locks only the page, and copies the row into the buffer area for display to the screen. Note that tablespace locks prohibit anyone from accessing any table in the entire tablespace, whether or not that table is part of the query. A page is a 4K section of the tablespace and contains the rows of a table.

For queries with ORDER BY, DB2 sorts the contents of the buffer area before displaying the data. Because this buffer is a memory area, the sorting routine uses a memory sort which is sometimes very slow. Therefore, use ORDER BY only on queries accessing fewer than 500 to 1000 rows. Before doing larger sorts, perform a utility sort, COBOL sort, or some other routine to presort the data. Without a sort in a query, the data appears in the order DB2 accesses it, producing unpredictable sequencing.

You can generate a subsort on a sort by listing multiple columns in ORDER BY. For example, to sort all the cities by state for table ADDRESSES you would:

```
SELECT LASTNAME, FIRSTNAME, CITY, STATE, ZIP
       FROM ADDRESSES
       ORDER BY STATE DESC, CITY
```

which produces the following:

```
LASTNAME      FIRSTNAME   CITY          STATE   ZIP

ADAMS         SAMUEL      CINCINATTI    OH      43000
WASHINGTON    MARTHA      CINCINATTI    OH      43211
WASHINGTON    GEORGE      COLUMBUS      OH      13211
LINCOLN       ABE         COLUMBUS      OH      13212
FRANKLIN      BEN         CHICAGO       IL      20011
JEFFERSON     TOM         CHICAGO       IL      20001
KENNEDY       JOHN        SPRINGFIELD   IL      22010
```

Now you have states sorted in descending order and cities in each state sorted in ascending order. The DESC clause causes the sort on the field it follows to be in descending order; ascending order is the default.

The available operators for comparisons in WHERE are given in TABLE 4-1. Other operator keywords you can use include AND, OR, and NOT.

Sample queries using different comparison operators and keywords include:

```
SELECT LASTNAME, FIRSTNAME, CITY
       FROM ADDRESSES
       WHERE STATE NOT = 'NY'

SELECT LASTNAME, FIRSTNAME, CITY
       FROM ADDRESSES
       WHERE STATE = 'OH' AND AGE > 50
```

```
SELECT LASTNAME, FIRSTNAME, CITY
      FROM ADDRESSES
      WHERE STATE = 'OH' OR AGE > 50

SELECT LASTNAME, FIRSTNAME, CITY
      FROM ADDRESSES
      WHERE (STATE = 'OH' OR AGE > 50) AND SEX = 'F'
```

Table 4-1. Valid WHERE operators.

Type of comparison	Operator	Type of comparison	Operator
equal	=	not equal	NOT =
greater than	>	not greater than	NOT >
less than	<	not less than	NOT <
less than or equal to	< =		
greater than or equal to	> =		

The first query selects all non-New Yorkers. The second query selects everyone who is over 50 years old from Ohio. The third query selects everyone who either lives in Ohio or is over 50 years old. The last query selects all the females who either live in Ohio or are over 50.

Note that when we mix the keywords AND and OR in the same WHERE clause, we separate them using parentheses using the same convention as COBOL.

Exercises

For the following EQUIPMENT table:

PRODID	PRODNAME	PRODTYPE	INITCOST	VENDOR	NUMBBOUGHT
4211	WRENCH	ST	4.23	KMART	6
5318	TRUCK	HM	15983.22	GM	2
3402	DRILL	LM	4532.99	ARGON	5
7321	PRESS	LT	165.66	DARGO	1
0900	CHAIR	FU	230.00	LITTLES	4
0901	TABLE	FU	500.00	LITTLES	2
0790	PRINTER	CE	650.00	IBM	2
2100	FAN	ET	125.00	KMART	2

4-1. Write the DML statement to read all columns in the table.

4-2. Write the DML statement to list product id, name, and initial cost for all rows in the table

- **a.** From KMART.
- **b.** Whose initial cost is greater than $500.00.
- **c.** With initial cost less than $200.00 from KMART.

4-3. Write the DML statement to list the id, name, and cost of all items in the table with the listing

- **a.** Alphabetized by PRODNAME.
- **b.** Sorted on PRODID in descending order.
- **c.** Sorted on INITCOST with most expensive items listed first.

4-4. Write the DML statement to list the id, name, cost, vendor, and number bought with the following condition:

- **a.** All items are from ARGON, LITTLES, or GM.
- **b.** The items are listed in sorted order by vendor and per vendor by product name.
- **c.** Items are not from LITTLES or GM and each item costs more than $100.00

The Keywords BETWEEN, IN, LIKE, and IS NULL

SELECT has several other keywords you can use to make the query easier to read, write, and understand. Many queries want data with the condition that a certain parameter is between two given values, inclusive. For these type queries, use BETWEEN in the WHERE clause. Its general form is:

```
WHERE parameter BETWEEN a AND b
```

For example, if you want to extract all the product IDs from the EQUIPMENT table in Exercises 4-1 through 4-4 above where the initial cost is between $100.00 and $500.00, you can use either of the following two queries:

```
SELECT PRODID, PRODNAME, INITCOST
    FROM EQUIPMENT
    WHERE INITCOST >=100 AND INITCOST <=500

SELECT PRODID, PRODNAME, INITCOST
    FROM EQUIPMENT
    WHERE INITCOST BETWEEN 100 AND 500
```

Still other queries might want data with the condition that a certain parameter is from a list of values. For these queries, you would use IN in the WHERE clause. Its general form is:

```
WHERE parameter IN (list)
```

Here, "list" is a specific list of values separated by commas, or another query called a *subquery* (see the discussion later in this chapter). For CHAR and VARCHAR parameters, each value in the list must include apostrophes on each side of the value. For example, if you want to extract all the product IDs from the

EQUIPMENT table where the items are from KMART, GM, or IBM, you can use either of the following queries:

```
SELECT PRODID, PRODNAME, INITCOST
   FROM EQUIPMENT
   WHERE VENDOR = 'KMART' OR VENDOR = 'GM' OR VENDOR = 'IBM'

SELECT PRODID, PRODNAME, INITCOST
   FROM EQUIPMENT
   WHERE VENDOR IN ('KMART', 'GM', 'IBM')
```

Note that you can list an item more than once and include items in the list which may or may not be in the column. The query:

```
SELECT PRODID, PRODNAME, INITCOST
   FROM EQUIPMENT
   WHERE VENDOR IN ('KMART', 'GM', 'IBM', 'FORD', 'IBM')
```

is a valid query and, in this case as far as the display appears, equivalent to the above two queries. (Note that the vendor name "FORD" is not in the table.)

The third keyword, LIKE, permits the use of a wildcard in the WHERE clause search criteria. Its general form is:

```
WHERE parameter LIKE 'name_'
```

or

```
WHERE parameter LIKE 'name%'
```

Here the underscore symbol is a wildcard for any one character, the percent symbol is a wildcard for 0 to 254 characters, and "name" is any character string. You can only perform LIKE searches on CHAR and VARCHAR columns. TABLE 4-2 contains sample search arguments using LIKE and their meaning.

Table 4-2. Sample search arguments using LIKE.

Search Argument	Extraction Criteria Meaning Search for:
WHERE NAME LIKE 'CA_'	Any three-character value beginning with the letters CA (e.g., CAT, CAD, CAG).
WHERE NAME LIKE '_O_	Any three-character value with the letter O in the middle (e.g., DOG, GOG, HOH).
WHERE NAME LIKE 'CA%'	Any two-or-more character value where the first two characters are CA (e.g., CA, CAT, CARPOOL).
WHERE NAME LIKE '%OO%'	Any two-or-more character value where the characters OO appear anywhere in the column (e.g., OO, MOON, SWOON, TOO).

These two examples illustrates the use of LIKE in WHERE.

First, a sample query listing all rows in the EQUIPMENT table where the product name is two characters long beginning with the letter S is given by:

```
SELECT PRODID, PRODNAME, INITCOST
    FROM EQUIPMENT
    WHERE PRODNAME LIKE ('S_')
```

The query listing all the rows in the same table where the vendor's name can be any length but must begin with the letters AR is given by:

```
SELECT PRODID, PRODNAME, INITCOST
    FROM EQUIPMENT
    WHERE VENDOR LIKE ('AR%')
```

To check for nulls in a column, use the fourth keyword IS NULL. Its general form is

```
WHERE parameter IS NULL
```

Note that the syntax demands that you use the phrase "IS NULL." A WHERE clause containing the phrase "=NULL" as in:

```
WHERE LASTNAME = NULL
```

is a common mistake and it generates an error message, causing the query to fail.

A check for a null character in a column might be necessary on columns that can contain nulls. Typical usage of nulls is in data for phone number or zip codes because people either forget information or are reluctant to provide it. To check if a column name in a table contains null values, you would enter the query:

```
SELECT * FROM tablename
WHERE columnname IS NULL
```

After observing the results, you can eliminate the null values by updating the row and column or by including IS NOT NULL as part of the query selection criteria. That is, before you issue the query:

```
SELECT LASTNAME, FIRSTNAME, CITY
       FROM ADDRESSES
       WHERE STATE = 'OH'
```

and make management decisions on the results, you would enter the query:

```
SELECT LASTNAME, FIRSTNAME, CITY
       FROM ADDRESSES
       WHERE STATE IS NULL
```

to identify all the rows that have STATE as nulls. If any rows are found, you should immediately modify the row by inserting a value for the null character—there might be "OH" rows improperly entered as nulls. Generally, when making queries on a table, rows containing nulls are:

- Data entry mistakes generated by hitting the Return key too quickly during data entry.
- Rows that need to be updated due to some data capturing problems.
- Column values that have not been entered due to the addition of the column to the table using ALTER.
- Created deliberately to exclude the value from the results.

In most cases, before end-users start querying the database, null values in columns and rows should be resolved. Valuable data can be lost due to DB2 queries ignoring null values and thereby generative erroneous results. You must be careful in dealing with nulls because DB2 even allows the loading of one null value in a column defined with a UNIQUE INDEX.

Obviously, you can use NOT with any of the above mentioned keywords. Such statements as:

```
SELECT PRODID, PRODNAME, INITCOST
    FROM EQUIPMENT
    WHERE INITCOST NOT BETWEEN 100 and 500

SELECT PRODID, PRODNAME, INITCOST
    FROM EQUIPMENT
    WHERE VENDOR NOT IN ('KMART', 'GM', 'IBM')

SELECT PRODID, PRODNAME, INITCOST
    FROM EQUIPMENT
    WHERE PRODNAME NOT LIKE ('S_', 'L_')

SELECT PRODID, PRODNAME, INITCOST
    FROM EQUIPMENT
    WHERE PRODNAME IS NOT NULL
```

are valid queries.

Note that you are not restricted to using just a single keyword in a query. Here is an example of a query containing multiple keywords:

```
SELECT LASTNAME, FIRSTNAME, CITY, STATE, ZIP
      FROM ADDRESSES
      WHERE ZIP LIKE '00___' AND
            CITY NOT IN ('NEW YORK', 'BUFFALO') AND
            STATE IS NOT NULL
```

Here you will find rows where the zip codes begin with the two characters "00," that are not in NEW YORK city or BUFFALO, and where STATE contains no null values.

We use LIKE for zip code since ZIP is a CHAR(5) column. Remember, unless you plan to perform arithmetic operations on a column, it should be defined as CHAR or VARCHAR.

Exercises

The following exercises use the EQUIPMENT table found preceding Exercise 4-1.

4-5. Write the DML statement to list the id, name, cost, vendor, and number bought with the following condition:

a. All items are from ARGON, LITTLES, or GM.
b. Only product IDs beginning with 42 are listed.
c. Only cost of between $50 and $350 are listed.

4-6. Write the DML statement to list the id, name, cost, vendor, and number bought with the following condition:

a. The items are not from vendors IBM, FORD, or GM.
b. Only product types ending with M or K are listed.
c. Items listed include only those where 2, 3 or 4 were bought.

4-7. Redo Exercise 4-5 but display the results in ascending order by vendor name and for items from the same vendor, by product name in descending order.

4-8. Suppose you do not want null values in the results of your queries in Exercises 4-5 and 4-6. What must you do?

Arithmetic Operations in Queries

Column names in SELECT can be:

- Column names as defined in the DB2 catalog.
- Column synonyms created by a VIEW.
- One or more column names separated by the arithmetic operations of +, –, *, and /, with or without constants.
- A summary function (discussed later in this chapter).

The SQL statement

```
SELECT PRODID, PRODNAME, (INITCOST+5.00)*NUMBBOUGHT
    FROM EQUIPMENT
    WHERE VENDOR IN ('LITTLES', 'IBM')
```

displays the product ID, its name, and the total cost of the purchase including shipping charges of $5.00 per item for items purchased from LITTLES or IBM. The results look like

```
PRODID      PRODNAME

0900        CHAIR          942
0901        TABLE         1010
0790        PRINTER       1310
```

Here DB2 only displays two column headings using the column names as they are defined in the DB2 catalog. Note that DB2 does not generate a column heading for columns containing an arithmetic operation.

Obviously, you have a problem if you want to sort the data in a column that contains an arithmetic operation. Because the column does not have a name, you have to put something in the ORDER BY option. The solution is to use the relative location of the column in ORDER BY. That is, to sort in descending order the data in the third column in the above display you would use:

```
SELECT PRODID, PRODNAME, (INITCOST+5.00)*NUMBBOUGHT
   FROM EQUIPMENT
   WHERE VENDOR IN ('LITTLES', 'IBM')
   ORDER BY 3 DESC
```

This query produces the display

```
PRODID      PRODNAME

0790        PRINTER       1310
0901        TABLE         1010
0900        CHAIR          942
```

Here DB2 extracts the data from the database, places it in a buffer, sorts the buffer, and displays the results on the screen. If you want a heading over the third column, you would have to enter the statement in QMF instead of DB2I's SPUFI screen. Remember, programmers and other technicians typically write SQL statements in the SPUFI screen while end-users typically write statements in QMF. Generally, in SPUFI you are only testing the DML statement for syntax errors and accuracy so you can later embed it in code. Consequently, because there is no facility to format the results, SPUFI only displays raw unformatted data. For sophisticated displays or printed reports, end-users enter DML statements in QMF's QUERY screen so they can format the results in QMF's FORMS screen.

You can use parentheses in arithmetic expressions to separate multiple operations. In fact, the rules for using parentheses in SQL are the same rules for using them in COBOL, Fortran, or other higher level languages.

You can also use arithmetic operations in WHERE and HAVING to select rows based on a calculated result. An example of an arithmetic operation in WHERE is:

```
SELECT PRODID, (INITCOST+20.00)/(YRSDEP-1)
   FROM EQUIPMENT
   WHERE NUMBBOUGHT*100 < INITCOST + 50.00
```

Summary Functions

SQL has several built-in functions to aid in summarizing results. These functions, called *summary functions,* include MAX, MIN, SUM, AVG, COUNT (DISTINCT), and COUNT (*). TABLE 4-3 lists each function and its meaning.

Summary functions return a single value and summarize data in a column. TABLE 4-4 gives examples for each of the summary functions using columns in the EQUIPMENT table.

The output generated by using a summary function in SELECT might look rather strange at times. Remember, in DB2I's SPUFI screen, the data is not formattable. Hence, when you use AVG, SQL returns the single value as a number sometimes with eight digits to the right of the decimal (i.e., 129.00933833, 30.09333333). Also, the data type of the result will be the same as the data

Table 4-3. Summary functions and their meaning.

Summary function	Meaning
`MAX(column name)`	Finds largest value in a column.
`MIN(column name)`	Finds smallest value in a column.
`SUM(column name)`	Finds the sum of all the values in a column.
`AVG(column name)`	Finds the average of all the values in a column.
`COUNT(DISTINCT column name)`	Counts the number of different values in a column.
`COUNT(*)`	Counts the number of rows in the result.

Table 4-4. Examples of summary function usage and their results.

Find the total number of rows.

```
SELECT COUNT(*)
FROM EQUIPMENT
```

Sample result:

```
1238
```

Find the total number of different vendors.

```
SELECT COUNT(DISTINCT VENDOR)
FROM EQUIPMENT
```

Sample result:

```
139
```

Find the average size and cost of an order from IBM.

```
SELECT AVG(NUMBBOUGHT), AVG(INITCOST)
FROM EQUIPMENT
WHERE VENDOR = 'IBM'
```

Sample result:

```
8 129.00933833
```

Find the cost of the most expensive item.

```
SELECT MAX(INITCOST)
FROM EQUIPMENT
```

Sample result:

```
15983.22
```

Find the cost of the least expensive item not from KMART.

```
SELECT MIN(INITCOST)
FROM EQUIPMENT
WHERE VENDOR NOT = 'KMART'
```

Sample result:

```
1.09
```

Table 4-4 cont.

Find the total number of items bought from DARGO, ARGON, or GM costing over $1000.00.

```
SELECT SUM(NUMBBOUGHT)
FROM EQUIPMENT
WHERE VENDOR IN ('DARGO', 'ARGON', 'GM') AND
      INITCOST > 1000.00
```

Sample result:

```
B2
```

Find the number of different product types, different vendors, and the average cost of an item in stock.

```
SELECT COUNT(DISTINCT PRODTYPE),COUNT
(DISTINCT VENDOR),
   AVG(INITCOST)
FROM EQUIPMENT
```

Sample result:

```
17 92 30.09333333
```

---

type of the column. That is, if the column is defined as SMALLINT, the value for AVG will be an integer between −32768 and 32767 with truncation occurring, if necessary.

For the function SUM, the actual sum of the column cannot go beyond the limits of the data type (−32768 or +32767 for SMALLINT, and −2,147,483,648 or +2,147,483,647 for INTEGER).

Before you use summary functions indiscriminately, you must first look at some problems they create, especially if null values exist in the rows. For COUNT(*), DB2 includes all rows it accesses via the WHERE clause, even rows with nulls. However, for COUNT (DISTINCT column name), DB2 considers all the null values in the column as the same value and counts them as one item.

The summary function AVG excludes all null values from the computation. Hence the computation:

$$\text{average} = \frac{\text{sum of the items in a column}}{\text{count of the items in a column}} = \frac{\text{SUM(column name)}}{\text{COUNT }(*)}$$

might not equal the value given by AVG. Because COUNT(*) includes rows with nulls and AVG averages the data excluding nulls, possible discrepancies can occur if null values exist in the summarizing column.

Note that summary functions do not generate column headings in the SPUFI screen. Also, each column must contain numbers (SMALLINT, INTEGER, FLOAT, DECIMAL) for the summarization of AVG, SUM, MAX, and MIN to perform properly.

The GROUP BY Option

Another way to summarize data is to use the summary functions on groups of identical data with a column. Such summarizations as finding the average sales by department, total sales by product type, average salary per job classification, average salary in each department, total purchases per vendor supplier, or total sales per customer require the grouping of identical items in one column using the GROUP BY option in SELECT. If you want to list the total number of items purchased by product name in the EQUIPMENT table, you would use:

```
SELECT PRODNAME, SUM(NUMBBOUGHT)
FROM EQUIPMENT
GROUP BY PRODNAME
ORDER BY PRODNAME
```

This query produces the following display:

```
PRODNAME

CHAIR          34
DRILL           8
FAN           123
PRINTER       229
PRESS          32
TABLE         392
TRUCK           2
WRENCH         10
```

Here, DB2 extracts PRODNAME and NUMBBOUGHT data from the TABLE equipment, places it in a buffer, uses a second buffer to find the sum per identical product name, sorts the results, and then displays the answer. All queries on tables are handled through buffer areas, leaving the table intact and unaffected on the database. You can sort the grouping using ORDER BY because GROUP BY only finds the value by groups without sorting the results.

Like ORDER BY, a GROUP BY column must also be a SELECTed column for display. That is, the query:

```
SELECT VENDOR, SUM(INITCOST)
FROM EQUIPMENT
GROUP BY PRODTYPE
```

produces an error and the query fails.

Note that when you use GROUP BY, you can display only summary information, or information that has a single value because only a single line displays per grouping. If you try, for example, to display the PRODIDs for each vendor, you could not use GROUP BY since multiple PRODID for the same vendor cannot physically display in one line.

You can use a combination of GROUP BY and WHERE to restrict the summary information. To find the number of males and females from OHIO in the table ADDRESSES, use:

```
SELECT SEX,COUNT(*)
FROM ADDRESSES
```

```
WHERE STATE = 'OH'
GROUP BY SEX
ORDER BY SEX
```

which gives the display:

```
SEX

FEMALE    3222
MALE      2398
```

Note that you would use COUNT(*) to count the number in each grouping. If you use COUNT(DISTINCT SEX), only the value 2 (for two sexes) would display on each line. Remember. COUNT DISTINCT counts the number of different items in a column while COUNT(*) counts all the items in a column, including nulls. To verify that you do indeed have 3222 females and 2398 males, you can enter the query:

```
SELECT LASTNAME,SEX,CITY,STATE
FROM ADDRESSES
WHERE STATE = 'OH' AND
      SEX IS NULL
```

to list anyone from OHIO with nulls in SEX. However, this problem would not exist if you had created the table ADDRESSES with SEX as NOT NULL which requires data to be entered for sex at load time.

Exercises

Given the following WEEKLYPAYROLL table containing the social security number, last name, first name, sex, department code, pay based on 40-hour week, additional renumeration for overtime, additional renumeration for piece work, and the week ending date:

FICA	LNAME	FNAME	SEX	DEPT	REGPAY	OVERPAY	PIECEPAY	DATE1
23456789	SMITH	JOHN	M	A10	345.00	45.00	12.50	10/06
34567890	JONES	MARY	F	A10	422.00	0.00	0.00	10/06
45678901	DOE	JIM	M	B15	310.00	89.00	0.00	10/06
56789012	ADAMS	KAREN	F	A15	439.00	22.00	44.00	10/06
67890123	LINCOLN	SUSAN	F	B10	676.00	0.00	0.00	10/06
89012345	DAVIS	SAM	M	B15	124.00	20.00	105.00	10/06
90123456	FRANKLIN	TONY	M	B15	345.00	45.00	55.50	10/06
01234567	FORD	SHARON	F	B10	440.00	56.00	0.00	10/06
12345678	JONES	MARK	M	A10	780.00	0.00	0.00	10/06
23456789	SMITH	JOHN	M	A10	345.00	15.00	5.00	10/13
34567890	JONES	MARY	F	A10	422.00	0.00	0.00	10/13
45678901	DOE	JIM	M	B15	310.00	19.00	0.00	10/13
56789012	ADAMS	KAREN	F	A15	439.00	67.00	44.00	10/13
67890123	LINCOLN	SUSAN	F	B10	676.00	0.00	0.00	10/13
89012345	DAVIS	SAM	M	B15	357.00	0.00	65.00	10/13
90123456	FRANKLIN	TONY	M	B15	345.00	0.00	15.50	10/13
01234567	FORD	SHARON	F	B10	440.00	56.00	0.00	10/13
21212121	JOHNSON	BOB	M	A10	330.00	30.50	20.25	10/13

4-9. Write the DML statement to list each employee's last name, first name, and total salary for week ending on 10/06.

4-10. Write the DML statements to find the average amount paid all employees for regular pay, overtime pay, and piecemeal pay for each of the two weeks.

4-11. Write the DML statement to find:

a. The total renumeration paid each employee in week 10/13.
b. The number of employees on the payroll for week ending 10/06.
c. The total number of different employees on the payroll.
d. The total renumeration of each employee for week ending 10/13 if the employees received a 10 percent increase in regular and overtime pay.

4-12. Write the DML statement(s) to find:

a. The average renumeration paid each male each week.
b. The number of female employees on the payroll for week ending 10/06.
c. The average overtime pay for females for each of the two weeks.
d. The maximum regular pay for any male and for any female.

4-13. Write the DML statement to find:

a. The total amount each employee earned for the two weeks.
b. The number of total employees grouped by sex.
c. The total salary outlay for each department per week.
d. The total paid all employees for the two weeks.

The HAVING Option

Because DB2 uses buffers to handle the intermediate steps in GROUP BY, you can further restrict the results by limiting which groups finally display. When you listed all the product names and how many were purchased, you listed all the product names. You could limit the listing to only products with an initial cost greater than $50.00 using

```
SELECT PRODNAME, SUM(NUMBBOUGHT)
FROM EQUIPMENT
WHERE INITCOST > 50.00
GROUP BY PRODNAME
ORDER BY PRODNAME
```

Now when DB2 extracts data from the table, it only uses those items whose initial cost is greater than $50.00, and the same set of groupings display. This query produces the following results:

```
PRODNAME

CHAIR        34
DRILL         8
FAN         123
PRINTER     229
PRESS        32
TABLE       392
TRUCK         2
WRENCH        0
```

But suppose you want to restrict the groupings that finally display. In this case, you might only want to view the groupings where 20 or more items were purchased. Here, you must first group the items and find the sum before you know which groupings to display. The HAVING option restricts what groupings display from GROUP BY. The query

```
SELECT PRODNAME, SUM(NUMBBOUGHT)
FROM EQUIPMENT
WHERE INITCOST > 50.00
GROUP BY PRODNAME
HAVING SUM(NUMBBOUGHT) >= 20
ORDER BY PRODNAME
```

produces the display

```
PRODNAME

CHAIR       34
FAN        123
PRESS       32
PRINTER    229
TABLE      392
```

Remember, HAVING affects the result after the grouping has occurred. To affect what is accessed before you group, place the selection criteria in the WHERE statement.

The UNION Option

On occasion, you might need to combine the rows from one table with rows from another table. The UNION option in SELECT combines multiple tables with the same number of columns and with identical data types in each column. If the column size and type in one table does not exactly match the respective column size and type in the second table, the query fails. You can combine tables EMPLONE and EMPLTWO using:

```
SELECT EMPLOYID, LASTNAME, FIRSTNAME, SALES
    FROM EMPLONE
    WHERE SALES >100.00 AND DEPTNUMB = 'Q111'
 UNION
SELECT EMPLID, LNAME, FNAME, SALES
 FROM EMPLTWO
 WHERE SALES >100.00 AND DEPTNO = 'Q111'
ORDER BY 2
```

Here, the employee ID, last name, first name, and amount of sales for employees in department Q111 having over $100.00 in sales from table EMPLONE combines with similar data from table EMPLTWO with the final result sorted by last name. Although each table has different names for the columns, the respective columns must be the same size and type. Here EMPLOYID and EMPLID, LASTNAME and LNAME, FIRSTNAME and FNAME, and SALES are defined as CHAR (9), VARCHAR (20), VARCHAR (20), and DECIMAL (7,2), respectively.

The INSERT Statement

You use INSERT to load data into tables. INSERT has two formats. The first format identifies both the column names and the data that goes into each column. To load data for the ADDRESSES table, you would use:

```
INSERT INTO ADDRESSES
        (LASTNAME, FIRSTNAME, CITY, STATE, ZIP)
VALUES ('DOE', 'JOHN', 'BOSTON', 'MA', '10222')
```

Note that the data in VALUES align one-to-one with the respective column names. In this example, "DOE" is loaded into LASTNAME, "JOHN" into FIRSTNAME, "BOSTON" into CITY, "MA" into STATE, and "10222" into ZIP. Here, it doesn't matter how the table was physically constructed using CREATE; the data is loaded into the table based on the one-to-one relationship between the names in the list and the data in VALUES. Only columns in the list will contain data; all other columns in the row are set to nulls. Obviously, if a column in the table description is defined as NOT NULL, that column name must appear in the list in INSERT. That is, if you created table ADDRESSES with EMPLOYID set as NOT NULL, the above INSERT statement would fail and an error message will display.

The second format for INSERT identifies the data that goes into each column and uses the predefined structure of the table to identify the column's names. For example,

```
INSERT INTO ADDRESSES
 VALUES ('123456', 'DOE', 'JOHN', 'BOSTON', 'MA', '10222',
 NULL, ' ')
```

aligns the indicated values with their corresponding columns in the ADDRESSES table as defined by CREATE and changed by ALTER. Here, "123456" loads into the first column in the table, "DOE" into the second column, and so on. If a table has 12 columns, for example, you must include 12 items in VALUE, otherwise the INSERT fails. Note that you use NULL to load nulls into a column and ' ' to load a space into a column. Omit the apostrophes if the data you want to insert is numeric data. The statement

```
INSERT INTO PAYROLL
 VALUES ('123456', 'DOE', 'JOHN', 40.00,12.00)
```

loads both alphanumeric and numeric data in table PAYROLL.

You can insert multiple rows into a table by using multiple INSERT statements. The following five INSERTs load five rows into the table ADDRESSES using SPUFI:

```
INSERT INTO ADDRESSES
 VALUES ('123456', 'DOE', 'JOHN', 'BOSTON', 'MA', '10222',
 NULL, ' ');
INSERT INTO ADDRESSES
 VALUES ('234567', 'SMITH', 'SUE', 'DENVER', 'CO', '32177',
 'F', ' ');
INSERT INTO ADDRESSES
```

```
VALUES ('345678', 'JONES', 'BOB', 'PEORIA', 'IL', '54366',
'M', '');
INSERT INTO ADDRESSES
VALUES ('456789', 'DOE', 'MARY', 'BOSTON', 'MA', '10222',
'F', '');
INSERT INTO ADDRESSES
VALUES ('567890', 'ACRE', 'TIM', 'DALTON', 'IN', '76666',
NULL, '')
```

If the table has a unique index on a column and you attempt to insert a duplicate value into the table, the insert fails.

Another way to load multiple rows into a table is to use a SELECT as part of the INSERT statement. In many cases, you must merge a series of daily transactions into a weekly transaction table. To accomplish this type merger, you would use the following general form of INSERT:

```
INSERT INTO tablename
  SELECT list FROM tablename
```

For example, to accumulate the daily transactions for an address table into the weekly address table WEEK05, you would:

```
INSERT INTO WEEK05
  SELECT * FROM ADDRESSMON;
INSERT INTO WEEK05
  SELECT * FROM ADDRESSTUES;
INSERT INTO WEEK05
  SELECT * FROM ADDRESSWED;
INSERT INTO WEEK05
  SELECT * FROM ADDRESSTHUR;
INSERT INTO WEEK05
  SELECT * FROM ADDRESSFRI
```

Because WEEK05 is a combination of each of the daily tables, you can perform the necessary queries on WEEK05 to produce weekly reports and have the daily transaction tables still intact.

Another advantage of using SELECT in INSERT is to create a smaller table for a user from a larger main table. Suppose Department "M122" wants a copy of the preceding day's sales results for each salesman in the department. Rather than use the main table MAINSALES which contains data on all departments, you can create a smaller table using:

```
INSERT INTO TEMPSALES
  SELECT * FROM MAINSALES
   WHERE DEPTNUMB = 'M122'
```

This INSERT statement extracts only information about department M122 and places it in TEMPSALES. Obviously, when you created TEMPSALES using DDL commands, it had to have the same definitions for the column as the table MAINSALES. Now the user department can make inquires on TEMPSALES without affecting any data on the main table MAINSALES.

If data already exists in the table, INSERT loads new data into the table placing it in the first available space in the tablespace containing the table. To prevent duplicate data from entering the table, you must place unique indexes on a column or columns. With a unique index on a column, all duplicate values fail to load.

If the table is a view and the view does not contain all the columns created as NOT NULL, then all INSERTs on that view will fail. Obviously, if the user does not have a view of a column that requires data at INSERT time, the user cannot load that row into the table. Hence, you must be careful in establishing views for users. If you create a table containing NOT NULL as a clause in CREATE TABLE, all users who want to INSERT rows into that view must have a view of all NOT NULLed columns.

The DELETE Statement

Obviously, if the user department wants only the previous day's data in the table, all older data must be erased before you INSERT the desired data into the table. DELETE erases one or more rows of data in tables. Unlike the DROP command in DDL, DELETE keeps the structure of the table intact and erases only the data. The general form of DELETE is:

```
DELETE FROM tablename
  criteria
```

To delete all the rows in a table, you use:

```
DELETE FROM tablename
```

For example, if user department M122 wants to use a temporary table to hold data, they would use

```
DELETE FROM TEMPSALES;

INSERT INTO TEMPSALES
       SELECT * FROM MAINSALES
           WHERE DEPTNUMB = 'M122'
```

Here, all data that was in TEMPSALES is erased before new data is loaded into it.

You must be careful in deleting data because:

```
DELETE FROM MAINSALES
```

erases all data in table MAINSALES. In the next chapter, we discuss how to selectively give users the power to delete data because you might not want all users to have the capability of destroying all the data in a table.

You can delete individual rows from a table by using WHERE in DELETE. That is, to delete all rows in table ADDRESSES having zip codes starting with 122, you use:

```
DELETE FROM ADDRESSES
   WHERE ZIP LIKE '122__'
```

Note that all the options and criteria for WHERE from the SELECT statement are also valid for the DELETE statement. That is, the statement:

```
DELETE FROM ADDRESSES
  WHERE (ZIP LIKE '122__' AND LASTNAME IN ('JONES',
  'ADAMS'))
        OR PHONE IS NULL
```

is a valid statement.

The UPDATE Statement

The UPDATE statement changes values in tables. Its general form is:

```
UPDATE tablename
SET column name = value,
    column name = value,
    column name = value,
    .
    .
    .
    WHERE criteria
```

Note that you can modify either a single column or multiple columns and either a single row or multiple rows within the table. To modify the city, state, and zip code for employee 123456 in the ADDRESSES table, you would use:

```
UPDATE ADDRESSES
SET CITY  = 'CHICAGO',
    STATE = 'IL',
    ZIP   = '13093'
WHERE EMPLOYID = '123456'
```

Here you must be careful of the synatx. Each statement in SET ends with a comma, except for the last statement. Statements to the right of the equal sign can be any valid statement. Hence, then you can double an employee's salary by using:

```
UPDATE PAYROLL
SET SALARY = SALARY * 2
WHERE EMPLOYID = '123456'
```

You can modify multiple rows by changing the criteria in WHERE. If Boston, for example, annexed several areas having zip codes 18902, 18903, and 18904, you can change those area's city names to Boston using:

```
UPDATE ADDRESSES
SET CITY = 'BOSTON'
WHERE ZIP IN ('18902', '18903', '18904')
```

Note that you use UPDATE to change or modify existing row values and INSERT to load initial values. Typically, you load data into tables using INSERT, review the data using SELECT, and change incorrect data using UPDATE. You modify only one row by providing a unique criteria in WHERE to access it. In most cases, the column will have a unique index and you use that column in WHERE.

Restrictions on INSERT, DELETE, and UPDATE

Most users will have a view of a table rather than having access to the entire table. Hence, there are some restrictions on using INSERT, DELETE, and UPDATE on these views. Because most views are conceptual, there may not be an actual table containing the rows and columns as seen by the user of the view. This is particularly true if you create a view using:

- A summary function
- A computed column
- A join
- A GROUP BY clause

On the views shown below, you cannot insert, update, or delete data from the view tables because they are conceptual in nature and do not exist as a unit anywhere in a tablespace:

- View table created with computed column.
- View table created with summary function.
- View table created by a join.
- View table created with a GROUP BY clause.

Referential integrity requirements might also impose restrictions on table inserts, deletes, or updates. For parent tables, you cannot update primary key columns for rows that have dependents that refer to them. You also cannot update primary key columns for more than one row at a time, so you must code a WHERE clause in your UPDATE statement that is satisfied by only one row in the table. (The easiest way to do this will probably be to reference the primary key in the WHERE clause.) Finally, you cannot delete a row with dependents if you coded ON DELETE RESTRICT for any dependent tables.

For dependent tables, you cannot insert rows unless they either have foreign key values which match those of some row of their parent or are NULL. Of course, if you created the dependent table with the NOT NULL clause for foreign keys, then you cannot even insert rows with NULL foreign keys. You also cannot update a dependent table's foreign keys unless you either set them to values which match those of some row of their parent or set them to NULL. Again, you might not be able to use NULL values.

Exercises

Given the WEEKLYPAYROLL table for Exercises 4-9 through 4-13:

4-14. Write the DML statement to find:

a. The average regular salary for each department for the week of 10/06. List only those departments having 3 or more employees.

b. The average overtime pay for each department for the week of 10/13. List only those departments with less than 3 employees.

4-15. Write the DML statement to insert the following rows in the WEEKLY-PAYROLL table:

CA	LNAME	FNAME	SEX	DEPT	REGPAY	OVERPAY	PIECEPAY	DATE
2121212	Lincoln	Abe	M	B15	500.00	50.00	0.00	10/13
3131311	Adams	John	M	B15	400.00	0.00	30.00	10/13

4-16. Write the DML statement to delete all males with regular pay less than 400.00 and no piecework pay in any week.

4-17. Susan Lincoln married George Washington and wants her employment record to reflect her new name, Susan Washington. Write the DML statement to modify all rows containing her old name.

4-18. The vice-president of corporate research wants a table called RESEARCH containing data on all employees who worked for the company the week of 10/06. This table should be in tablespace "USERBOSS," which is in database "USERBASE." Write the DDL and/or the DML commands to create the table and extract the desired data from WEEKLYPAYROLL.

5

Control Language and Security

Everything within the DB2 product is protected by the DB2 software system and users must be given authorization to use not only the product itself but its individual features. That is, if a user has not been granted authorization to use an item in DB2, that user is denied use of that item. This authorization to use DB2 items is granted either explicitly or implicitly. Some of the resources you need authorization for include the following:

- Using the DB2 menus (e.g., SPUFI)
- Creating and using databases, tablespaces, tables
- Using the SQL commands (SELECT, INSERT, GRANT, etc.)
- Using the utilities
- Using the commands
- Generating a PLAN and doing a BIND
- Executing load modules needing a PLAN

TABLE 5-1 contains a list of all the items protected in DB2.

Table 5-1. Protected items in DB2.

STORAGE GROUP	VIEW	BIND	CATALOG
DATABASE	INDEX	EXECUTE	UTILITIES
TABLESPACE	GRANT	BUFFER POOL	COMMANDS
TABLE			

Obviously, the first step in using DB2 is accessing it through TSO, IMS, or CICS. A user must logon to one of these three subsystems before accessing DB2. Because these subsystems might be configured to require each user to have a unique authorization ID, the subsystem logon process provides the first level of security for DB2. The second level of protection requires each user in these subsystems to have additional authorization to use DB2 and the items within it.

The three sources for receiving authorization in DB2 are through an administrative level, through the Control Language command of GRANT, and by creating an object.

Authorization through Administrative Levels

The five administrative levels in DB2—SYSADM, DBADM, DBCTRL, DBMAINT, and SYSOPR—form a hierarchy of control as illustrated in FIG. 5-1. Each level automatically possesses certain individual authorities as shown in FIG. 5-2. These individual authorities can then be GRANTed to other individuals as the need arises.

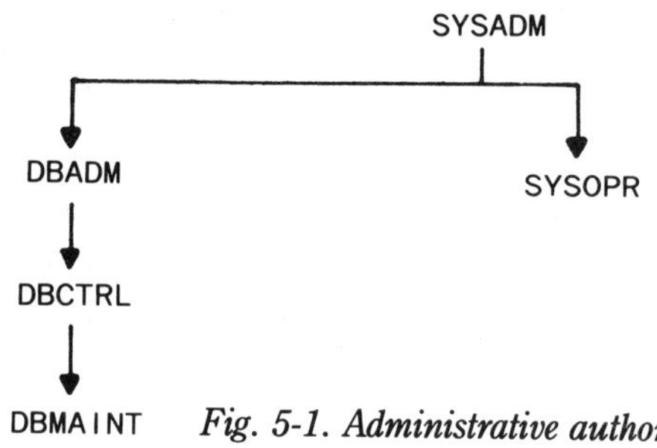

Fig. 5-1. Administrative authorities.

System Administrator (SYSADM)

When an organization first installs DB2 onto their system, whoever installs the product creates an installer SYSADM account.

This account has control over all the DB2 resources and is used to install the product on various DASD devices. The installer SYSADM then creates one or more other SYSADM accounts to manage and supervise future usage of DB2. This System Administrator (SYSADM) then creates Database Administrators (DBADMs) to manage and supervise the individual databases on DB2. SYSADM also creates SYSOPR who issues the system operations commands of TRACE, RECOVER, DISPLAY, STOPALL, and IMAGCOPY.

After DB2 is installed, it is managed by the System Administrator who is either one person or a group of people. The SYSADM is specially trained in DB2 and has the following main functions:

- *Coordination of users*. The SYSADM coordinates the users of the databases by creating one or more DBADMs for each database defined on the system. In fact, a user cannot use DB2 unless the user is given DBADM authorization or assigned to an already existing DBADM.

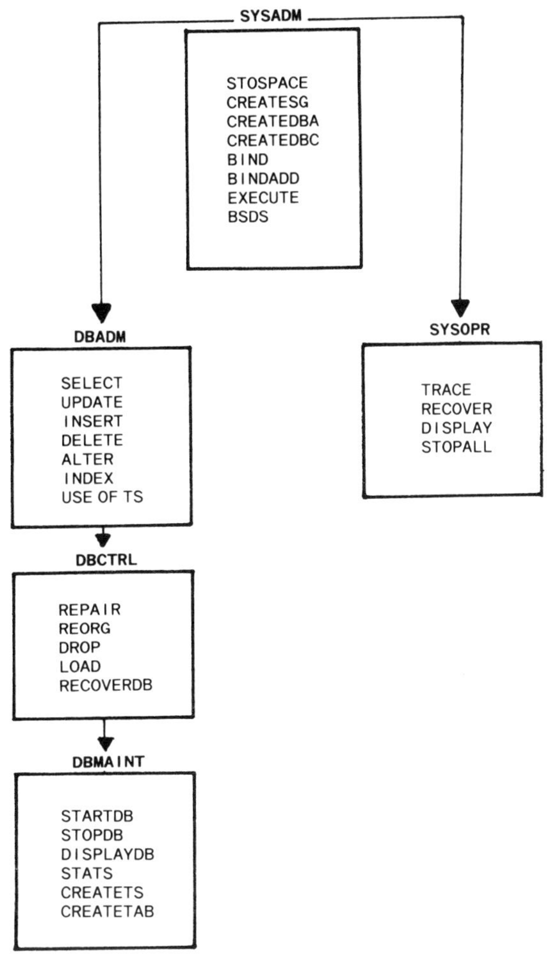

Fig. 5-2. Individual authorities for SYSADM, DBADM, DBCTRL, DBMAINT, and SYSOPR.

- *Monitoring performance.* The SYSADM continually monitors the performance of the database. When problems develop with the DB2 software package, it is the responsibility of the SYSADM to fix them. When necessary, the SYSADM consults with the systems team and IBM's DB2 technical support team for problem resolution.
- *Designing standards.* The SYSADM designs standards and procedures for the use of the databases in DB2. The SYSADM distributes and enforces standards and procedures relating to DB2.
- *Providing backup and recovery.* The SYSADM is responsible for providing controls and procedures for the systematic backup of the databases in DB2.

- *Control over all DB2 resources*. The SYSADM controls who has access to DB2's resources by issuing GRANTS and creating various administrative levels within DB2. In particular, the SYSADM creates the storage group for the database and a database name in that storage group and then creates a DBADM for that database. Typically, SYSADM controls the DB2 product and leaves the day-to-day managing of the databases to the DBADMs.

Database Administrator (DBADM)

The DBADM has authority for a particular database. A user responsible for multiple databases must be granted DBADM authority for each database. The SYSADM creates a DBADM using the following statement:

```
GRANT DBADM
ON DATABASE database name
TO username
```

Here, "username" is any user ID and "database name" is an eight-character database name. For example, for user $TONY to be the DBADM for the database PAYROLL, SYSADM issues the following:

```
GRANT DBADM
ON DATABASE PAYROLL
TO $TONY
```

Once a user is a DBADM, he or she can then create tablespaces, tables, and other items in DB2. Figure 5-2 contains a brief list of some of a DBADM's authorizations. Note that a DBADM also has authorization for DBCTRL and DBMAINT.

Once the SYSADM creates the database name and one or more DBADMs for that database, DBADM uses DDL to CREATE one or more tablespaces to hold the user department's tables. After creating the tablespace, the DBADM then GRANTs authorization to access the tablespace to each individual user.

Each DBADM has his or her own database to manage and control. Some DBADMs might want to control the entire table creation process by creating all tables and then GRANT the users authorization to use specific commands on specific tables and views. Other DBADMs might want to make the programming staff responsible for table creation. In this case, the DBADM GRANTs them the authorization of CREATETAB. If a user wants to create tables, those users must also be given CREATETAB authorization. Because tables reside in tablespaces and because tablespaces are a protected item, each user who creates tables must also be GRANTed privilege to use the tablespace that holds the table. For example, the following two commands authorize users $TONY and $MARY the privilege of using tablespace EPTFTS1 and creating tables on the database PAYROLL:

```
GRANT USE OF TABLESPACE EPTFTS1
TO $TONY, $MARY
```

```
GRANT CREATETAB
ON DATABASE PAYROLL
TO $TONY, $MARY
```

Note that the SYSADM usually creates the database and one or more DBADMs to manage it.

DBCTRL, DBMAINT, and SYSOPR

Database Control (DBCTRL) has the following authorizations:

- REPAIR—used to repair tablespaces and indexes.
- REORG—used to reorganize tablespaces and indexes.
- DROP—used to drop databases.
- LOAD—used to load tables.
- RECOVERDB—used to recover tablespaces and indexes and modify certain DB2 catalog tables.
- all the authorizations of DBMAINT.

DBCTRL does not access data in tables. He or she simply manages certain objects within DB2. Note that DBCTRL also has the authorizations of DBMAINT which has the following authorizations:

- STOPDB—used to make specific database unavailable for applications.
- STARTDB—used to make the database available after it was stopped.
- DISPLAYDB—used to display the status of a database.
- STATS—used to run the RUNSTATS utility to update statistics on database and its objects.
- CREATETS—used to create tablespaces.
- CREATETAB—used to create tables.

Both DBCTRL and DBMAINT administrative levels manage the day-to-day use of the database. We generally create these two levels whenever the database goes into production mode and the Operations Team needs authorization to manage it.

DBCTRL and DBMAINT are administrative levels for a particular database. While DBCTRL and DBMAINT are created by a DBADM, the SYSADM is the only one that has the power to create SYSOPRs. The System Operator (SYSOPR) has the following authorizations:

- TRACE—used to start or stop a trace in DB2.
- RECOVER—used to recover tablespaces or pages to the current state.
- DISPLAY—used to display the status of a database or to display information about DB2 connections.
- STOPALL—used to stop DB2 subsystem.

The SYSOPR's responsibility is to manage the DB2 system and not a particular database.

The three levels DBCTRL, DBMAINT, and SYSOPR do not have access to the data in the database. To access data in a particular database, they must be specifically granted authorization to use the necessary DML command. Note that the main purpose of these three levels of authorization is to manage and administer the databases rather than actively seek work with the data in them.

Authorization through Control Language

Control Language is part of the security feature for DB2. You can GRANT users access to databases, tablespaces, tables, views and other DB2 objects. GRANT also restricts the user's usage of both the Data Definition Language and the Data Manipulation Language.

GRANT and REVOKE

GRANT gives the user certain privileges while REVOKE takes them away. However, you can revoke only those privileges specifically granted. That is, if SYSADM creates a DBADM, for example, the SYSADM cannot revoke specific authorizations assigned to the administrative level of DBADM. In particular, SYSADM could not revoke DBADM's power to DELETE since that command is an integral part of being a DBADM. Also, if a user creates a table, no one can revoke that user's right to use the table because an owner of a table has inherent rights to a table independent of GRANT and REVOKE.

Table privileges with GRANT authorization. You grant privileges on tables using:

```
GRANT authority
ON tablename
TO username
```

Here, ''authority'' is SELECT, INSERT, DELETE, INDEX, or ALTER; ''tablename'' is one or more simple or fully qualified table names; and ''username'' is one or more user IDs or PUBLIC.

Suppose $EPTF creates tables EMPLOYEE, CLASSES and ROOMS. Some examples of $EPTF granting access to his or her tables include

- Authorizing $MARY and $CHARLES to use SELECT and UPDATE on table EMPLOYEE:

  ```
  GRANT SELECT, UPDATE
  ON EMPLOYEE
  TO $MARY, $CHARLES
  ```

- Authorizing $SOMEONE to use UPDATE on table ROOMS. Also, allow $SOMEONE to pass that privilege on to other users:

  ```
  GRANT UPDATE
  ON ROOMS
  TO $SOMEONE
  WITH GRANT OPTION
  ```

- Authorizing $ROBERT to update only columns LASTNAME and FIRSTNAME in table EMPLOYEE:

```
GRANT UPDATE (LASTNAME, FIRSTNAME)
ON EMPLOYEE
TO $ROBERT
```

- Authorizing anyone to SELECT on table CLASSES:

```
GRANT SELECT
ON CLASSES
TO PUBLIC
```

- Authorizing $KAREN to have all accessing privileges (SELECT, UPDATE, DELETE, INSERT) on table EMPLOYEE:

```
GRANT ALL
ON EMPLOYEE
TO $KAREN
```

WITH GRANT OPTION authorization. Because $SOMEONE has the power of GRANT OPTION in one of the above examples, he or she can grant other users the right to also update table CLASSES. That is, $SOMEONE could issue the following GRANT to allow $BETH to update $EPTF's table CLASSES:

```
GRANT UPDATE
ON $EPTF.CLASSES
TO $BETH
```

In fact, the GRANT OPTION clause can be issued to other users permitting them to authorize still further users to update $EPTF's table CLASSES.

For example, $SOMEONE can pass the authority of GRANT OPTION on $EPTF's table CLASSES for UPDATE by using the statement:

```
GRANT UPDATE
ON $EPTF.CLASSES
TO $BETH
WITH GRANT OPTION
```

Here, $BETH not only has the authority to update $EPTF's table CLASSES, but also has the authority to let other users have that same authority.

Note that you can give any user the authorization to access tables you create, and you can let them pass that authorization on to other users by adding WITH GRANT OPTION to the command of GRANT. However, there are two exceptions to using GRANT OPTION. You cannot use WITH GRANT OPTION in a GRANT for partial column updates. That is, the statement:

```
GRANT UPDATE (LASTNAME, FIRSTNAME)
ON EMPLOYEE
TO $ROBERT
WITH GRANT OPTION
```

generates an error message and GRANT fails. The second exception is that you cannot use WITH GRANT OPTION when you grant TO PUBLIC. For the statement:

```
GRANT SELECT
ON CLASSES
TO PUBLIC
WITH GRANT OPTION
```

the grant is allowed and the system ignores the WITH GRANT OPTION clause.

Note that only the specific authorization originally granted can be passed on to other users. A user with only UPDATE authority has only UPDATE authority and no others. If that user is also given GRANT OPTION authority, he or she can only pass on to other users those items in the GRANT statement containing the GRANT OPTION clause. Suppose, for example, $SOMEONE issues the following two GRANTS:

```
GRANT UPDATE
ON $EPTF.CLASSES
TO $BETH
WITH GRANT OPTION

GRANT DELETE
ON $EPTF.CLASSES
TO $BETH
```

Here, $BETH has the authority to UPDATE and DELETE on the table $EPTF.CLASSES but can only issue GRANTs for UPDATE privilege.

Exercises

5-1. Users $TOM11 and $SUE45 want to access the table PAYABLES in $MARY's account. What command must $MARY issue to give these two users complete access to the table?

5-2. $BILL created the view SUMMARY on table BONDS. He wants users $KAREN, $MIKE, and $ANDY to only see the data in the view but not change it. What command does $BILL issue to accomplish this task?

5-3. User $SALLY wants to create tables in a tablespace. What commands must you issue if $SALLY has never used DB2 before?

5-4. $CRISTY owns the table MEDICAL. She wants the two physicians on her staff, $MARGE and $TRACY, to access only the columns LASTNAME, FIRSTNAME, MEDHISTORY, and DATE_TREATED in the table. Their access includes the right to read the data and change it but not delete it. What command does she issue to accomplish this task?

5-5. $ROBERT has just been promoted to Accounting Manager and does not have current access to DB2. $ROBERT wants to have the power to control who uses the three tables PAYABLES, RECEIVABLES, and CONTROLLERS assigned to his department. What commands do you issue to give $ROBERT this power?

5-6. A company has created a table called VACATIONS containing data on each employee's time used for vacations. What command do you issue to let every employee view data in the table but not change it?

REVOKE authorization. You can REVOKE any GRANTed table privilege using the general form:

```
REVOKE authority
ON tablename
FROM username
```

Some examples include:

```
REVOKE SELECT
ON CLASSES
FROM PUBLIC

REVOKE SELECT, UPDATE
ON EMPLOYEE
FROM $MARY, $CHARLES

REVOKE ALL
ON EMPLOYEE
FROM $TONY, $MIKE

REVOKE UPDATE
ON $EPTF.CLASSES
FROM $BETH
```

Note that when you revoke an UPDATE privilege, it revokes the authorization to update all columns on the table. You cannot REVOKE an UPDATE on only a specific column. That is,

```
REVOKE UPDATE (LASTNAME, CLASSTIME)
ON $EPTF.CLASSES
FROM $BETH
```

generates an error message and the REVOKE fails.

Database privileges. You can grant and revoke privileges on databases using:

```
GRANT authority
 ON DATABASE dbname
 TO username
```

and

```
REVOKE authority
ON DATABASE dbname
FROM username
```

A SYSADM, for example, creates a DBADM for database PAYROLL using:

```
GRANT DBADM
ON DATABASE PAYROLL
TO $EPTF
```

and revokes that authority using:

```
REVOKE DBADM
ON DATABASE PAYROLL
FROM $EPTF
```

A DBADM for database PAYROLL can issue:

```
GRANT CREATETS, CREATETAB
ON DATABASE PAYROLL
TO $STEVE, $CHRISTINE, $MIKE
```

to give $STEVE, $CHRISTINE, and $MIKE the authority to create tablespaces and tables within those tablespaces in database PAYROLL.

Note that if the SYSADM wanted to create a DBADM but not let him or her have the power to create tablespaces (CREATETS), the SYSADM must separately and individually GRANT each and every authorization for DBADM, DBCTRL, and DBMAINT given in FIG. 5-2. That is, if SYSADM issues the statement:

```
GRANT DBADM
ON DATABASE PAYROLL
TO $EPTF
```

and then issued the statement:

```
REVOKE CREATETS
ON DATABASE PAYROLL
FROM $EPTF
```

DB2 generates an error message and the REVOKE fails.

Use of bufferpool, storage group, and tablespace privileges. Although a user has been given authorization to create items in a database, they must also be given the authorization to use bufferpools, storage groups, and tablespace. You can grant and revoke use of these objects using:

```
GRANT USE OF objectname itemname
TO username
```

and

```
REVOKE USE OF objectname itemname
FROM username
```

where "objectname" is the word BUFFERPOOL, STOGROUP, or TABLESPACE. Some examples include:

```
GRANT USE OF STOGROUP EU8001
TO $LARRY
```

```
GRANT USE OF BUFFERPOOL BP2
TO $EPTF

GRANT USE OF TABLESPACE EPTFTS1
TO $MARK

REVOKE USE OF TABLESPACE EPTFTS2
FROM $SARA
```

DBADM and User Authorization Creation

Typically, the SYSADM creates a storage group, a database in the storage group, and a DBADM for the database using the CREATE STOGROUP, the CREATE DATABASE, and the GRANT DBADM ON DATABASE commands, respectively. Next, the SYSADM issues a series of grants which authorizes DBADM to use the storage group and bufferpools assigned by the CREATE DATABASE command. That is, if the SYSADM used:

```
CREATE DATABASE EPTFEDUC
       STOGROUP EU8001
       BUFFERPOOL BP1
```

to create a database, he or she then issues the following GRANTs:

```
GRANT USE OF STOGROUP EU8001
       TO $EPTF

GRANT USE OF BUFFERPOOL BP1
       TO $EPTF.

GRANT DBADM
ON DATABASE EPTFEDUC
TO $EPTF
```

The DBADM then creates tablespaces for his or her account and for any user who needs to create tables. After the tablespaces are created, the DBADM then issues a series of GRANT USE OF TABLESPACE commands to all users who will access the tablespaces. DBADM or the development team then creates tables and views in the tablespaces. Finally, each user is given authorization to use the tables by issuing a series of GRANT commands. For users who want to create their own tables, DBADM issues a GRANT CREATETAB ON DATABASE command for each such user.

Owners of tables privileges. The SYSADM, the DBADM, or the owner of an entity gives explicit authorization to another user by issuing a GRANT to that user. The user also receives implicit authorization by the DB2 system when he or she creates certain entities or performs certain tasks in DB2 (such as creating a table or performing a BIND). For example, when you create a table, you own that table and DB2 assigns you certain inherent privileges while using it. Some of these privileges include the right to:

- SELECT, UPDATE, DELETE, INSERT on the table.
- GRANT and REVOKE the use of these four commands on the table to other users.

- CREATE views and indexes on the table.
- DROP, or ALTER the table.
- LOAD data into the table using the LOAD utility.

These rights and privileges are independent of the SYSADM or DBADM and require no intervention by them.

A creator of a table is the owner of a table and can DROP or ALTER the table whenever he or she wishes. No additional authorization needs to be generated because DROP and ALTER are implicit authorities. The owner of a table can also use the LOAD utility to load data into the table because LOAD is also an implicit authority. However, the owner needs specific authority from SYSADM, DBADM, or DBCTRL to use the LOAD utility on tables he or she does not own.

Creating Tables for Other Uses

Creating tables in your account. Once you create a table, you can create views on the table and GRANT other users the right to use the table or view. Remember, by creating a view or table, you use the table's or view's simple name when you access it in your account. However, other users of your table or view will have to use the fully qualified name of it. To avoid using the fully qualified name, each user of your table could create a synonym in their account for your table or view. Once they create a synonym in their account, they can then use the synonym name instead of the fully qualified name.

Remember also, after you create a table or view, no one can use it unless you grant them authorization to use it. We should be careful in doing this because a user with UPDATE and DELETE authorization on your table can severely damage it or destroy all the data in it. Also, authorized users of your table with INSERT ability can contaminate the data by inserting erroneous or invalid data on it. Before you haphazardly authorize someone to use your table or view, you must adequately document what they are to do and not do to the table or view, and you should adequately train them on using DML commands.

Creating tables in another account. If you have SYSADM, DBADM, or DBCTRL authority, you can create tables in another user's account. The other user becomes the owner of the table and has all the rights and privileges that table owners enjoy. You can create the table in another account by using the other user's account ID in the CREATE TABLE command. For example, the DBADM $EPTF can create a table in $SAM's account by issuing the command:

```
CREATE TABLE $SAM.SAMPLE
(ID          CHAR (5)    NOT NULL,
 LASTNAME    CHAR (20)   NOT NULL,
 FIRSTNAME   CHAR (20),
 ADDRESS     CHAR (20),
 YTDPAYMENT  DECIMAL (8,2))
 IN EDUCBASE.EPTFTS4
```

Here, $SAM becomes the owner of table SAMPLE. Note that DBADM has the authority to see all data in the databases assigned him or her. It does not matter whether DBADM created the table or some other user created the table. If the table exists in the database, DBADM can access it. DBCTRL can also create a table in another user's account. Remember, DBCTRL has no power to manipulate data in tables unless he or she is explicitly GRANTed authorization to do so. Therefore, DBCTRL will not be able to access the data in the other user's account.

Creating Views

$SAM as the owner of the table in the above example can create a view on the table using the following:

```
CREATE VIEW PAYMENTS
AS SELECT ID, LASTNAME, FIRSTNAME, YTDPAYMENT
FROM $SAM.SAMPLE
```

He can then authorize several users to access the view by issuing:

```
GRANT SELECT, UPDATE(LASTNAME, FIRSTNAME, YTDPAYMENT)
  ON TABLE PAYMENTS
  TO $STEVE, $PHIL, $ROBERT
```

$STEVE can then access data in the table by using:

```
SELECT ID, YTDPAYMENT
FROM $SAM.PAYMENTS
```

or by issuing the command:

```
CREATE SYNONYM MYPAY FOR $SAM.PAYMENTS
```

and then accessing the data using

```
SELECT ID, YTDPAYMENT
FROM MYPAY
```

Remember, $STEVE issues the CREATE SYNONYM command one time, and thereafter uses the synonym name in all future accessing of $SAM'S view.

Although a DBADM and DBCTRL have the power to create tables in other user's accounts, they cannot create views in other user's accounts. Only the SYSADM can create both tables and views in other accounts.

When you create a view and grant someone authority to use it, that person can access the table via that view. If DBADM or someone else modifies your authority on the table by giving you additional privileges, those users you authorized do not automatically have the new privileges. Similarly, if DBADM or someone else removes some of the privileges from a base table, those privileges are also removed from the views automatically.

Cascading Effect in REVOKE

Whenever you revoke an authorization, DB2 treats the revoke as if the original GRANT never occurred. That is, a revoke of a grant also revokes all other GRANTs resulted from the original. For example, suppose $MARY issues the command:

```
GRANT SELECT
ON CLASSES
TO $KAREN
WITH GRANT OPTION
```

followed by $KAREN issuing the command:

```
GRANT SELECT
ON CLASSES
TO $RALPH
```

Now if $MARY issues:

```
REVOKE SELECT
ON CLASSES
FROM $KAREN
```

the revoke cascades downward and automatically revokes $RALPH's SELECT authority on table CLASSES. Here, the granting lineage is:

$MARY → $KAREN → $RALPH.

By breaking the lineage from $MARY to $KAREN, all successive grants are lost. You can rectify the problem by issuing multiple GRANTs to $KAREN from multiple sources. If you had two DBADMs $MARY and $TONY issue separate GRANTS to $KAREN, you can circumvent the cascading effect. Here, both $MARY and $TONY issues:

```
GRANT SELECT
ON CLASSES
TO $KAREN
WITH GRANT OPTION
```

The grant lineage looks like

```
$MARY →
          $KAREN → $RALPH
$TONY →
```

Here, $KAREN can still authorize anyone she wants. If $MARY revokes her authorization, $KAREN still has authority from $TONY and $RALPH still maintains his granted authority. Note that timing is essential. $RALPH continues having authority because both $MARY and $TONY granted $KAREN authority before $KAREN passed it on to $RALPH. $KAREN had a double GRANT when she authorized $RALPH. However, suppose $MARY grants $KAREN who then grants $RALPH and later $TONY grants $KAREN. $KAREN only had one grant authority when she granted $RALPH. Now, when $MARY revokes $KAREN's authority, $RALPH is automatically revoked also since DB2 treats the revoke as if the original grant never occurred—in this case $KAREN lost her power to pass the authority on, so $RALPH's authority is revoked. However, now $KAREN still has authority from $TONY and can re-GRANT $RALPH his authority. Note that if $RALPH had passed on the authority to another user, he would have to also re-grant those users.

Cascading revokes are particularly troublesome when you issue authority to user departments who will be using the database for years. DBADM might grant the manager of a user department the authority to do certain things with GRANT OPTION. That manager might in turn authorize subordinates to access tables and produce reports. Those subordinates might in turn authorize still other users, such as sales representatives, field personnel, and the like. When someone in the user department resigns, is promoted, or changes job functions, DBADM may revoke that person's authorization which in turn could generate a cascading effect. Therefore, whenever you grant authorizations, we should document who is authorized and what authorizations they have. Although the DB2 catalog keeps track of authorizations in DB2 system tables, with hundreds or perhaps thousands of users accessing hundreds or thousands of tables, having a DBADM query DB2 catalogs is time consuming and sometimes not practical. This is especially true in a dynamic environment where promotions are frequent or employee turnover is high.

Exercises

5-7. $CHARLES has retired from the company and was DBADM to the database EMPLOYEES. What command does SYSADM issue to revoke $CHARLES's authority on the database? How does this affect the other users of the database? What are other alternatives for SYSADM?

5-8. $SHARON created the table HOUSES and granted $TOM, $FELICIA, and $TONY the right to SELECT any column and update only columns PURCHASER and SELLER in the table. She now wants to revoke these users' right to view and update the column PURCHASER. What commands does she issue to revoke their authority?

5-9. DBADM $SUSAN gave $STEVE the right to create tables on database EDUCATE. She now wants to revoke his right to create any additional tables on the database. What command does she issue to revoke his authority?

5-10. DBADM $CHARLES gave $HARRY the right to create tables on database PAYROLL. He now wants to revoke $HARRY's right to view all tables on the database. What command does $CHARLES issue?

6

Advanced SQL Topics

Most of the discussions on DML in this book have been on how to query a single table. However, in many cases, the data you need is not available in only one table and requires the spanning of multiple tables to extract it. When you combine data that exists in one table with data that exists in another table, you perform a process called *joining*. Each of the tables that are to be joined must contain at least one column of data common to both tables. You can create this common column when you design the tables.

Joining Two Tables

You join two tables together by:

- Listing in SELECT the column names that you want from both tables.
- Listing the names of the two tables in FROM.
- Listing the relationship between the two tables in WHERE.

The column names you use in SELECT are the simple column names from each table. However, if two tables contain the exact same name, you need to use the fully qualified name for that column. The table names you use in FROM are the simple names if you own the tables or the fully qualified names if you do not own the tables. Note that if you do not own a table, you must be given authorization to use it. Remember, whoever creates the table owns the table, and that owner GRANTS other users authorization to use it.

The relationship you specify in WHERE is called the *join condition* and has the form:

```
WHERE table1.columnname = table2.columnname
```

The following SELECT statement joins the EQUIPMENT table and SALVAGE table from Exercise 3-6:

```
SELECT PRODID, PRODNAME, TYPENAME
FROM EQUIPMENT, SALVAGE
WHERE EQUIPMENT.PRODTYPE = SALVAGE.PRODID
```

This query produces the following results:

```
PRODID        PRODNAME      TYPENAME

4211          WRENCH        SMALL TOOL
5318          TRUCK         HEAVY MACHINERY
3402          DRILL         LIGHT MACHINERY
7321          PRESS         LARGE TOOL
0900          CHAIR         FURNITURE
0901          TABLE         FURNITURE
0790          PRINTER       COMPUTER EQUIPMENT
2100          FAN           SMALL ELECTRIC TOOL
```

You can further restrict the query by including additional conditions in WHERE. A similar query to the one above extracts only those items that have an initial cost of over $400.00. The query becomes:

```
SELECT PRODID, PRODNAME, TYPENAME
FROM EQUIPMENT, SALVAGE
WHERE EQUIPMENT.PRODTYPE = SALVAGE.PRODID
      AND INITCOST > 400.00
```

and produces the following results:

```
PRODID        PRODNAME      TYPENAME

5318          TRUCK         HEAVY MACHINERY
3402          DRILL         LIGHT MACHINERY
0901          TABLE         FURNITURE
0790          PRINTER       COMPUTER EQUIPMENT
```

When DB2 executes a join query, it places the two tables in a buffer area and tests the join condition. Therefore, the buffer area you defined in CREATE must be large enough to contain both tables. If the combined lengths of the two tables exceed the 4K buffer size, you must increase it to 32K using ALTER.

If you fail to put the join condition in WHERE, DB2 extracts all possible combinations from the two tables. This combination is called the *Cartesian product* and generally is not meaningful.

Note that you are not restricted to joining just two tables. You can join more than two tables by placing multiple column names in SELECT and the joining criteria for the multiple tables in WHERE, separating them with AND.

Synonyms in Join

You can create a synonym in the join by including the synonym name in the FROM clause. For example, you can use the synonym E for the table name $EPTF.EQUIPMENT using:

```
SELECT PRODID, PRODNAME, TYPENAME
FROM $EPTF.EQUIPMENT E, SALVAGE
WHERE E.PRODTYPE = SALVAGE.PRODID
      AND INITCOST > 400.00
```

Here, DB2 performs a simple algebraic substitution of replacing all Es with $EPTF.EQUIPMENT before it executes the query. Similarly, you can use the synonym S for SALVAGE and rewrite the above query as:

```
SELECT PRODID, PRODNAME, TYPENAME
FROM $EPTF.EQUIPMENT E, SALVAGE S
WHERE E.PRODTYPE = S.PRODID
      AND INITCOST > 400.00
```

Here, DB2 duplicates the data into two areas, one called E and the other called S, both of which reside in a buffer area.

This technique is particularly useful if you join two tables that have many columns with the same name. Figure 6-1 contains two tables having multiple occurrences of the same column name. A query to display the department name and the employee's name and address using the tables in FIG. 6-1 becomes:

```
SELECT DEPTNAME, LASTNAME, FIRSTNAME, E.ADDRESS,E.CITY
       E.STATE, E.ZIP
  FROM EMPLOYEE E, DEPARTMENT D
  WHERE E. DEPTNUMB = D.DEPTNUMB
```

giving what you see in FIG. 6-2.

EMPLOYEE TABLE

IDNUMB	LASTNAME	FIRSTNAME	ADDRESS	CITY	STATE	ZIP	DEPTNUMB
12345	DOE	JOHN	12 E. 3RD	DUNLAP	TN	12345	D12
23456	SMITH	SUE	RT 2	DONLEY	TX	87655	D12
34567	CANARY	LARRY	RT 1 BOX 123	ADA	AR	43432	A10
45321	BIRD	KAREN	123 WARWICK	SPENCER	NJ	92929	A11

DEPARTMENT

DEPTNUMB	DEPTNAME	ADDRESS	CITY	STATE	ZIP
D12	COMPUTER CENTER	TETROL BLDG	NASHVILLE	TN	12221
A10	ENGINEERING	234 E. 23RD	OAK RIDGE	TN	12224
A11	NUCLEAR CONTROL	456 FAIRFAX	OAK RIDGE	TN	12222

Fig. 6-1. Two tables with multiple occurrences of the same column names.

DEPTNAME	LASTNAME	FIRSTNAME	ADDRESS	CITY	STATE	ZIP
COMPUTER CENTER	DOE	JOHN	12 E. 3RD	DUNLAP	TN	12345
COMPUTER CENTER	SMITH	SUE	RT 2	DONLEY	TX	87655
ENGINEERING	CANARY	LARRY	RT 1 BOX 123	ADA	AR	43432
NUCLEAR CONTROL	BIRD	KAREN	123 WARWICK	SPENCER	NJ	92929

Fig. 6-2. The product of the join of the two tables in Fig. 6-1.

Here, DB2 replaces each E in the query for EMPLOYEE and each D for DEPARTMENT. This query extracts the department name, the employee's last name, first name, address, city, state, and zip. The linkage between the two tables is found in the join condition

```
WHERE EMPLOYEE.DEPTNUMB = DEPARTMENT.DEPTNUMB
```

Note that if the two tables had different names for the department number, you would not have to use its fully qualified name in WHERE. That is, if you created one table with DEPTNO and the other table with DEPTNUMB as the name of the department's number then the join condition would be:

```
WHERE DEPTNO = DEPTNUMB
```

Subselects

A second technique to access more than one table in the same query is to create a SELECT within a SELECT called a subselect.

Subselects in arithmetic operations. The query:

```
SELECT LNAME, FNAME, SALARY
FROM PAYROLL
WHERE SALARY > (SELECT AVG(SALARY) FROM PAYROLL)
```

finds the employees whose salary is larger than the average salary of all employees. Here, DB2 performs the innermost SELECT first and computes the average salary of all employees in the PAYROLL table. This value is then used by the outermost SELECT to query the database. That is, after the above subquery executes, the main query is equivalent to the intermediate step

```
SELECT LNAME, FNAME, SALARY
FROM PAYROLL
WHERE SALARY > (1234.99)
```

Note that if you use a subselect as part of an arithmetic operation, the subselect must return only a single value. Obviously, the statement:

```
WHERE SALARY > (1234.56, 3522.88,  32626.88)
```

created when multiple values are returned from a subquery is meaningless. Therefore, when using a subselect, use MAX, MIN, AVG, COUNT(DISTINCT), and COUNT(*) if the subselect is part of an arithmetic operation.

You are not restricted to using the same table in the subquery. You can write queries to retrieve rows from one table based on some condition in another table. The queries:

```
SELECT LASTNAME, FIRSTNAME, EMPLID, SALARY
FROM PAYROLL
WHERE HOURS > 20 + (SELECT AVG(HOURS) FROM PAYWEEK1)

SELECT LASTNAME, FIRSTNAME, EMPLID, SALARY
FROM PAYROLL
```

```
WHERE  HOURS > 20 + (SELECT AVG(HOURS) FROM PAYWEEK1
                     WHERE OVERPAY <= 100.00)

SELECT AVG(SALARY), MAX(SALARY), MIN(SALARY)
FROM PAYROLL
WHERE  HOURS > (SELECT AVG(HOURS) FROM PAYWEEK1
                WHERE OVERPAY <= 100.00)

          AND
          RATE < 2 * (SELECT MIN(RATE) FROM PAYWEEK2
                      WHERE SEX = 'F' AND BIRTHDATE <
                      380101)
```

are examples of using subselects in arithmetic operations based on data in another table.

Subselects using IN. If it is possible for multiple values to return from a subquery, you must use the IN option in WHERE of SELECT. That is, a query to extract the employee's name and ID from a PAYROLL table who were employed in payweek #1 in departments whose name begins with the letters "D" or "E" becomes:

```
SELECT LNAME, FNAME, EMPLID
FROM PAYROLL
WHERE DEPTNO  IN (SELECT  DEPTNO FROM PAYWEEK1
                  WHERE  DEPTNO LIKE 'D_' OR
                         DEPTNO LIKE 'E_')
```

Remember, with the IN option of SELECT, the values inside the parentheses can be any values including duplicates. If the subquery:

```
SELECT DEPTNO FROM PAYWEEK1
```

returns the values D11, D12, E32, D11, D11, E34, and D12, the previous query has the intermediate result of:

```
SELECT LNAME, FNAME, EMPLID
FROM PAYROLL
WHERE  DEPTNO  IN ('D11', 'D12', 'E32', 'D11', 'D11', 'E34',
       'D12')
```

Remember, for subqueries, DB2 extracts the data from the table and places the results in a buffer area. The values in the buffer area are then used to evaluate the main query statement. Subqueries are evaluated from the innermost query to the outermost query or from bottom to top.

You must be careful in writing complex queries. If you use too many subqueries in the same statement or if the query contains a combination of subqueries and multiple join operations, you might get an error message indicating that the query is too complex to be evaluated. Obviously, a query containing 20 subqueries is not only difficult to write but it also will result in an error message. As a general rule, you might want to limit the number of subqueries in the same query to some small number, perhaps 5 or less. It is frustrating to enter a large, and complicated query only to have DB2 return an error message. Here, common sense and experience will dictate the length and complexity of queries.

You can use subselects in the WHERE or HAVING clause of SELECT. However, all subselects must be on the right side of the search condition and must appear in parentheses. DB2 starts at the innermost parentheses and works its way outward to the outermost parentheses when multiple subselects appear in the same statement. Note that you cannot use UNION or ORDER BY in a subselect. However, you can union the results of a statement containing a subselect with another statement or use ORDER BY on the final results of query. The queries:

```
SELECT LASTNAME, FIRSTNAME, SALARY
FROM PAYMONTH1
WHERE DEPTNO IN (SELECT DEPTNUMB FROM PAYWEEK1)

UNION

SELECT LASTNAME, FIRSTNAME, SALARY
FROM PAYMONTH2
WHERE DEPTNO IN (SELECT DEPTNUMB FROM PAYWEEK2)
```

and

```
SELECT LASTNAME, FIRSTNAME, SALARY
FROM PAYROLL
WHERE DEPTNO IN (SELECT DEPTNUMB FROM PAYWEEK 2)
ORDER BY LASTNAME
```

are valid statements.

Duplicate Rows and the DISTINCT Option

You can eliminate the extraction of duplicate or identical rows in a table by using the keyword DISTINCT in SELECT. The query:

```
SELECT PRODID, PRODNAME, PRODTYPE, VENDOR
FROM EQUIPMENT
DISTINCT
```

displays only unique rows. That is, if the data in all the columns in two or more rows is identical, only one row will be extracted from the table (see FIG. 6-3).

PRODID	PRODNAME	PRODTYPE	VENDOR	NUMBBOUGHT	
4211	WRENCH	ST	KMART	6	(4.23)
5318	TRUCK	HM	GM	2	(15983.22)
3402	DRILL	LM	ARGON	5	(4532.99)
7321	PRESS	LT	DARGO	1	(165.66)
0900	CHAIR	FU	LITTLES	4	(230.00)
0901	TABLE	FU	LITTLES	2	(500.00)
0790	PRINTER	CE	IBM	2	(650.00)
2100	FAN	ET	KMART	2	(125.00)

Fig. 6-3. Duplicate rows eliminated from retrieval.

Note that the data from one row must be an exact duplicate of the data from another row including the columns that are not part of the user's view. Hence, two rows could appear identical to a user if data in columns hidden from a user contains non-identical data (see FIG. 6-4). Note that in both FIGS. 6-3 and 6-4, values in parentheses are not included in the user's view and therefore, are not visible to him or her.

PRODID	PRODNAME	PRODTYPE	VENDOR	NUMBBOUGHT	
4211	WRENCH	ST	KMART	6	(4.23)
4211	WRENCH	ST	KMART	6	(4.55)
4211	WRENCH	ST	KMART	6	(4.66)
5318	TRUCK	HM	GM	2	(15983.22)
5318	TRUCK	HM	GM	2	(13453.68)
3402	DRILL	LM	ARGON	5	(4532.99)
7321	PRESS	LT	DARGO	1	(165.66)
0900	CHAIR	FU	LITTLES	4	(230.00)
0901	TABLE	FU	LITTLES	2	(500.00)
0790	PRINTER	CE	IBM	2	(650.00)
2100	FAN	ET	KMART	2	(125.00)
2100	FAN	ET	KMART	2	(154.90)

Fig. 6-4. User's view restrictions not eliminating duplicate rows.

The EXISTS Option

On occasion, you might need to test for the existence of a certain condition to guarantee that at least one row satisfies the query conditions. Remember, if no rows exist for a given query, DB2 returns a null value. This can lead to undesirable results if the query is a subquery. For example, the query:

```
SELECT LNAME, FNAME, EMPLID
FROM PAYROLL
WHERE DEPTNO  IN  (SELECT DEPTNO FROM PAYWEEK1
                    WHERE  DEPTNO LIKE 'D_' OR
                           DEPTNO LIKE 'E_')
```

contains the subquery:

```
SELECT DEPTNO
FROM PAYWEEK1
WHERE  DEPTNO LIKE 'D_' OR
       DEPTNO LIKE 'E_')
```

If no departments exist in table PAYWEEK1 satisfying the WHERE clause, the subquery returns a null value. The original query is then equivalent to:

```
SELECT LNAME, FNAME, EMPLID
FROM PAYROLL
WHERE DEPTNO IN (NULLS)
```

You can insert the keyword EXISTS in the WHERE clause giving the query:

```
SELECT LNAME, FNAME, EMPLID
FROM PAYROLL
```

```
WHERE EXISTS DEPTNO IN (SELECT DEPTNO FROM PAYWEEK1
                        WHERE DEPTNO LIKE 'D_' OR
                              DEPTNO LIKE 'E_')
```

Now, if no row satisfies the subquery, the first query is not executed, saving processing time.

The ALL/ANY Option

Sometimes you might want to query a table and find data that is larger or smaller than some value in a list. For example, a Dean of a College might want to find the names of all faculty members whose salary is greater than any Department Chairman's salary. Suppose FIG. 6-5 represents the salaries of four academic departments.

DEPARTMENT TABLE

DEPTNAME	LASTNAME	FIRSTNAME	SALARY	RANK
ENGLISH	TOMAS	KAREN	56000.00	1
ENGLISH	SMITH	MARK	31000.00	3
ENGLISH	STEVENS	MARY	35000.00	3
ENGLISH	MARTIN	DANIEL	45000.00	0
MATH	BIRD	STEVE	43000.00	0
MATH	WASHINGTON	GEORGE	38000.00	2
MATH	LINCOLN	SUE	35000.00	2
MATH	ADAMS	JOHN	28000.00	3
CHEMISTRY	JEFFERSON	BETTY	40000.00	4
CHEMISTRY	ADAMS	HARRY	55500.00	0
CHEMISTRY	FORD	GINGER	55000.00	1
COMPUTER SCI.	JOHNSON	MARGARET	51000.00	1
COMPUTER SCI.	JONES	MIKE	44000.00	0
COMPUTER SCI.	GRANT	COLLIN	59000.00	2

TITLE TABLE

RANK	TITLE
0	CHAIRMAN
1	INSTRUCTOR
2	ASSISTANT PROFESSOR
3	ASSOCIATE PROFESSOR
4	PROFESSOR

Fig. 6-5. Academic salaries and ranks tables.

The query:

```
SELECT *
FROM DEPARTMENT
WHERE RANK = '0'
```

produces the following results:

DEPTNAME	LASTNAME	FIRSTNAME	SALARY	RANK
ENGLISH	MARTIN	DANIEL	45000.00	0
MATH	BIRD	STEVE	43000.00	0
CHEMISTRY	ADAMS	HARRY	55500.00	0
COMPUTER SCI.	JONES	MIKE	44000.00	0

To find all the faculty members whose salaries are greater than any of the Department Chairmen, you would use:

```
SELECT LASTNAME, FIRSTNAME, SALARY
FROM DEPARTMENT
WHERE  SALARY > 43000.00 AND
       RANK NOT = '0'
```

Here, we wrote two queries; one to find a list of salaries, and another to extract the needed result. You can combine these two queries into a single statement using ANY as a keyword. The query satisfying the Dean's requirements is:

```
SELECT LASTNAME, FIRSTNAME, SALARY
FROM DEPARTMENT
WHERE  SALARY  >  ANY  (SELECT SALARY
                        FROM DEPARTMENT
                        WHERE RANK = '0')
```

which produces the following results:

LASTNAME	FIRSTNAME	SALARY
TOMAS	KAREN	56000.00
FORD	GINGER	55000.00
JOHNSON	MARGARET	51000.00
GRANT	COLLIN	59000.00

Now suppose the Dean of the College wants a list of all faculty members whose salaries exceed the largest salary of any Department Chairman. You can use the keyword ALL in WHERE giving:

```
SELECT LASTNAME, FIRSTNAME, SALARY
FROM DEPARTMENT
WHERE  SALARY  >  ALL  (SELECT SALARY
                        FROM DEPARTMENT
                        WHERE RANK = '0')
```

Now the results contain a list of all faculty members whose salary is greater than 55500.00 and includes

LASTNAME	FIRSTNAME	SALARY
TOMAS	KAREN	56000.00
GRANT	COLLIN	59000.00

Exercises

Given the following tables containing sample data:

STUDENTFEE TABLE

STUDENT ID	LAST NAME	FIRST NAME	COURSE FEES OWES	COURSE FEES PAID	DORM FEE OWES	DORM FEE PAID
X(5)	X(20)	X(20)	9(4)V99	9(4)V99	9(5)V99	9(5)V99
12345	DOE	JOHN	450.44	890.00	1200.00	2200.00
23456	SMITH	MARY	300.00	900.00	2400.00	0.00
34567	BROWN	SUE	0.00	1000.00	0.00	1200.00
45667	ADAMS	KAREN	300.00	900.00	2400.00	0.00

DORMASSIGN TABLE

STUDENT ID	BUILDING ASSIGNED	ROOM # ASSIGNED	TYPE ROOM	SEX	STUDENT'S STATUS
X(5)	X(15)	XXX	X	X	X
12345	PERKINS HALL	120	P	M	Active
23456	SCOTT HALL	211	D	F	Active
34567	SCOTT HALL	230	Q	F	Active
67890	PERKINS HALL	101	P	M	Active
43215	SCOTT HALL	200	D	F	Quit

TYPECODE TABLE

TYPE ROOM	DESCRIPTION	CAPACITY
X	X(20)	9
P	PRIVATE	1
D	DOUBLE	2
Q	QUAD	4
S	SUITE	1
E	PENTHOUSE	2
F	FAMILY	4

6-1. Write the SQL statement(s) to give users $ADMTR and $ADMDE a view of the STUDENTFEE table where they have access to the student name, ID, and amounts owed. Also, write the control statements to grant them access to the views.

6-2. Write the following DML commands:

a. List all the males including each name, ID, and total amount each owes.
b. List all students in PERKINS HALL who are female—include each name and ID.
c. List all the rooms that are private.

d. List all rooms in each building—list the building and then rooms in that building, all in ascending order.

6-3. Write the DML commands to:

a. List each building, each room and all the students in them listing each ID, name, room number, and building—sort the results on building, room number in descending order, and last name.

b. Identify if students of different sexes have been assigned the same dorm room—omit those assigned to family rooms.

c. Produce a financial listing of all students, the total amount each paid, and the total amount each owe—sorted by amount owed.

7

The DB2 Catalog

In this chapter, we look at several important catalog tables and investigate how to use DML on the catalog to extract needed information. Obviously, in a dynamic company using DB2, many users will have access to tables, views, and other objects within the numerous databases created by both the program development team and other support personnel.

Because multiple users will have access to multiple tables and because owners of objects can pass onto other users certain rights and privileges, you will need to know who has access to a particular table and who is authorized to access objects within certain databases. You particularly need this information if you intend to drop a table or revoke someone's authorization to use an object. Remember, when you drop an object, you could lose valuable information about other objects. For example, when you drop a table, you lose all views based on that table along with all that table's synonyms and the synonyms for those views.

Catalog Information about Databases

The DB2 catalog is composed of a set of tables containing information about all the objects within DB2. These include descriptions about each database structure, the tablespaces, tables, views, authorizations, plans, views, and other objects. TABLE 7-1 lists many of the tables in the DB2 catalog. You can access the DB2 tables using the SQL language; in particular, DML. Note that the DB2 catalog is a dynamic catalog where the DB2 system constantly accesses the catalog to:

- Verify accessing authorizations for DML commands (SELECT, UPDATE, DELETE, and INSERT).

- Update itself when users CREATE, ALTER, or DROP objects.
- Modify authorization tables when users GRANT and REVOKE authorizations or CREATE or DROP tables.
- Identify indexes and use views.
- Create plans.
- Perform any other activity relating to the structure of DB2 entities.

Table 7-1. List of tables in the DB2 catalog.

SYSCOPY	SYSSYNONYMS	SYSRESAUTH
SYSCOLUMNS	SYSTABLES	SYSDBRM
SYSFIELDS	SYSTABAUTH	SYSPLAN
SYSINDEXES	SYSTABLEPART	SYSPLANAUTH
SYSINDEXPART	SYSTABLESPACE	SYSPLANDEP
SYSKEYS	SYSDATABASE	SYSUSERAUTH
SYSFOREIGNKEYS	SYSDBAUTH	SYSVIEWS
SYSLINKS	SYSTOGROUP	SYSVIEWDEP
SYSRELS	SYSVOLUMES	

You can only use the SELECT clause of DML to access the DB2 catalog. The DB2 system updates, deletes, and inserts entries into the DB2 catalog and prohibits all users from issuing the corresponding DML commands to perform these functions on tables in the DB2 catalog. The only direct insertion of data into a catalog table by a user is the placing of a comment on an object—which is explained later in this chapter.

Database Structure Information

If you want to list all the database names on the system, you can query the DB2 catalog table SYSIBM.SYSDATABASE using:

```
SELECT *
FROM SYSIBM.SYSDATABASE
```

Here DB2 lists the database name, the authorization ID of its creator, name of the storage group for the database, what buffer pool it uses, and other information. Query SYSDATABASE when you want to identify on which storage group a database resides or to list the database names in the catalog to verify that a proposed database name does not already exist in DB2. TABLE 7-2 contains selected column descriptions for the SYSDATABASE table.

Column Name	Description
NAME	Database name.
CREATOR	ID of database creator.
STGROUP	Name of storage group.
BPOOL	Name of buffer pool.

Table 7-2. Selected column names and their description for SYSIBM.SYSDATABASE.

Database Authorization Information

While the SYSDATABASE table contains data about the structure of the database, the SYSDBAUTH table contains data about the five administrative authorizations and authorizations on using the various utility programs within DB2. You can query the SYSDBAUTH table to identify which users are SYSADM, DBADM, DBCTRL, DBMAINT, and SYSOPR by using the statement:

```
SELECT GRANTOR, GRANTEE, CREATETABAUTH, DBADMAUTH,
       DBCTRAUTH, DBMAINTAUTH
FROM SYSIBM.SYSDBAUTH
WHERE NAME = 'EDUCBASE'
```

Here, the query extracts data on who granted the privilege, who received the privilege, and what privileges that user has on database EDUCBASE. The columns CREATETABAUTH, DBADMAUTH, DBCTRLAUTH, and DBMAINTAUTH contain a one-character code where a space indicates the user does not have the privilege, a G indicates the user has the privilege with GRANT OPTION, and a Y indicates the user has the privilege without GRANT OPTION. See TABLE 7-3 for a breakdown of the codes.

Table 7-3. Selected column names and their description for SYSIBM.SYSDBAUTH.

Column Name	Description
GRANTOR	ID of user who granted the authorization.
GRANTEE	ID of user who received the authorization.
NAME	Name of database.
AUTHHOWGOT	Administrative level of grantor (S = SYSADM, D = DBADM, C = DBCTRL, M = DBMAINT, " " = none).
CREATETABAUTH	Code to indicate grantee can create tables (G = has GRANT OPTION, Y = doesn't have GRANT OPTION, blank = not authorized).
CREATETSAUTH	Code to indicate grantee can create tablespaces (G = has GRANT OPTION, Y = doesn't have GRANT OPTION, blank = not authorized).
DBADMAUTH	Code to indicate grantee has DBADM authority (G = has GRANT OPTION, Y = doesn't have GRANT OPTION, blank = not authorized).
DBCTRLAUTH	Code to indicate grantee has DBCTRL authority (G = has GRANT OPTION, Y = doesn't have GRANT OPTION, blank = not authorized).
DBMAINTAUTH	Code to indicate grantee has DBMAINT authority (G = has GRANT OPTION, Y = doesn't have GRANT OPTION, blank = not authorized).

Catalog Information about Tablespaces

To identify what tablespaces exist within DB2 and each tablespace's major characteristics, you can query the SYSIBM.SYSTABLESPACE table. See TABLE 7-4 for a list of selected columns in the table and a brief description of their meanings.

Table 7-4. Selected column names and their descriptions for SYSIBM.SYSTABLESPACE.

Column Name	Description
NAME	Tablespace name.
CREATOR	ID of tablespace creator.
DBNAME	Name of database containing tablespace.
BPOOL	Bufferpool used for tablespace.
LOCKRULE	Code for locking strategy for tablespace (A = any, P = page, S = tablespace).
ERASERULE	Code for erasing datasets when tablespace is dropped (N = not erased, Y = erased).
CLOSERULE	Code for closing datasets when tablespace not used (N = not closed, Y = closed).
NTABLES	Number of tables defined in the tablespace.
NACTIVE	Number of pages active in tablespace.

Tablespace Structure Information

The statement:

```
SELECT NAME, DBNAME, LOCKRULE, ERASERULE, CLOSERULE,
  BPOOL
FROM SYSIBM.SYSTABLESPACE
WHERE CREATOR = '$EPTF'
```

extracts data on all the tablespaces user $EPTF created within DB2. This data includes the tablespace name, the database name, the locking strategy (any, page, tablespace), file erasing indicator (yes, no), file closing indicator (yes, no), and buffer pool name. Note that this data was once entered by a user when he or she created the tablespace using the CREATE TABLESPACE command or altered using the ALTER command.

To find all the tablespaces within the database EDUCBASE, you can use:

```
SELECT NAME, LOCKRULE, ERASERULE, CLOSERULE, BPOOL
FROM SYSIBM.SYSTABLESPACE
WHERE DBNAME = 'EDUCBASE'
```

Here, the results from the query identify several of the parameters used in the CREATE TABLESPACE command issued on database EDUCBASE. You can also extract statistical data from the catalog which DB2 updates and maintains either through a continuous process or through the implementation of a utility program. For example, you can identify how many tables exist in tablespace EDUCTS1 and the number of active pages in the tablespace using:

```
SELECT NTABLES, NACTIVE
FROM SYSIBM.SYSTABLESPACE
WHERE NAME = 'EDUCTS1'
```

Tablespace Authorization Information

On occasion, you might need to identify all the users who can create objects within the database. For example, you can list all the users who can create tablespaces by querying the SYSIBM.SYSDBAUTH table using:

```
SELECT GRANTOR, GRANTEE, NAME, AUTHHOWGOT, CREATET-
SAUTH
FROM SYSIBM.SYSDBAUTH
WHERE CREATETSAUTH NOT = ' '
```

Here, the query extracts data on who granted the privilege, who has CREATETS authority, the name of the database for the CREATETS privilege, the administrative level (SYSADM, DBADM, etc.) of the grantor of the privilege, and a code for identifying if the grantee has WITH GRANT OPTION (G = has GRANT OPTION, Y = doesn't have GRANT OPTION).

Catalog Information about Tables and Views

When users create tables, DB2 accesses the SYSIBM.SYSTABLES table and stores various parameters in the columns within the table. In addition to storing data found in the CREATE TABLE statement, DB2 maintains statistical data about the table in other columns within SYSTABLES. This data is used by the system to manage DB2 and generate algorithms to handle the data in a database.

Table and View Structure Information

TABLE 7-5 contains a list of selected columns in SYSIBM.SYSTABLES and a brief description of their meanings. You can use the statement:

```
SELECT NAME, COLCOUNT, CARD, NPAGES
FROM SYSIBM.SYSTABLES
WHERE (CARD > 0 OR
       NPAGES > 0) AND
       DBNAME = 'EDUCBASE' AND
       TSNAME = 'EDUCTS1'
```

to extract the name of the table, the number of columns in the table, the total number of rows in the table, and the number of pages containing rows. Here, we tested for CARD and NPAGES for being a positive number since if either

Table 7-5. Selected column names and their description for SYSIBM.SYSTABLES.

Column Name	Description
NAME	Table or view name.
CREATOR	ID of table or view creator.
DBNAME	Name of database containing table or view.
TSNAME	Name of tablespace containing the table.
TYPE	Code for view or table (T = table, V = view).
COLCOUNT	Number of columns in table or view.
CARD	Total number of rows in table.
NPAGES	Total number of pages containing rows.
EDPROC	Name of the EDITPROC for table.
VALPROC	Name of the VALIDPROC for table.
REMARKS	Comments on the table.

contain the value −1 either the row describes a view or the statistics for the row are not currently available.

You can also extract data about the editing and validation routines attached to tables. The statement:

```
SELECT NAME, CREATOR, EDPROC, VALPROC
FROM SYSIBM.SYSTABLES
WHERE DBNAME = 'EDUCBASE' AND
      TYPE NOT = 'V'
```

identifies all tables in database EDUCBASE, who created them, and the names of all editing and validation routines attached to them. When you want to drop a table or view, you can use the results of this query to notify the various owners of the tables so they can take the appropriate action to ensure the recovery of their data. In addition, the programming staff will need the information to re-attach the EDITPROCs and VALIDPROCs to maintain the integrity of the inputted data.

You can identify who created each table in a database using

```
SELECT CREATOR, NAME, TYPE, TSNAME, DBNAME
FROM SYSIBM.SYSTABLES
```

Similarly, you can either identify all the tables a particular user created using:

```
SELECT NAME, TSNAME, DBNAME
FROM SYSIBM.SYSTABLES
WHERE CREATOR = '$EPTF' AND
      TYPE = 'T'
```

or identify all the views a user created using:

```
SELECT NAME, TYPE, TSNAME, DBNAME
FROM SYSIBM.SYSTABLES
WHERE  CREATOR = '$EPTF' AND
       TYPE = 'V'
```

Because some users can create views on views, we can list all the users who have created a view of a view using:

```
SELECT NAME, CREATOR
FROM SYSIBM.SYSTABLES
WHERE TSNAME = 'SYSVIEWS'
```

Here, when a view of a view is created, DB2 sets TSNAME to the value SYSVIEWS.

Table and View Authorization Information

You can identify all the users who can create tables (using the CREATETAB authorization) on a particular database by querying the DB2 catalog table SYSIBM.SYSDBAUTH. The statement:

```
SELECT GRANTOR, GRANTEE, AUTHHOWGOT, CREATETABAUTH
FROM SYSIBM.SYSDBAUTH
WHERE  CREATETTABAUTH NOT = ' ' AND
       NAME = 'EDUCBASE'
```

extracts information about all the users who have CREATETAB authority on database EDUCBASE. Here, the extracted data includes who granted the privilege, who received CREATETAB authority, the administrative level (SYSADM, DBADM, etc.) of the grantor, and a code for identifying if the grantee has WITH GRANT OPTION (G = has GRANT OPTION, Y = doesn't have GRANT OPTION).

In addition, you can query SYSIBM.SYSTABAUTH to identify users who can access data in tables or views on a particular database. See TABLE 7-6 for a list of selected columns in the table SYSIBM.SYSTABAUTH and a brief description of their meanings. Note that SYSTABLES contains information on who can create objects while SYSTABAUTH contains information on who has authorization to access data in the database. The statement:

```
SELECT TTNAME, STNAME
FROM SYSIBM.SYSTABAUTH
WHERE  GRANTEE = '$EPTF' AND
       DBNAME = 'EDUCBASE'
```

extracts the name of all the tables and views in database EDUCBASE that user $EPTF can access.

Table 7-6. Selected column names and their description for SYSIBM.SYSTABAUTH.

Column Name	Description
GRANTOR	ID or user who granted the authorization.
GRANTEE	ID or user who received the authorization.
SCREATOR	If CREATE VIEW was used to create this authorization, then SCREATOR is the ID in the CREATE VIEW statement.
STNAME	If CREATE VIEW was used to create this authorization, then STNAME is the view name in the CREATE VIEW statement.
TTNAME	Name of table or view.
ALTERAUTH	Code for authorization to ALTER table (G = has GRANT OPTION, Y = doesn't have GRANT OPTION, blank = not authorized).
SELECTAUTH	Code for authorization to SELECT rows in table (G = has GRANT OPTION, Y = doesn't have GRANT OPTION, blank = not authorized).
UPDATEAUTH	Code for authorization to UPDATE rows in table (G = had GRANT OPTION, Y = doesn't have GRANT OPTION, blank = not authorized).
INSERTAUTH	Code for authorization to INSERT rows in table (G = has GRANT OPTION, Y = doesn't have GRANT OPTION, blank = not authorized).
DELETEAUTH	Code for authorization to DELETE rows in table (G = has GRANT OPTION, Y = doesn't have GRANT OPTION, blank = not authorized).
INDEXAUTH	Code for authorization to create an index on table (G = has GRANT OPTION, Y = doesn't have GRANT OPTION, blank = not authorized).
GRANTEETYPE	Code to indicate grantee is a plan (P) or user (blank).

You can modify the query to include the type of authorization user $EPTF has on each table or view using:

```
SELECT TTNAME, STNAME, SELECTAUTH, UPDATEAUTH,
       DELETEAUTH, INSERTAUTH
FROM SYSIBM.SYSTABAUTH
WHERE GRANTEE = '$EPTF' AND
      DBNAME = 'EDUCBASE'
```

Here, the extraction contains the names of the tables and views along with a code (blank, G, or Y) in each of the last four columns indicating whether user $EPTF has SELECT, UPDATE, DELETE, and INSERT authorization on that table.

You can also list all the users who have access to a particular table by using the query:

```
SELECT GRANTEE
FROM SYSIBM.SYSTABAUTH
WHERE  TTNAME = 'PAYROLL' AND
       DBNAME = 'EDUCBASE' AND
       GRANTEETYPE = ' '
```

Note that you eliminate all plans from the list of users by restricting the column GRANTEETYPE to blanks or spaces.

Similarly, you can extract all the users who have a view of the table PAYROLL in database EDUCBASE by using the statement

```
SELECT GRANTEE
FROM SYSIBM.SYSTABAUTH
WHERE  TTNAME = 'PAYROLL' AND
       DBNAME = 'EDUCBASE' AND
       GRANTEETYPE = ' ' AND
       STNAME NOT = TTNAME
```

Note that when a user creates a view, STNAME contains the view name and TTNAME contains the table name. If, however, no view is created for the table, STNAME contains the table name located in column TTNAME.

You can also query SYSIBM.SYSVIEWS directly to identify who created a view. See TABLE 7-7 for column definitions for SYSIBM.SYSVIEWS. The query:

```
SELECT NAME, CREATOR
FROM SYSIBM.SYSVIEWS
WHERE CREATOR LIKE '$EP_'
```

lists all the views where the first three characters of the creator ID are $EP.

Table 7-7. Selected column names and their description for SYSIBM.SYSVIEWS.

Column Name	Description
NAME	View name.
CREATOR	ID of view creator.
CHECK	Code for CHECK OPTION (Y or N).
TEXT	254 character remark.

Catalog Information about Synonyms

You can list all the synonyms for a table or view by querying the SYSIBM. SYSSYNONYMS table (see TABLE 7-8). The statement:

```
SELECT NAME, CREATOR
```

```
FROM SYSIBM.SYSSYNONYMS
WHERE TBNAME = 'PAYROLL' AND
TBCREATOR = '$EPTF'
```

identifies all synonyms for the table or view $EPTF.PAYROLL. Similarly, you can identify all the synonyms created by $EPTF using:

```
SELECT NAME, TBNAME, TBCREATOR
FROM SYSIBM.SYSSYNONYMS
WHERE CREATOR = '$EPTF'
```

Table 7-8. Selected column names and their description for SYSIBM.SYSSYNONYMS.

Column Name	Description
NAME	Synonym name for the table or view.
CREATOR	ID of synonym's creator.
TBNAME	The name of the table or view.
TBCREATOR	ID of creator of table or view.

Catalog Information about Columns

The DB2 catalog table SYSIBM.SYSCOLUMNS contains one row for every column in each table and view (see TABLE 7-9).

Table 7-9. Selected column names and their description for SYSIBM.SYSCOLUMNS.

Column Name	Description
NAME	Column name.
TBNAME	Name of table or view containing column.
TBCREATOR	ID of creator of table or view.
COLNO	Numeric code for relative place of column in table or view.
COLTYPE	Type of column (SMALLINT, INTEGER, FLOAT, DECIMAL, CHAR, VARCHAR, etc.).
LENGTH	Length of column attribute (2, 4, 4, n, 1 to 254, 1 to 254) respective to COLTYPE list.
NULLS	Nulls allowed in column (N or Y).
UPDATES	Is column updateable (N or Y).
REMARKS	Contains 0 to 254 byte character string from COMMENT ON statement.

Column Structure Information

The statement:

```
SELECT NAME, COLTYPE, NULLS, REMARKS
FROM SYSIBM.SYSCOLUMNS
WHERE TBNAME = 'EMPLOYEE' AND
      TBCREATOR = '$EPTF'
```

lists all the columns in table $EPTF.EMPLOYEE, the type of column it is, whether it can contain nulls, and any comments about the column (from COMMENT ON). Note that after you create a table using the CREATE statement, you can verify the table definiton using the above query.

Using COMMENT ON

You can place text, usually in the form of documentation, about columns, views, and tables in the following DB2 catalog tables:

```
SYSIBM.SYSTABLES
SYSIBM.SYSVIEWS
SYSIBM.SYSCOLUMNS
```

The text can be up to 254 characters in length. You place the text in the corresponding catalog table using COMMENT ON for columns, tables, and views. In particular, you can place documentation text for a table in SYSIBM.SYSTABLES using:

```
COMMENT ON TABLE EMPLOYEE IS
'employee table contains data about all employees in
 XYZ corporation'
```

Note that if the table is a view, DB2 places the documentation text in the TEXT column of SYSIBM.SYSVIEWS instead of the REMARKS column of SYSIBM-.SYSTABLES.

You can place documentation text about a particular column into SYSIBM-.SYSCOLUMNS using:

```
COMMENT ON COLUMN EMPLOYEE.SEX IS
'SEX column in EMPLOYEE table can be either M, F, or
 nulls'
```

It is a good idea to tag remarks to a particular column especially if certain column parameters are confusing. For example, if you create a column in the EMPLOYEE table for STATE and want to include the abbreviations for PR and DC for Puerto Rico and Washington D.C., respectively, you can use:

```
COMMENT ON COLUMN EMPLOYEE.STATE IS
 'STATE column can contain any of 52 abbreviations-the
 abbreviations for the 50 states plus PR and DC for
 Puerto Rico and Washington D.C.'
```

You can retrieve the documentation about column remarks using the statement:

```
SELECT NAME, REMARKS
FROM SYSIBM.SYSCOLUMNS
WHERE TBNAME = 'EMPLOYEE' AND
      TBCREATOR = '$EPTF'
```

Here, you extract all the columns in table $EPTF.EMPLOYEE along with the remarks about each column. You must have SYSADM or DBADM authority or be the creator of the table to store documentation remarks using COMMENT ON. However, any user with access to SYSIBM.SYSCOLUMNS can query the table and list the remarks. This is particularly helpful for the project leader on computer systems with no data dictionary. The project leader can place documentation in the DB2 catalog about each table and column in his or her database using COMMENT ON. The programming staff can then retrieve the documentation as they need it using SELECT on the appropriate table.

You can list all the tables and their remarks for which user $EPTF created using:

```
SELECT NAME, REMARKS
FROM SYSIBM.SYSTABLES
WHERE TBCREATOR = '$EPTF'
```

Similarly, you can extract all of $EPTF's views and remarks about the view using:

```
SELECT NAME, TEXT
FROM SYSIBM.SYSVIEWS
WHERE CREATOR = '$EPTF'
```

Column Authorization Information

When you grant someone UPDATE privilege on a column, DB2 makes an entry in SYSIBM.SYSCOLAUTH (see TABLE 7-10). You can identify all users who have UPDATE privilege on any column in a table by querying SYSCOLAUTH. For example, the query:

```
SELECT GRANTEE
FROM SYSIBM.SYSCOLAUTH
WHERE CREATOR = '$EPTF' AND
      TNAME = 'EMPLOYEE' AND
      COLNAME = 'SEX'
```

extracts all the users who have update privilege on $EPTF.EMPLOYEE.SEX.

Exercises

7-1. Write the SELECT statement:

  a. Find all users who have a view of $EUTR.EMPLOYEE.

  b. Find all users who can create tables in database PRODPAY.

  c. Find all DBADMs on DB2.

Table 7-10. Selected column names and their description for SYSIBM.SYSCOLAUTH.

Column Name	Description
GRANTOR	ID of user who granted the authorization.
GRANTEE	ID of user who received the authorization.
CREATOR	ID of the creator of the table or view.
TNAME	Name of the table or view.
COLNAME	Column name for which UPDATE applies.

d. List all the columns in tables $EPTF.DEPARTMENT and $ERF-T.EMPLOYEE.

7-2. DB2 user $QWTY is retiring from the company. What procedure should SYSADM establish to prohibit $QWTY's access to DB2 without dropping all items he or she created.

7-3. Write the SELECT statement:

a. Find all the tables user $EPTF can access.

b. Find all the tables user $EPTF created.

c. Find all the tables user $EPTF created containing the column STATE.

7-4. Write the SELECT statement:

a. List all the columns defined as CHAR on the system and created having more than 15 characters.

b. Does the table $IUYT.TABLE1 have any views of views?

c. List all the users of database EDUCBASE.

8

Program Development and Preparation

To use DB2 efficiently, you cannot simply rely exclusively on entering SQL statements directly into the system one line at a time. This is particularly evident if you try to insert data about 10,000 customers into the system. To enter data on each customer by typing the INSERT statement and its parameters 10,000 times is not only inefficient, it is also tedious and time-consuming work. Therefore, you must rely on computer programs containing SQL statements to handle the bulk of your data entry activity. You can then enter SQL statements directly into the system only when you want to extract specific information about a topic.

In this chapter, we discuss the procedures and steps to process embedded SQL statements in COBOL code, and in the next chapter, we discuss the requirements and coding procedures to embed SQL statements in COBOL. We chose COBOL for the language because most commercial sites are COBOL shops. You can embed SQL code in other languages as well, including PL/I, Fortran, APL2, C, and IBM 370 assembler, to name a few. The SQL statements you can embed in code include all the DML, DDL, and CL commands.

Program Preparation

It is obvious you cannot simply place the statement:

```
DELETE FROM PAYROLL
WHERE ID = '1234'
```

into COBOL since the COBOL compiler will flag the SQL statement as an error. Also, you must provide a link between the variables in the COBOL code and the table and column descriptions in the DB2 catalog. The steps you must follow are:

1. Test the SQL statement in DB2I for accuracy.
2. Embed the SQL statement into the COBOL program.
3. Perform a precompile to convert the SQL statements to COBOL statements or to CALLs which the COBOL compiler can interpret.
4. Compile the program to create an object module.
5. Link edit the program to produce a load module.
6. BIND the program to interface the COBOL code to DB2.
7. Run the resultant load module.

Figure 8-1 graphically represents the steps you must take to process SQL statements in COBOL code—or any supported language.

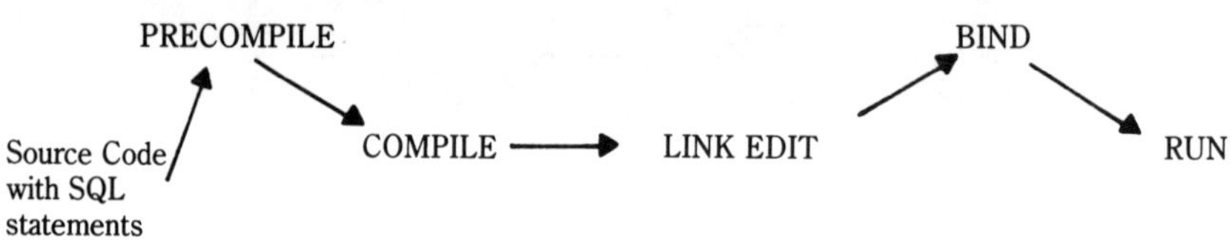

Fig. 8-1. Steps to process SQL in COBOL.

Note that you can write code, precompile it, compile it, and link it without DB2 being online. Only at BIND time must DB2 be online to the system because the BIND uses the DB2 catalog to interface and verify items in the code with the database description in the DB2 catalog.

Source Code with SQL Statements

You can embed SQL statements in COBOL by first checking the SQL statement in DB2I (DB2 Interactive) to verify that the statement works in DB2. Here, you can check for syntax errors and verify the fact that the statement performs the desired function properly. After you are satisfied the SQL statement is correct, you can then embed it into the COBOL code. Place the delimiter EXEC SQL before the SQL statement to indicate its beginning and place the delimiter END-EXEC after the statement to indicate its end. For example, to place the statement:

```
DELETE FROM PAYROLL
WHERE ID = '1234'
```

in COBOL you would use

```
EXEC SQL
DELETE FROM PAYROLL
WHERE ID = '1234'
END-EXEC.
```

Here, EXEC SQL identifies the beginning of the SQL statement and END-EXEC identifies its end. Note that if you have multiple SQL statements, one after the other, you must embed each statement separately. That is, to embed the two consecutive statements

```
DELETE FROM PAYROLL
WHERE ID = '1234';
SELECT LASTNAME, FIRSTNAME
FROM PAYWEEK1
```

you would use:

```
EXEC SQL
DELETE FROM PAYROLL
WHERE ID = '1234'
END-EXEC.
EXEC SQL
SELECT LASTNAME, FIRSTNAME
FROM PAYWEEK1
END-EXEC.
```

Embedding SQL statements in COBOL requires the three layers:

```
EXEC SQL          (the beginning delimiter)
SQL statement
END-EXEC.         (the ending delimiter)
```

Precompile, Compile, and Link Edit

Once you embed all the SQL code within your program, you are ready to perform the precompile. The precompiler creates two objects: the massaged original code minus the SQL statements, and the Database Request Module (DBRM). Note that the precompile option is one of several options in DB2I. You can access DB2I from MVS system software using menus provided by the DB2 software product. A submenu of DB2I is a SPUFI option which you select to write SQL statements to query DB2 databases.

The precompiler "massages" the embedded SQL instructions within the source code by

1. Making them comments within the source code.
2. Converting them to CALLs or language instructions.
3. Writing each SQL statement to a sequential file (called a Database Request Module, or DBRM).
4. Placing either a time tag or a version tag on the results of the precompile, which is the modified source code and the DBRM.

The precompiler analyzes each SQL statement and validates its syntax. Note that because you can precompile without DB2 being online, the precompiler does not check the DB2 catalog for verification of variable names. That is, the precompiler would not verify the column names and table name in the DB2 catalog for the statement:

```
SELECT LASTNME, FIRSTNME, ADRESS
FROM PAYRULL
```

Here, the precompiler assumes that LASTNME, FIRSTNME, and ADRESS are valid column names and PAYRULL is a valid table name. The actual process of verifying each SQL statement in COBOL against the DB2 catalog descriptions occurs at BIND time, not precompile time.

After the precompiler verifies the syntax, it transforms each SQL statement into a COBOL comment and converts the SQL statement to COBOL code (one or more CALLs with parameters). In addition, the precompiler places a copy of each SQL statement in a sequential file, called a Database Request Module. The DBRM will later be processed when you perform the BIND.

The BIND

After you finish with the precompile, you can then perform a normal compile on the precompiled source code and link it to produce a load module. If the original code did not contain SQL statements, you could now run the resultant load module. However, because the program does contain SQL statements, you must perform an additional step called a BIND to prepare the program's DBRM. The issues mandating this extra process are:

- DB2's security requirements demand that you have authorization for using the DB2 entities (such as tables, views, etc.) and statements (SELECT, DELETE, etc.).
- The code specifies what you want to access but does not contain instructions on how to navigate through the database.
- The names and descriptions in the code have not been verified against the names and descriptions in the DB2 catalog.

The BIND validates the authorizations for using DB2's entities and statements, generates an access strategy based on the SQL request and the physical characteristics of the database, compares the table definitions in the DB2 catalog with SQL statements in the code, and determines the locking strategy (page or tablespace).

After you resolve all BIND errors and redo the BIND if needed, you can then run the load module. Note that if you fail to perform the BIND, the load module will ABEND whenever it tries to execute a compiled SQL statement in the code.

The BIND uses the DBRM as an input file and creates two files as output: the processed DBRM and a PLAN. Remember, the DBRM is a sequential file of all the SQL statements in the code. The BIND processes the DBRM one SQL statement at a time and produces another file called a *PLAN*. The PLAN contains the results of the BIND and is accessed each time the load module executes an SQL statement in the code. When the BIND creates the PLAN, it stores it in the DB2 catalog for referencing by the load module. When the load module accesses SQL statements in the code, DB2 accesses the PLAN to validate security, finds the accessing strategy for the database, finds the locking strategy for it, and verifies that the DB2 items accessed in the code still exist in the DB2 catalog. Note that the DB2 catalog is an active catalog because the PLAN must access it each and every time it processes an SQL statement in the code.

Whoever binds the code has automatic EXECUTE privilege. That is, whoever binds the code can execute the code. All other users must be given explicit authorization to execute the code and access the plan.

The PLAN

Both the processed DBRM and the plan are stored in the DB2 catalog and DB2 software manages them. Other files that you have created include:

- The source code with embedded SQL (a product of coding).
- The source code with converted SQL code (a product of the precompiler).
- The DBRM (also a product of the precompiler).
- The object module (a product of the compiler).
- The load module (a product of the linkage editor).

Each of these files is found in some user or systems library.

The Binder produces one of the following four types of plans:

- A FAILED bind where no plan is produced.
- A VALID plan where the plan works.
- An INVALID plan where some existing resource is lost.
- An INOPERATIVE plan where a rebind was unable to build a plan since the DB2 catalog needs some additional resource.

Obviously, a FAILED bind requires you to modify the code, supply additional resources to the DB2 catalog, and start anew at the precompile step. A VALID plan indicates that the COBOL code containing SQL statements has interfaced with the DB2 catalog definitions accurately. You then must execute the load module and test and debug the logic of the COBOL code you wrote.

An INVALID plan occurs when some DB2 resource used by an existing plan disappears from the DB2 catalog. For example, if you drop an index or a table, DB2 immediately invalidates all plans using that index or table. You must then resupply the resource and perform a REBIND. Note that you have three options in DB2I concerning binding: BIND ADD, BIND REPLACE, and REBIND.

Use the option BIND ADD when you perform the original BIND. After BIND ADD creates the plan and processes DBRM, use the option BIND REPLACE if you change any SQL statement in the COBOL code. Note that you must perform a second BIND to generate a new plan whenever you change the original code. That is, after you reprecompile, recompile, and relink the modified code, you must use BIND REPLACE to generate a new plan for the code and a new processed DBRM.

Use the REBIND option when you lose resources from the DB2 catalog but have not changed the original COBOL code. This occurs when you drop a

DB2 resource and the DB2 software automatically invalidates the plan making it INOPERATIVE. Because the only thing affected is the DB2 resource, you can simply resupply it, if appropriate, and REBIND. For example, if you DROP a table and then recreate it, you must REBIND all plans using that table or views of that table. However, if you drop an index, you can either resupply the index using CREATE INDEX or REBIND without the use of the index. Here, because the original resource was lost, the accessing strategies and locking procedures are no longer valid, hence DB2 invalidates the plans. When you REBIND, DB2 uses the processed DBRM to generate a new PLAN. Because none of the COBOL code has been affected, the processed DBRM contains all the instructions and parameters the REBIND needs to generate the new plan (see FIG. 8-2).

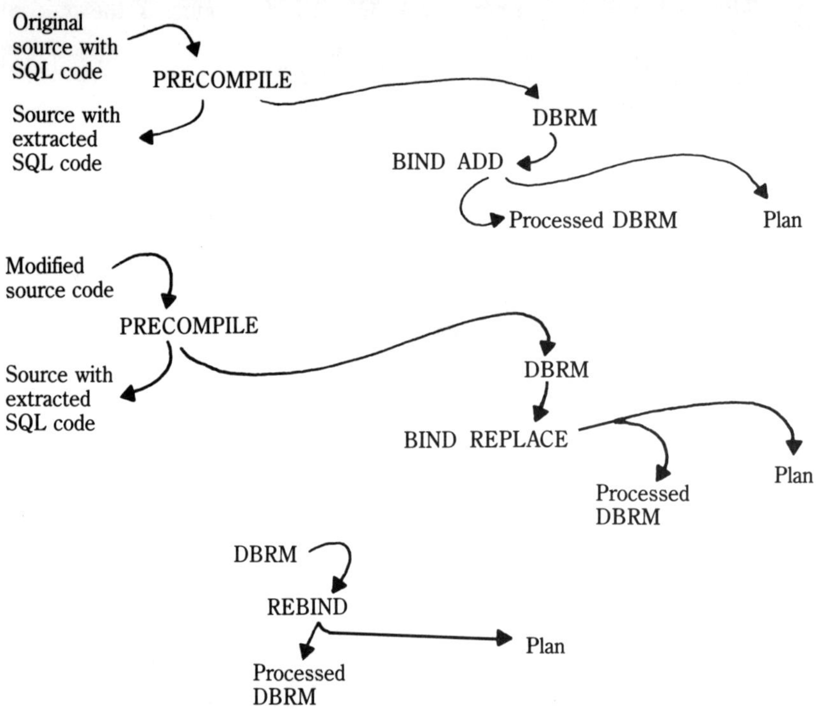

Fig. 8-2. Using BIND ADD to create processed DBRM and plan after writing the original source code; using BIND REPLACE to create new processed DBRM and new plan after modifying the source code; and using REBIND to create new processed DBRM and new plan after supplying missing DB2 catalog resource.

Note that if an executing load module references an invalid plan (for instance, a resource is lost), DB2 will initiate one REBIND automatically. If at the end of this automatic run-time rebind, DB2 continues to have a problem with the DB2 resource, it will then ABEND the program. In most cases, you would not want the system to perform an automatic run-time REBIND because a user is probably accessing the program. For very large programs or for programs containing many SQL statements, the REBIND process could take a considerable amount of time to complete. This is particularly true when other users are online to DB2 and accessing the DB2 catalog and locking its tables.

Binding and rebinding should occur during non-peak computer usage times because the process may be slow. Before you drop a DB2 resource, you should check the DB2 catalog tables and identify all plans that depend on that resource. You can then REBIND those plans either at non-peak times dynamically or in a batch file. Remember, most users are unfamiliar with the mechanics of binding, and it may be a futile effort to try to explain to an uninformed user why his or her program is pausing to perform a rebind at run-time.

In summary, use BIND ADD whenever you BIND for the first time. Use BIND REPLACE whenever you change the program, and use REBIND whenever you change a DB2 resource (drop or add an index, drop then add a table, etc.). If you do anticipate changing a DB2 resource, you should query the DB2 catalog beforehand to identify the plans affected by the change. After you change the DB2 resource, you then rebind to create a new plan. If possible, use a batch file to perform the rebind during non-peak usage time.

Time Stamps and Level Numbers

Note that DB2 keeps copies of both the original DBRM and the processed DBRM. Because the original DBRM contains all the SQL statements found in the code, if you modify only a COBOL language instruction, logically you should not be required to redo the BIND because none of the SQL code has changed—and the plan should still be valid. However, to ensure that all load modules access the plan based on that module's BIND, DB2 places a time stamp on all files created by the system. When you write the code and eventually BIND, all the produced files contain the same time stamp. At run time (when we execute the code), the time stamp on the load module must match the time stamp on the plan. If the time stamps match, the system executes the instructions. If, however, they have different time stamps, the system ABENDs the program (see FIG. 8-3).

Whenever you make a change in the code, a new time stamp is placed on the results of the precompile. Hence, when you link the code, the load module's time stamp will be different than the plan's time stamp, forcing the system to abend the program. To resolve the time stamp dilemma so that you don't have to bind each time you make a small change in the COBOL code, you can use level numbers rather than time stamps (see FIG. 8-4). Now you can change the non-SQL COBOL code in the source code, precompile, compile, link, and execute. Because you did not affect the SQL code in the source, you do not have to BIND REPLACE. At precompile time, simply tell the precompiler to use the previous level number forcing the plan and the load module to have the same level numbers.

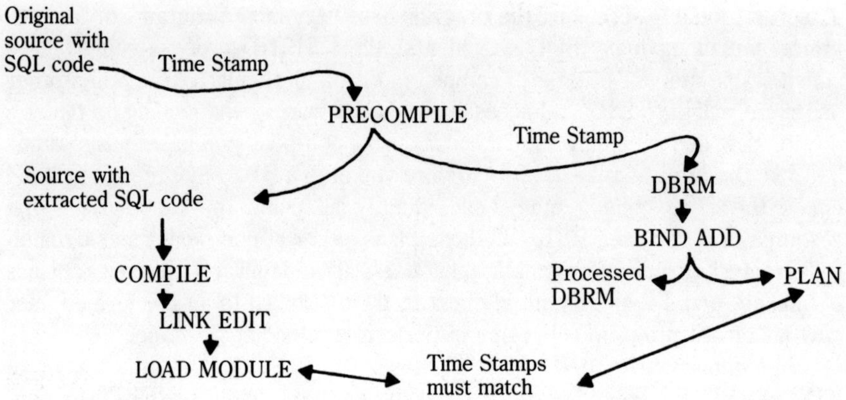

Fig. 8-3. Using time stamps to verify SQL code in load module matches SQL accessing strategy in plan.

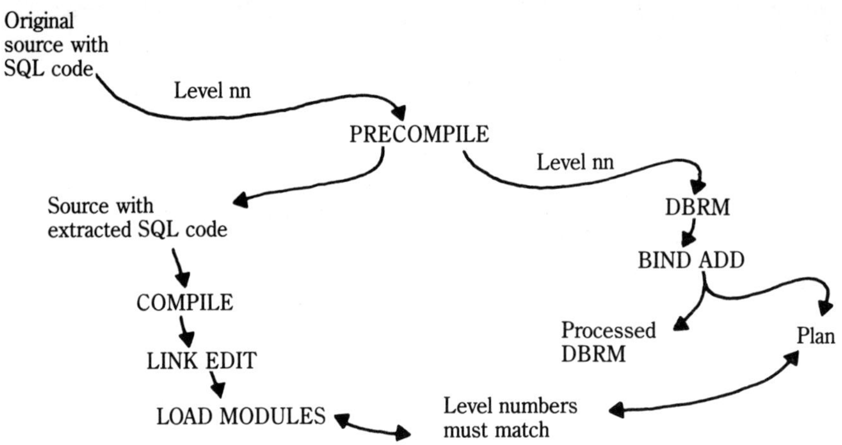

Fig. 8-4. Using level numbers to verify SQL code in load module matches SQL accessing strategy in plan.

Destroying the Plan

You can erase the plan and processed DBRM from the DB2 catalog by using FREE. DB2 drops both the plan and the processed DBRM from the DB2 catalog. However, the original copy of the DBRM that remains is in the user's copy library. If you want to also destroy the original DBRM, use normal systems utilities to delete the file. Note that DB2 software package keeps the files in the DB2 catalog secure. However, entities such as source code, object code, load modules, and the DBRM created by precompiling are all found in some user library which is not part of the DB2 system. Hence, these objects have only RACF (Resource Access Control Facility) protection. Because the plan and processed DBRM reside in the DB2 catalog, you cannot erase them using typical system file deletion utilities. Remember, if DB2 creates an object, it also manages that object and requires a specific DB2 command to alter or erase it.

Authorizations to BIND

Only the SYSADM has BIND and BINDADD authorization. He or she must either GRANT to individual users the authorization to perform the bind or GRANT to the public the right to bind. Whoever performs the bind or rebind must have authorization to perform every SQL statement in the code that is to be bound. That is, if the code creates tables, then whoever binds must have CREATETAB authority and if the code creates a tablespace, whoever binds must have CREATETS authorization.

Program Areas

One of the first steps in writing a COBOL program is to create in WORKING-STORAGE definitions of the data areas you will use in the code.

SQLCA Area

If you embed SQL statements in the COBOL code you must include an SQL Communication Area (SQLCA) in WORKING-STORAGE. This area is used during the communications between DB2 and the program and includes several status fields. In the PROCEDURE DIVISION, you must check the variables defined in this area subsequent to each execution of an SQL instruction. You can create the SQLCA area in WORKING-STORAGE by placing the statement

```
EXEC SQL
INCLUDE SQLCA
END-EXEC.
```

in the WORKING-STORAGE SECTION.

DCLGEN

When you precompile the program, the precompiler does not reference the DB2 catalog. That is, at precompile time, the variables in the SQL code are not checked for accuracy against their definitions in the DB2 catalog. Such mistakes as misspelling a table name or placing a column name in the wrong table will go unchecked by the precompiler. The precompiler assumes everything between the EXEC SQL and the END-EXEC to be accurate SQL statements. Only at BIND time will the system check the SQL statements in the code against the database definitions in the DB2 catalog. Because the binder does not function like a compiler, any one error will abort the binding of the code. Therefore, multiple errors in an SQL statement require that you one-by-one correct, reprecompile, recompile, relink, and reBIND REPLACE the code. Obviously, this is very time consuming and a waste of valuable resources.

You can speed up the process of error-identification by including a table or view DECLARE statement in WORKING-STORAGE. Here, the DECLARE clause is an SQL statement containing a description of the table or view and is used to check the validity of the table and column names and their data types. For example, if you created the table CUSTITEMS using:

```
CREATE TABLE CUSTITEMS
    (CUSTID    CHAR(10)           NOT NULL,
     AMTOWED   DECIMAL(7,2)       NOT NULL,
     AMTPAID   DECIMAL(7,2)       NOT NULL,
     HIGHBAL   DECIMAL(10,2)              ,
     NUMBORD   SMALLINT                   ;
     ITEMNAME  CHAR(15)                   )
IN   USERBASE.USERTS1
```

You can define it in WORKING-STORAGE using the following DECLARE statement in WORKING-STORAGE:

```
EXEC SQL
DECLARE CUSTITEMS TABLE
    (CUSTID    CHAR(10),
     AMTOWED   DECIMAL(7,2),
     AMTPAID   DECIMAL(7,2),
     HIGHBAL   DECIMAL(10,2),
     NUMBORD   SMALLINT,
     ITEMNAME  CHAR(15))
END-EXEC.
```

Now, the precompiler will check the table and column names and their data types for accuracy in all SQL statements in the PROCEDURE DIVISION. Any discrepancies that exist will be flagged and listed when the precompile terminates. You can then correct all the errors and redo the precompile until you get an error-free precompile. Then proceed with the normal compile, linkage, and BIND. Now the BIND identifies only errors resulting in discrepancies between the definitions in the DECLARE clause and the definitions that actually exist in the DB2 catalog.

Note, however, you can still have problems with the DECLARE statement not accurately portraying the actual definitions in the catalog. When you type the DECLARE statement, you could still make typographical errors and misspell the table and column names. To create an accurate DECLARE statement that reflects the table definition as it actually exists in the DB2 catalog, you perform a DCLGEN. A DCLGEN is a DB2I option that converts the table definition into a series of COBOL 01 and 05 levels and places the results in a preselected Include library (see FIG. 8-5). You then can use the statement:

```
EXEC SQL
INCLUDE dclgen name
END-EXEC.
```

in the WORKING-STORAGE SECTION. When you use the DB2I DCLGEN option, you identify the name of the table (CUSTITEMS), the Include library it will reside in, and its name in the Include library (for example, DCLGCUST for FIG. 8-5). You can place this name in a DECLARE statement using:

```
EXEC SQL
```

```
INCLUDE DCLGCUST
END-EXEC.
```

and place this statement in WORKING-STORAGE.

When you precompile, the precompiler copies any members in the Include library that appear as statements in the code. Now the code contains the actual descriptions of the tables and columns as they were created and later altered. The precompiler will now check all the table and column definitions and flag any errors for later resolution.

DB2 catalog description
CUSTITEMS TABLE

```
CUSTID      CHAR(10)
AMTOWED     DECIMAL(7,2)
AMTPAID     DECIMAL(7,2)
HIGHBAL     DECIMAL(10,2)
NUMBORD     SMALLINT
ITEMNAME    CHAR(15)
```

DCLGEN→

Includes library description

```
01 CUSTITEMS.
   05 CUSTID PIC X(10).
   05 AMTOWED PIC S9(5)V99
        COMP-3.
   05 AMTPAID PIC S9(5)V99
        COMP-3.
   05 HIGHBAL PIC S9(8)V99
     COMP-3.
   05 NUMBORD PIC S9(4)
        COMP.
   05 ITEMNAME PIC X(15).
```

Fig. 8-5. Using DCLGEN to create a COBOL definition of the table CUST ITEMS in an include library.

Authorizations

Note that you must be given authorization by SYSADM to use the DCLGEN option. In many cases, the DCLGENs are performed by either SYSADM or DBADM, and the option is not available to the remaining programming staff. Because every installation has its own standards, you must check with your SYSADM to determine if you have access to DCLGEN.

Recall, only SYSADM can create a PLAN unless he or she explicitly authorizes other users to use the BINDer. BIND, BINDADD, and EXECUTE are authorizations automatically given to each SYSADM and to no other user. A SYSADM can use the command

```
GRANT BIND, BINDADD, EXECUTE TO PUBLIC
```

to authorize everyone to use these three privileges. Because each installation has its own criteria and standards for BINDing, you should check with SYSADM before trying a BIND.

You must be authorized to use all resources needed by the plan. That is, if the program creates tables and tablespaces, whoever BINDs the DBRM must have CREATETAB and CREATETS authority. In addition, you can GRANT the EXECUTE authority to whoever runs the program using:

```
GRANT EXECUTE ON PLAN planname TO userid
```

Also, if SYSADM did not GRANT to the PUBLIC the power to BIND, he or she must use:

```
GRANT BIND ON PLAN planname TO userid
```

to authorize a user to BIND. Note that a GRANT BIND also includes the authorization to BIND REPLACE, REBIND, and FREE.

You can identify who has authorization on PLANs by querying the DB2 catalog table SYSIBM.SYSPLANAUTH (see TABLE 8-1).

Table 8-1. Selected column names and their descriptions for SYSIBM.SYSPLAN.

Column Name	Description
NAME	Name of plan.
CREATOR	ID of user who created the plan.
VALID	Is plan valid (Y, N).

The query:

```
SELECT NAME, CREATOR
FROM SYSIBM.SYSPLAN
WHERE VALID = 'Y'
```

lists all the valid plans in the DB2 catalog. The query:

```
SELECT NAME, VALID
FROM SYSIBM.SYSPLAN
WHERE CREATOR ='$TONY' AND VALID = 'Y'
```

lists all the valid plans user $TONY created. You can also query SYSIBM.SYSPLANAUTH to identify all users who are authorized to execute a certain plan (see TABLE 8-2). The query:

```
SELECT   GRANTEE
FROM SYSIBM.SYSPLANAUTH
WHERE  NAME = 'PAYPLAN' AND
        (EXECUTEAUTH = 'Y' OR EXECUTEAUTH = 'G')
```

identifies all users who can execute plan PAYPLAN.

You can revoke a user's authorization to BIND or EXECUTE plans using:

```
REVOKE BIND, EXECUTE
ON PLAN planname
FROM username
```

The statement:

```
REVOKE BIND
ON PLAN PAYPLAN
FROM $SUSAN
```

revokes $SUSAN's authorization to BIND the plan PAYPLAN.

Table 8-2. Selected column names and their descriptions for SYSIBM.SYSPLANAUTH.

Column Name	Description
GRANTOR	ID of user who granted the authorization.
GRANTEE	ID of user who received authorization.
NAME	Name of the plan.
BINDAUTH	Code for BIND, REBIND, and FREE authorization: blank = not authorized, Y privilege held without GRANT option, G privilege held with GRANT option.
EXECUTEAUTH	Code for EXECUTE authorization: blank = not authorized, Y privilege held without GRANT option, G privilege held with GRANT option.

Exercises

8-1. When do you use BIND ADD, BIND REPLACE, and REBIND?

8-2. What is the function of the DCLGEN? Who performs the DCLGEN?

8-3. Suppose you want to use three different tables in your application program. Briefly describe what INCLUDE statements you must include in your program.

8-4. An application development team is using account $TYRE to create and write computer programs and DB2 entities. However, the user department wants the production version of the application to be executed in account $ACCT. Briefly explain the procedures the application team will follow to BIND and EXECUTE both the testing version and the production version of the program (such as when and in which account will the application team BIND and EXECUTE the testing and production versions of the application?).

8-5. The SYSADM granted to PUBLIC both the BIND and EXECUTE privilege. The SYSADM now wants to query the DB2 catalog to find all the users who have a plan in the DB2 catalog. What is DML statement to generate this information?

8-6. The SYSADM wants a list of all plans in the DB2 catalog and who created them. Write the DML statement to extract this data.

8-7. The DBADM for database PAYROLL wants to drop an index for table EXECUTIVES. Write the DML statement to find all plans based on this table.

9

SQL and COBOL

In the last chapter, we discussed the procedures and steps to process embedded SQL statements in a computer program. In this chapter, we discuss how to embed SQL statements in COBOL programs. We begin coding SQL statements in a COBOL program by first defining in WORKING-STORAGE the INCLUDE statements containing the SQLCA and the DCLGEN includes library member names for the table descriptions.

Using Host Variables

The SQLCA area contains status codes for the results of DB2 accesses via the embedded statements. The DCLGEN contains the WORKING-STORAGE descriptions for the column variables in the tables we will use. In place of constants used in interactive SQL you normally use variables in embedded SQL statements. Such variables are defined in WORKING-STORAGE. For example, the statement:

```
SELECT LASTNAME, FIRSTNAME, EMPLID
FROM EMPLOYEE
WHERE SEX = 'M' AND STATE = 'TX'
```

converts to the following statement containing variables:

```
SELECT LASTNAME, FIRSTNAME, EMPLID
FROM EMPLOYEE
WHERE SEX = :INPUT-SEX AND STATE = :INPUT-STATE
```

Variables you use in SQL statements must conform to COBOL naming and syntax rules. These (non-DB2 table) variables are called *host variables* and are placed in 01 levels within the WORKING-STORAGE SECTION of the COBOL code. In most cases, the data types for columns in DB2 are either CHAR, VARCHAR, SMALLINT, INTEGER, or DECIMAL. You must define their corresponding host variables using the appropriate PICTURE clause conforming to the criteria in FIG. 9-1.

Table definition	COBOL PICTURE clause equivalent	
INTEGER	PIC S9(9)	COMP
SMALLINT	PIC S9(4)	COMP
DECIMAL (n, d)	PIC S9(n-d)V9(d)	COMP-3
CHAR(n)	PIC X(n)	
VARCHAR(n)	PIC X(n)	

Fig. 9-1. Identifying PICTURE definition for host variables.

Note that for table columns defined as CHAR and VARCHAR, we use a corresponding PIC X (n) clause for the host variable. Here, "n" is a positive integer between 1 and 254. Figure 9-2 contains the WORKING-STORAGE descriptions for the host variables in the SQL statement:

```
EXEC SQL
  SELECT LASTNAME, FIRSTNAME, ADDRESS
    INTO :READIT-LASTNAME,
         :READIT-FIRSTNAME,
         :READIT-ADDRESS
  FROM EMPLOYEE
  WHERE EMPLID = :SCREEN-EMPLID
END-EXEC.
```

Column name in table	CREATE TABLE description	Host variable name in COBOL	COBOL description
EMPLID	CHAR(9)	SCREEN-EMPLID	PIC X(9)
LASTNAME	CHAR(25)	READIT-LASTNAME	PIC X(25)
FIRSTNAME	CHAR(20)	READIT-FIRSTNAME	PIC X(20)
ADDRESS	CHAR(30)	READIT-ADDRESS	PIC X(30)

Fig. 9-2. Host variable descriptions for corresponding EMPLOYEE column variables.

In the above query, the embedded statement uses the value in SCREEN-EMPLID as a key to access the table EMPLOYEE. DB2 extracts data in columns LASTNAME, FIRSTNAME, and ADDRESS for that row and places it in the COBOL variables READIT-LASTNAME, READIT-FIRSTNAME, and READIT-ADDRESS, respectively (see FIG. 9-3 for a typical 01 level host variable definition).

```
01  EMPLOYEE-TABLE-HOST-VARIABLES.
    05 SCREEN-EMPLID                      PIC X(9).
    05 READIT-DEMOGRAPHIC-DATA.
       10 READIT-LASTNAME                 PIC X(25).
       10 READIT-FIRSTNAME                PIC X(20).
       10 READIT-ADDRESS                  PIC X(30).
       10 READIT-CITY                     PIC X(25).
       10 READIT-STATE                    PIC X(2).
       10 READIT-ZIP                      PIC X(5).
```

Fig. 9-3. Host variables defined in working storage for EMPLOYEE table.

You process numeric data in much the same way as you process alphanumeric data. Figure 9-4 contains the host variable's PICTURE clauses for the embedded statement:

```
EXEC SQL
   SELECT HOURSWORKED, RATEOFPAY, NUMBDEPENDENTS
      INTO :READIT-HOURS-WORKED,
           :READIT-RATE-OF-PAY,
           :READIT-NUMBER-DEPENDENTS
   FROM SALARY
   WHERE EMPLID = :SCREEN-EMPLID
END-EXEC.
```

Column name in table	CREATE TABLE description	Host Variable name in COBOL	COBOL description
HOURSWORKED	DECIMAL(6,1)	READIT-HOURS-WORKED	PIC S9(5)V9 COMP-3
RATEOFPAY	DECIMAL(7,2)	READIT-RATE-OF-PAY	PIC S9(5)V99 COMP-3
NUMBDEPENDENTS	SMALLINT	READIT-NUMBER-DEPENDENTS	PIC S9(4) COMP

Fig. 9-4. Host variable descriptions for corresponding table column variable.

Again, place the host-variable definition in an 01 level in WORKING-STORAGE (see FIG. 9-5).

```
01  SALARY-TABLE-HOST-VARIABLES.
    05 READIT-HOURS-WORKED           PIC S9(5)V9    COMP-3.
    05 READIT-RATE-OF-PAY            PIC S9(5)V99   COMP-3.
    05 READIT-NUMBER-DEPENDENTS      PIC S9(4)      COMP.
```

Fig. 9-5. Host variables defined in working storage for SALARY table.

Here, the above embedded SQL statement uses the value in SCREEN-EMPLID as a key to access the table SALARY. DB2 extracts data in columns HOURSWORKED, RATEOFPAY, and NUMBDEPENDENTS for that row and places it in the COBOL variables READIT-HOURS-WORKED, READIT-RATE-OF-PAY, and READIT-NUMBER-DEPENDENTS, respectively. The data descriptions in CREATE TABLE for the three numeric columns:

```
HOURSWORKED
RATEOFPAY
NUMBDEPENDENTS
```

must match the host variable descriptions in WORKING-STORAGE for:

```
READIT-HOURS-WORKED
READIT-RATE-OF-PAY
READIT-NUMBER-DEPENDENTS
```

respectively. Use the criteria in FIG. 9-1 to establish the match. If they mismatch, the precompiler generates either a warning message or an error message at precompile time.

Note that a host variable that appears in an embedded SQL statement has a colon preceding it. Any variable in the embedded SQL statement with a colon preceding it is considered a host variable. Not only does the precompiler check each embedded SQL statement for name and data type accuracy against the DB2 table definition, it also checks the data types of the host variables to ensure their data type accuracy. Use the criteria in FIG. 9-1 for defining them to ensure that proper communications exist between the data transmitted from DB2 tables (via DB2's accessing communications software) and the COBOL program.

You are not restricted to using host variables in just the SELECT statement. You can use host variables anywhere in any SQL statement that is appropriate. For example, when you write a COBOL routine to add records (rows) to a table (such as an ADD program), you use host variables in INSERT. A typical INSERT statement to load an employee's first name, last name, address, city, state, and zip is given in FIG. 9-6.

```
EXEC SQL
  INSERT INTO EMPLOYEE
    (LASTNAME, FIRSTNAME, ADDRESS, CITY, STATE, ZIP)
  VALUES (READIT-LASTNAME,
          :READIT-FIRSTNAME,
          :READIT-ADDRESS,
          :READIT-CITY,
          :READIT-STATE,
          :READIT-ZIP)
  WHERE EMPLID = :SCREEN-EMPLID
END-EXEC.
```

Fig. 9-6. Embedded SQL statement to INSERT data into EMPLOYEE table.

Typically, the ADD program would display a screen to the user and let him or her enter a name and other demographic data about an employee. In this case, the program must either use the variables in FIG. 9-3 as targets of input for data entered via the user or have MOVE statements to move the data from the input variables to the host variables in FIG. 9-3.

It is possible to use the group level name from WORKING-STORAGE for a host variable in an SQL statement. For example, the statement:

```
EXEC SQL
   SELECT LASTNAME, FIRSTNAME, ADDRESS, CITY, STATE, ZIP
        INTO :READIT-DEMOGRAPHIC-DATA
    FROM EMPLOYEE
    WHERE EMPLID = :SCREEN-EMPLID
END-EXEC.
```

is equivalent to the SQL statement in FIG. 9-7.

Note that you load the DB2 table data into the COBOL group-level name READIT-DEMOGRAPHIC-DATA. The variables must match up correctly.

```
EXEC SQL
  SELECT LASTNAME, FIRSTNAME, ADDRESS, CITY, STATE, ZIP
    INTO :READIT-LASTNAME,
         :READIT-FIRSTNAME,
         :READIT-ADDRESS,
         :READIT-CITY,
         :READIT-STATE,
         :READIT-ZIP
  FROM EMPLOYEE
  WHERE EMPLID = :SCREEN-EMPLID
END-EXEC.
```

Fig. 9-7. Embedded SQL statement to extract data from EMPLOYEE table.

That is, the number of variables returned from DB2 and their data type must match up exactly with the number of variables in the group level and their corresponding data types. Any mismatch results in an error being generated either at precompile time if you use a DECLARE or INCLUDE the table column definitions in the code or at run time if you do not DECLARE or INCLUDE the table column names. Obviously, the statement:

```
EXEC SQL
     SELECT *
         INTO :READIT-DEMOGRAPHIC-DATA
     FROM EMPLOYEE
     WHERE EMPLID = :SCREEN-EMPLID
END-EXEC.
```

creates the most problems. Because the precompiler does not access the DB2 catalog, it cannot verify the fact that * includes only those variables in the group level READIT-DEMOGRAPHIC-DATA. Consequently, the precompiler assumes they match. At BIND time, the binder accesses the DB2 catalog and checks the table definition with the code. It is at this time the BIND verifies the matching of the columns with the COBOL group level definition. Any error generates an error message and the BIND fails.

Note also that other problems exist with using the wildcard "*" in embedded SELECT statements. Even if the BINDer creates a valid plan for code containing an embedded

```
SELECT *
```

statement, there is no guarantee the program will execute properly. Remember, at run-time, you do not want the end-users getting upset with code that ABENDs or stops temporarily for REBINDing. When you use SELECT * in embedded statements, you risk the chance that someone could issue an ALTER TABLE command and add an extra column to the table that is being selected. When this occurs, DB2 extracts an extra value representing the newly added column, creating an ABEND at run time. This occurs because the extracted values from the table no longer match exactly with the host variable definition in the code. Therefore, even though you can use the wildcard * in SELECT in DB2I and QMF, you should avoid it in embedded SQL.

Number of Rows Returned Considerations

Note some problems that may exist with using the statement in FIG. 9-7. Here we assume EMPLID has a unique index created for it, and only a single row will be returned from DB2. If however, multiple rows return, you will get an error message and the program will ABEND at run time. Because the definition of the host variables includes only a definition for one set of values, you must ensure that only one row returns from DB2 for correct execution. You have three possibilities for your SQL statements:

- No row will return.
- A single row will return.
- Multiple rows will return.

No Rows Returned

Obviously, if no row returns from an embedded SQL statement, you do not have to bother with handling the returned data. Several SQL statements that do not return data from tables are given in FIG. 9-8.

```
EXEC SQL
  DELETE FROM EMPLOYEE
  WHERE EMPLID = :SCREEN-EMPL-ID
END-EXEC.
EXEC SQL
  INSERT INTO HISTORY
    (RATE, BIRTHDATE)
  VALUES (:SCREEN-CUSTOMER-RACE,
          :SCREEN-CUSTOMER-BDATE)
  WHERE EMPLID = :SCREEN-EMPLID
END-EXEC.
```

Fig. 9-8. Embedded SQL statements that do not return row values.

Single Row Returned

If you have a single row returning from DB2, you again have no problem. Simply use the host variables that are depository for the returned data and manipulate the variables as you would any COBOL variable in the program. Several examples of SQL statements that return a single row value are given in FIG. 9-9.

Multiple Rows Returned Using DECLARE CURSOR

When you have multiple rows returning from DB2, you must process each row separately. Therefore, you will identify any SELECT that can return multiple rows by using a DECLARE CURSOR statement in WORKING-STORAGE. This creates a buffer area for the data. Then FETCH each row from the buffer area for processing. The general form of the DECLARE CURSOR statement is:

```
EXEC SQL
     DECLARE variable name CURSOR FOR
          SQL statement
END-EXEC.
```

```
EXEC SQL
   SELECT LASTNAME, FIRSTNAME
      INTO :READIT-LASTNAME,
           :READIT-FIRSTNAME
   FROM EMPLOYEE
   WHERE EMPLID = :SCREEN-EMPLID
END-EXEC.
EXEC SQL
   SELECT AVG(SALARY), MIN(SALARY), MAX(SALARY)
      INTO :AVERAGE-SALARY-HOLD,
           :MINIMUM-SALARY-HOLD,
           :MAXIMUM-SALARY-HOLD
   FROM EMPLOYEE_SALARY
   WHERE DEPT = :DEPARTMENT-CODE
END-EXEC.
```

Fig. 9-9. Embedded SQL statements that return a single row.

That is, if you want to use the embedded statement:

```
EXEC SQL
    SELECT LASTNAME, FIRSTNAME, ADDRESS, CITY, STATE, ZIP
       INTO :READIT-LASTNAME,
              :READIT-FIRSTNAME,
              :READIT-ADDRESS,
              :READIT-CITY,
              :READIT-STATE,
              :READIT-ZIP
     FROM EMPLOYEE
     WHERE STATE= :SCREEN-STATE
END-EXEC.
```

in your program, place:

```
EXEC SQL
   DECLARE POINTER1 CURSOR FOR
    SELECT LASTNAME, FIRSTNAME, ADDRESS, CITY, STATE, ZIP
     FROM EMPLOYEE
     WHERE STATE = :SCREEN-STATE
END-EXEC.
```

in WORKING-STORAGE. The DECLARE statement informs DB2 that multiple rows could be returned when DB2 extracts data from a table. DB2 will create a buffer area to serve as a temporary storage area for the DB2 extraction process.

Note the restriction on using a cursor on tables that you must have defined as parent tables via the PRIMARY KEY clause. A cursor cannot be used in an UPDATE operation on any column that has been defined as part of a primary key. In such a case, you must code your SQL so that only one row can be returned at a time.

Selecting Multiple Rows from a Table Using FETCH, OPEN and CLOSE

To access the data in the buffer created by the DECLARE...CURSOR statement, OPEN the CURSOR, perform multiple FETCHes of the data, and then CLOSE the CURSOR. That is, after you insert the above DECLARE statement in WORKING-STORAGE, you use:

```
MOVE 'TN' TO SCREEN-STATE.
EXEC SQL
     OPEN POINTER1
END-EXEC.
```

when you want to read data from the DB2 table. DB2 will now access the table and extract a number of rows from the table and place them into the cursor's buffer area. Here you would force the value TN into the variable SCREEN-STATE. Obviously, you could initialize SCREEN-STATE in other ways. You could use:

```
EXEC SQL
    FETCH POINTER1
      INTO :READIT-LASTNAME,
           :READIT-FIRSTNAME,
           :READIT-ADDRESS,
           :READIT-CITY,
           :READIT-STATE,
           :READIT-ZIP
END-EXEC.
```

when you want to read each row from the buffer area. Here, you would process the buffer area much like you would process a sequential tape file or disk file. That is, you place the FETCH statement in a looping mechanism and continue to read each row (record) from the buffer until all rows (records) are processed.

Note that DB2 extracts data from the DB2 table when it processes the OPEN statement. At that time, DB2 accesses the table using the index (if one exists) and extracts data from the table. It uses the SELECT statement in the appropriate DECLARE clause in WORKING-STORAGE for the cursor you OPEN. DB2 extracts only enough rows from the table to fill the buffer area assigned for it. As you FETCH rows from the buffer area, DB2 extracts additional rows from the table and places them in a queue within the cursor's buffer area. This process ensures that a particular query will not exhaust the available virtual memory assigned to a particular user.

After you determine that all the rows have been read from the buffer area, you can terminate processing by closing the cursor using:

```
EXEC SQL
     CLOSE POINTER1
END-EXEC.
```

For the above FETCH, the program extracts the first row from the buffer area and places the extracted column values into the host variables READIT-LASTNAME, READIT-FIRSTNAME, READIT-ADDRESS, READIT-CITY, READIT-STATE, and READIT-ZIP, respectively. You can then use these variables in the program as you would any COBOL variable.

Determining End-of Buffer

Place FETCH in some looping routine and continue to process rows from the buffer until all rows are processed. Check the SQLCA variable SQLCODE for the value 100 to determine when all rows have been read from the cursor's buffer area. In fact, anytime you process an SQL statement in the program, you must check variables in the SQLCA region to verify that the SQL statement processed correctly. Figure 9-10 contains information on several SQLCA variables you can use to test for DB2 completion codes.

Variable	Meaning
SQLCODE	0 value indicates the statement executed successfully +100 value indicates no data exists −n value indicates an error occurred.
SQLERRD	A subscripted variable where SQLERRD(3) contains the number of rows inserted, deleted, or updated for INSERT, DELETE, and UPDATE, respectively.
NOT-FOUND	An 88 level variable for SQLCODE = 100.
SQLWARNO	Indicates a warning condition (i.e., SQLCODE > 0 and SQLCODE NOT = 100) if it contains a "W."
SQLWARNING	An 88 level variable for SQLWARNO containing a "W."
SQLERROR	An 88 level for SQLCODE < 0.
NOT FOUND	Special variable name for WHENEVER clause—same meaning as NOT-FOUND.

Fig. 9-10. Selected SQLCA variables and their meanings.

Use the statements:

```
FETCH...
IF SQLCODE = 100
      GO TO 290-CLOSE-AND-QUIT-ROUTINE
ELSE
      PERFORM 300-PROCESS-EMPLOYEE-ROW
      GO TO 205-READ-A-ROW-FROM-BUFFER.
```

to process rows in the same way you use:

```
READ FILEA INTO RECORDA
      AT END GO TO 290-CLOSE-AND-QUIT-ROUTINE.
PERFORM 300-PROCESS-EMPLOYEE-ROW
```

to process sequential records in standard COBOL files. That is, both groups of statements read sequential records and provide for end-of-file determination.

As a general summary, when you extract multiple rows from a table you must:

1. Declare a cursor in WORKING-STORAGE containing the appropriate SELECT statement.
2. OPEN the cursor to extract the rows from the table and place them into a buffer area.
3. FETCH each row from the buffer by placing the FETCH statement within a loop.

4. After FETCHing each row, check for end-of-file (or is SQLCODE = 100)
5. If not at end-of-file, process another row (go back to step 3).
6. CLOSE the cursor when end-of-file occurs.

Now look at a sample COBOL program in FIG. 9-11 to see how to use embedded SQL statements to extract multiple rows from a table.

```
    WORKING-STORAGE SECTION
            .
            .
            .
    01 EMPLOYEE-TABLE-HOST-VARIABLES.
           05 SCREEN-EMPLID                                    PIC X(9).
           05 READIT-DEMOGRAPHIC-DATA.
                        10 READIT-LASTNAME                     PIC X(25).
                        10 READIT-FIRSTNAME                    PIC X(20).
                        10 READIT-ADDRESS                      PIC X(30).
                        10 READIT-CITY                         PIC X(25).
                        10 READIT-STATE                        PIC X(2).
                        10 READIT-ZIP                          PIC X(5).
* DEFINE THE TABLE FROM DECLGEN PROCESS
          EXEC SQL
              INCLUDE DCLEMPL
          END-EXEC.
* DEFINE THE SQL COMMUNICATIONS REGION
          EXE SQL
              INCLUDE SQLCA
          END-EXEC.
          EXEC SQL
             DECLARE POINTER1 CURSOR FOR
                 SELECT LASTNAME, FIRSTNAME, ADDRESS, CITY
                        STATE, ZIP
                 FROM EMPLOYEE
                 WHERE STATE = :SCREEN-STATE
          END-EXEC.
              .
              .
              .
PROCEDURE DIVISION.
          .
          .
          .
*INITIALIZE EMPLOYEE TABLE'S KEY COLUMN (FIELD)
       MOVE 'TN' TO SCREEN-STATE.
200-ACCESS-SQL-TABLE-EMPLOYEE.
         EXEC SQL
             OPEN POINTER1
         END-EXEC.
          .
          .
          .
205-READ-A-ROW-FROM-BUFFER.
         EXEC SQL
           FETCH POINTER 1
              INTO :READIT-LASTNAME,
                   :READIT-FIRSTNAME,
```

Fig. 9-11. Sample COBOL code to FETCH multiple rows from EMPLOYEE table.

```
                    :READIT-ADDRESS,
                    :READIT-CITY,
                    :READIT-STATE,
                    :READIT-ZIP
           END-EXEC.
           IF SQLCODE = 100
                MOVE 'YES' TO PROCESSED-ALL-RECORDS
                GO TO 290-CLOSE-AND-QUIT-ROUTINE
           ELSE
                PERFORM 300-PROCESS-EMPLOYEE-ROW
                GO TO 205-READ-A-ROW-FROM-BUFFER.
       290-CLOSE-AND-QUIT-ROUTINE.
           EXEC SQL
                CLOSE POINTER1
           END-EXEC.
       299-ROUTINE-END.
           EXIT.
       300-PROCESS-EMPLOYEE-ROW.
```

Fig. 9-11 cont.

Note that after you fetch a row, the table values for that row are in the host variables READIT-LASTNAME, READIT-FIRSTNAME, READIT-ADDRESS, READIT-CITY, READIT-STATE, and READIT-ZIP and you process them as you would any COBOL variable.

Other Error-Trapping Mechanisms

You can use the keywords SQLWARNING, SQLERROR, and NOT FOUND in a WHENEVER clause to automatically trap warnings, errors, and not-found conditions. Typically, you place the WHENEVER clause immediately after the PROCEDURE DIVISION statement in the program. WHENEVER is to COBOL as ON ERROR is to BASIC. That is, whenever a particular condition arises anytime with the program, control reverts to the WHENEVER statement. For example, the statements:

```
PROCEDURE DIVISION.
      EXEC SQL
           WHENEVER SQLERROR PERFORM 9000-SQL-ERROR-
                          TRAP-ROUTINE
      END-EXEC.
      EXEC SQL
           WHENEVER SQLWARNING PERFORM 9100-SQL-WARNING-
                          ROUTINE
      END-EXEC.
      EXEC SQL
           WHENEVER NOT FOUND CONTINUE
      END-EXEC.
```

creates a trapping mechanism for errors and warnings. The error and warning routines in paragraphs 9000 and 9100 will contain error-handling or warning-handling procedures, if needed. You can use the condition CONTINUE for NOT FOUND because you will handle that condition as you FETCH the individual rows from the cursor's buffer area. Place the COBOL statement:

```
IF SQLCODE = 100
        MOVE 'EMPLOYEE NOT ON DATABASE' TO ERROR-MSG
        MOVE 'YES' TO HAVE-AN-ERROR
        GO TO END-OF-ROUTINE.
```

after each FETCH statement in the program to test for processing the last row from the cursor's buffer area. When you try to FETCH past the end of the buffer area, DB2 returns the status code 100 to the SQLCA variable SQLCODE.

Updating Using a Cursor

The process of updating a row involves the following six step operation:

1. DECLARE the cursor using the general form:

   ```
   EXEC SQL
        DECLARE variable name CURSOR FOR
             SELECT statement
        FOR UPDATE OF list of column names
   END-EXEC.
   ```

   Here, "list of column names" are the columns that are to be updated for the row or rows extracted by the SELECT statement. For example, the statement:

   ```
   EXEC SQL
        DECLARE POINTER1 CURSOR FOR
             SELECT LASTNAME, FIRSTNAME, ADDRESS, CITY
             FROM EMPLOYEE
             WHERE EMPLID = :SCREEN-EMPLID
        FOR UPDATE OF LASTNAME, FIRSTNAME, ADDRESS,
             CITY
        END-EXEC.
   ```

   not only identifies the row that is to be extracted (here, EMPLID = :SCREEN-EMPLID) but also identifies the columns that are to be updated (LASTNAME, FIRSTNAME, ADDRESS and CITY). Note that you must move a value to SCREEN-EMPLID before you OPEN the cursor so that you read the proper row from the table.
2. Open the cursor using the OPEN statement and the cursor's name.
3. Retrieve the row to be updated using the FETCH statement.
4. Use the following form of the UPDATE statement to modify the row:

   ```
   UPDATE tablename
        SET column name = value,
            column name = value,
            column name = value,
                 .
                 .
                 .
   WHERE CURRENT OF cursor name
   ```

5. Loop to step 3 and continue the cycle until all rows in the buffer area are processed (i.e., SQLCODE = 100).
6. CLOSE the cursor.

Obviously, between the third and fourth steps the program must query the user for the actual data that will be used to modify the columns in the row. The program then must verify that the entered data is valid data for the database. Use host variables in the UPDATE statement to move the modified data to the table column names. For example, the statement:

```
UPDATE EMPLOYEE
    SET LASTNAME  = :SCREEN-LASTNAME,
        FIRSTNAME = :SCREEN-FIRSTNAME,
        ADDRESS   = :SCREEN-ADDRESS,
        CITY      = :SCREEN-CITY
WHERE CURRENT OF POINTER1
```

uses the values in the host variables SCREEN-LASTNAME, SCREEN-FIRSTNAME, SCREEN-ADDRESS, and SCREEN-CITY to update the row for an employee in the table. The value in the host variable SCREEN-EMPLID in the DECLARE statement identifies which EMPLOYEE row is updated. Part of the COBOL program to perform an update is given in FIG. 9-12.

```
WORKING-STORAGE SECTION.
            .
            .
            .
     EXEC SQL
          DECLARE POINTER1 CURSOR FOR
               SELECT LASTNAME, FIRSTNAME, ADDRESS, CITY
               FROM EMPLOYEE
               WHERE EMPLID = :SCREEN-EMPLID
          FOR UPDATE OF LASTNAME, FIRSTNAME, ADDRESS, CITY
END-EXEC.
01 EMPLOYEE-TABLE-HOST-VARIABLES.
     05 SCREEN-EMPLID                                    PIC X(9).
     05 READIT-DEMOGRAPHIC-DATA.
          10 READIT-LASTNAME                             PIC X(25).
          10 READIT-FIRSTNAME                            PIC X(20).
          10 READIT-ADDRESS                              PIC X(30).
          10 READIT-CITY                                 PIC X(25).
          10 READIT-STATE                                PIC X(2).
          10 READIT-ZIP                                  PIC X(5).
01 EMPLOYEE-UPDATE-DATA.
     05 SCREEN-LASTNAME                                  PIC X(25).
     05 SCREEN-FIRSTNAME                                 PIC X(20).
     05 SCREEN-ADDRESS                                   PIC X(30).
     05 SCREEN-CITY                                      PIC X(25).
     05 SCREEN-STATE                                     PIC X(2).
     05 SCREEN-ZIP                                       PIC X(5).
     EXEC SQL
          INCLUDE DCLEMPL
     END-EXEC.
     EXEC SQL
```

Fig. 9-12. Selected code to update a table row using an embedded UPDATE statement.

```
        INCLUDE SQLCA
    END-EXEC.
          .
          .
          .
PROCEDURE DIVISION
          .
          .
          .
300-BEGIN-ROW-EXTRACTION.
        MOVE INPUT-ID TO SCREEN-EMPLID.
        EXEC SQL
             OPEN POINTER1
        END-EXEC.
*
        EXEC SQL
             FETCH POINTER1 INTO :READ-IT-DEMOGRAPHIC-DATA
        END-EXEC.
*
        IF SQLCODE = 100
             MOVE 'EMPLOYEE NOT ON DATABASE' TO ERROR-MSG
             MOVE 'YES' TO HAVE-AN-ERROR
             GO TO 399-END-ROUTINE.
*
        PERFORM 400-VERIFY-DATA-ROUTINE.
        IF DESIRED-ROW = 'NO'
              GO TO 399-END-ROUTINE.
*
        EXEC SQL
           UPDATE EMPLOYEE
                  SET
             LASTNAME    =  :SCREEN-LASTNAME,

             FIRSTNAME   =  :SCREEN-FIRSTNAME,

             ADDRESS     =  :SCREEN-ADDRESS,

             CITY        =  :SCREEN-CITY
           WHERE CURRENT OF POINTER1
        END-EXEC.
*
        IF SQLCODE NOT = 0
             MOVE 'CANNOT UPDATE ROW' TO ERROR-MSG
             MOVE 'YES' TO HAVE-AN-ERROR
             GO TO 399-END-ROUTINE.
*
        EXEC SQL
           CLOSE POINTER1
        END-EXEC.
399-END-ROUTINE.
```

Fig. 9-12 cont.

Note that you perform the routine 400-VERIFY-DATA-ROUTINE to verify that the extracted row is indeed the row the user wants to modify. Also, the values in SCREEN-LASTNAME, SCREEN-FIRSTNAME, SCREEN-ADDRESS, and SCREEN-CITY contain the modifications to the row for the respective columns.

Note that when you use the UPDATE command in an embedded statement:

1. You update only a single row.
2. You must point to the row to be updated using FETCH.
3. After you update the row, DB2 still points to that row until you FETCH another row.
4. Each column you update must be included in the DECLARE statement.

Deleting a Row or Rows

You can delete a single row or multiple rows using an embedded DELETE statement. Typically, you would want to view the records before you deleted them to verify that you are indeed deleting the proper rows in the table. The logic for deleting rows using an embedded DELETE and a cursor is similar to the logic to update a row using an embedded UPDATE statement. That is, the steps to follow are:

1. DECLARE a cursor for the rows you potentially want to delete.
2. OPEN the cursor.
3. Point to a row using FETCH.
4. Display it on the screen.
5. If you want to delete it, use the general form of the DELETE statement:

   ```
   EXEC SQL
       DELETE FROM tablename
       WHERE CURRENT OF cursor name
   END-EXEC.
   ```

6. Provide a looping mechanism to repeat steps three through five until all rows are extracted from the buffer area.
7. Close the cursor.

Place the DECLARE statement in WORKING-STORAGE to identify the multiple rows that are to be deleted. Note that in the DECLARE statement you identify the condition for extracting the multiple rows by using the WHERE clause in DELETE. For example, if you want to delete all employees in the EMPLOYEE table who are from Texas and view the data before you delete it, you could use the statements in FIG. 9-13.

Obviously the statement:

```
EXEC SQL
     DELETE FROM EMPLOYEE
     WHERE STATE = :SCREEN-STATE
END-EXEC.
```

will delete all the employees from Texas when SCREEN-STATE contains the value TX. In this case, DB2 deletes all the rows and with no user verification of the data in the rows occurring. However, in many cases, it is desirable to require the user to first verify the data before deleting it. Note also you could

```
WORKING-STORAGE SECTION.
          EXEC SQL
              INCLUDE DCLEMPL
          END-EXEC.
          EXEC SQL
              INCLUDE SQLCA
          END-EXEC.
          EXEC SQL
             DECLARE POINTER2 CURSOR FOR
                  SELECT LASTNAME, FIRSTNAME, ADDRESS, CITY
                  FROM EMPLOYEE
                  WHERE STATE = :SCREEN-STATE
          END-EXEC.
          .
          .
          .
PROCEDURE DIVISION.
          .
          .
          .
    MOVE 'TX' TO SCREEN-STATE.
    EXEC SQL
          OPEN POINTER2
    END-EXEC.
    *
START-ROUTINE.
    *
          EXEC SQL
                FETCH POINTER2 INTO :READ-IT-DEMOGRAPHIC-DATA
          END-EXEC.
          IF SQL-CODE = 100
                GO TO END-ROUTINE.
    *
          PERFORM DISPLAY-AND-VERIFY.
          IF DELETE-ROW = 'NO'
                GO TO START-ROUTINE
          ELSE
                EXEC SQL
                     DELETE FROM EMPLOYEE
                     WHERE CURRENT OF POINTER2
                END-EXEC.
          GO TO START-ROUTINE.
    *
END-ROUTINE.
    *
     EXEC SQL
           CLOSE POINTER2
     END-EXEC.
```

Fig. 9-13. Deleting multiple rows using a cursor.

simply SELECT the rows using a cursor, display them to the screen, and then ask the user:

DO YOU WANT TO DELETE ALL THE ABOVE ROWS?

If the user responds affirmatively, you can then use the above embedded DELETE statement to erase all the rows for the values just displayed.

Exercises

9-1. Suppose you used the following CREATE statement to create a table:

```
CREATE TABLE        CUSTITEMS
      (CUSTID       CHAR(10)            NOT NULL,
       AMTOWED      DECIMAL(7,2)        NOT NULL,
       AMTPAID      DECIMAL (7,2)       NOT NULL,
       HIGHBAL      DECIMAL (10,2)              ,
       NUMBORD      SMALLINT                    ,
       ITEMNAME     CHAR(15)                    )
IN USERBASE.        USERTS1
```

a. Write the embedded INSERT statement to load data into this table.

b. Write the embedded UPDATE statement to load data into this table.

c. Write the embedded DELETE statement to delete any row for a value in the host variable INPUT-CUSTID.

d. Write the 01 level definition for the host variables you will use for this table.

9-2. Write a COBOL program to create an add screen to insert data into the CUSTITEMS table in Exercise 9-1.

9-3. Write a COBOL program to create an update screen to modify data for the CUSTITEMS table in Exercise 9-1.

9-4. A user wants a program to read data from the CUSTITEMS table and to display it on the screen. After a row is displayed, the user wants the option to modify the row, delete the row, or look at the next row. Write a computer program to process this user's request.

10

Table and Index Space: Structure and Characteristics

Data is stored in rows within a logical unit called tables. These rows physically reside on pages in a tablespace in an area of disk reserved under a database name. The size of the data in a column is defined in parameters when you CREATE the table using DDL. The number of bytes each column uses is dictated by the data type and its length at CREATE time. DB2 creates the indexspace using parameters in the CREATE INDEX statement. If data already exists in the table, DB2 scans the tablespace and builds the index. However, if there is no data for the table in the tablespace, DB2 builds the index as you load data into the tablespace at INSERT or LOAD time.

Storing Data

When you enter data into the row of a logical table, DB2 physically loads the data into the first available space in the first available page in the tablespace. The first two bytes of the data contain two codes: one indicates whether or not it is a null value, and the other indicates its length in hexadecimal. The null-indicator byte contains the value hexadecimal 00 (low values) if the data is not nulls, or the value hexadecimal FF (high values) if it is a null value.

Obviously, because the first two bytes are reserved for DB2 codes, the maximum size of any column is 254 characters. In addition, because the first byte is either hex 00 for not-nulls or hex FF for nulls, when you use ORDER BY in a query on a column containing nulls, the null values appear last in the list for ascending order and first in the list for descending order.

Each row in DB2 contains a six-byte header and a two-byte pointer. Each page has a header of 19 bytes, an area to store rows, and an area to store multiple RID values. When you insert a row based on an indexed column into a page,

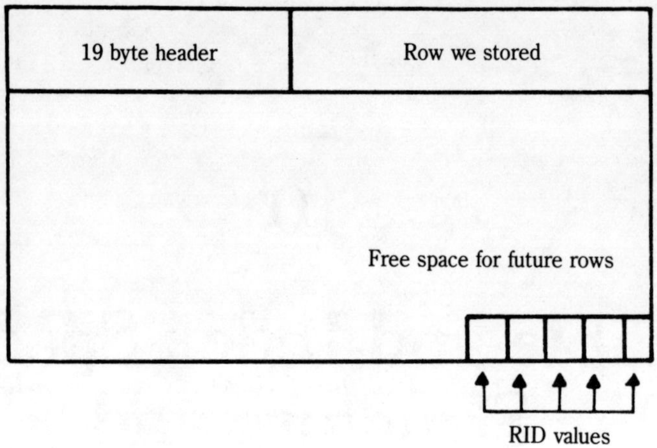

Fig. 10-1. Format of a page.

the index keeps track of the row's physical location by using a Record ID or RID value (see FIG. 10-1).

The RID values are pointers to the relative location of a row within a page. When accessing a row within a page DB2 uses the row's RID value to locate the row in the page (see FIG. 10-2).

Index

Index Key	Page #	RID value
123456789	1001	1
234567890	1001	3
345678901	1001	2

Page #1001

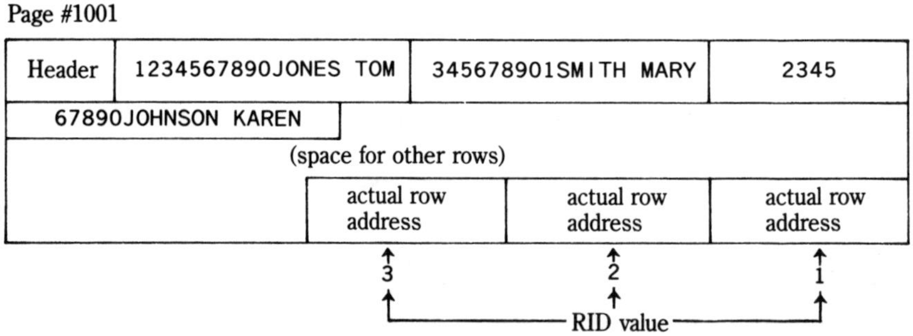

Fig. 10-2. Using RID values to locate a row on a page.

Thus to find a particular row in the tablespace, DB2 accesses the index and using the index key finds the row's page number and RID value. It then locates the page in the tablespace and extracts the row by using the actual address stored on the page referenced by the row's RID value. For example, in FIG. 10-2 to find a row where EMPLID = 234567890, DB2 goes to the index and extracts page number 1001 and RID value 3. It goes to the tablespace, and reads into memory page 1001. It then uses the relative address referenced by the third RID value on the page to extract the desired row. DB2 then places the row into a buffer area containing the data extracted for the query.

Note that you will have some problems with using this concept. First, DB2 stores the rows from any table on any page. That is, DB2 does not store a table as one contiguous piece of data but rather intermingles rows of one table with rows of another table. If you want all the rows of a particular table, DB2 either uses the index to load each row into the data buffer or it reads every row of every page in the tablespace to find the rows for that particular table. Hence, if you do not create an index for the table and use that index, DB2 locks the entire tablespace and then scans it looking for the needed data. Obviously, if you have multiple tables stored in the tablespace, when DB2 locks the tablespace, all data in that space is locked to other users. Therefore, if other tables exist in the tablespace, they will be locked to other users until DB2 completes its tablespace scan.

Types of Tablespaces

Tablespaces can be of one of three varieties: simple, shared, and partitioned. For a simple tablespace, you create and store a single table within a single tablespace. For a shared tablespace, you create multiple tables in one tablespace. In a partitioned tablespace, you create one table in one tablespace but place the tablespace in multiple areas of DASD.

Remember, when you place multiple tables in a tablespace, DB2 sequentially stores their rows in the tablespace as they are loaded via the DML INSERT or through the LOAD utility. In addition, when you have a shared tablespace and DB2 accesses a column that does not contain an index, DB2 locks the entire tablespace and scans it. Here, all rows (and consequently all logical tables) are locked in the tablespace. Also, DB2 performs a tablespace scan and reads all rows on all pages in the tablespace consuming both time and resources.

Partitioning a Tablespace and Using a Cluster Index

You can partition a tablespace when you use the keyword NUMBPARTS in the CREATE TABLESPACE statement. Partition the tablespace by using a range of key values for your primary key in the CREATE INDEX statement. Each partition you create can reside on different device types. For example, you can use the following CREATE statement to partition the tablespace EDUCTS1 into four parts, the first three on volume EU8001 and the fourth on volume EU8002:

```
CREATE TABLESPACE EDUCTS1
        IN EDUCBASE
        USING STOGROUP EU8001
                PRIQTY 30
```

```
            SECQTY 20
        ERASE YES
        NUMPARTS 4 (PART 4 USING STOGROUP EU8002
            PRIQTY 10
            SECQTY 5)
        LOCKSIZE ANY
        BUFFERPOOL BP2
        CLOSE YES
```

You can create the corresponding index on a table in the partitioned tablespace using:

```
    CREATE INDEX CUSTINDEX
    ON CUSTITEMS
    (CUSTID)
    USING STOGROUP EU8003
    PRIQTY 10
    SECQTY 5
    ERASE YES
    CLUSTER (PART 1 VALUES ('2000000000'),
             PART 2 VALUES ('4000000000')
             PART 3 VALUES ('6000000000'),
             PART 4 VALUES ('9999999999'))
```

Here, you can create an index on column CUSTID in the table CUSTITEMS and identify where the various rows will reside in the four tablespace partitions. Rows with CUSTID values between '0000000000' and '2000000000' inclusive will reside in partition 1; '2000000001' and '4000000000' inclusive will reside in partition 2; '4000000001' and '6000000000' inclusive will reside in partition 3; and '6000000001' and '9999999999' inclusive will reside in partition 4.

You can have only one cluster index per table. By clustering the index and partitioning the tablespace the Operations Team can perform backups and other utilities on the separate parts of the tablespace because they reside on different volumes. By having smaller segments to manipulate, utilities also finish faster, and backups are easier and quicker to create. Also, you minimize page accessing by clustering the indexes into partitions. Note that when you use CLUSTER, the rows are physically stored according to the key sequence for the various partitions.

Using Indexes

In the above example, you place the tablespace on the two volumes EU8001 and EU8002 and the index in an index space on volume EU8003. By separating the tablespace into partitions and creating an index on another volume, you are trying to minimize database or hardware contention problems. Obviously, you only create cluster indexes when you need them. Because you can ALTER tablespaces and indexes, you only modify the tablespace structure and indexes whenever problems arise.

Remember, DB2 creates the indexspace using parameters in the CREATE INDEX statement. If the table already has data, DB2 scans the tablespace and builds the index. However, if the table has no data, DB2 builds the index while you load data into the tablespace at INSERT or LOAD time. DB2 maintains the index and indexspace and decides (through various algorithms within the software package) whether to use the index to access rows in tables. Note that DB2 decides whether to use the index or not either when you BIND or RUN a query dynamically or in batch mode.

Also, if DB2 does not use the index, it performs a tablespace scan to find the values, thereby locking the tablespace against other users' access. This in effect overrides the LOCKSIZE PAGE option in the CREATE TABLESPACE statement since a lock of the tablespace is automatic if DB2 does not use the index.

Index Structure

When you create an index, DB2 creates an indexspace and places the table holding the index in the indexspace. The index is composed of *root pages* and *leaf pages*. The root page contains the page number of all leaf pages and a range of values for the key-values on that leaf page (see FIG. 10-3). When you access a row using an index, DB2 searches the root page looking for the access key among the range of keys in the root page. Once it identifies that the key falls within the range, it then accesses the necessary leaf page and searches for the access key given in the query. Once it finds the access key, it extracts the page number location and RID value for that row. DB2 then goes to the tablespace containing the row, finds the row's address using the RID number, and extracts the data in the row, placing it in a buffer. For example, assume you entered the query:

```
SELECT *
FROM PARTVALUE
WHERE PARTID = '12225'
```

with column PARTID having an index. Using the data in FIG. 10-3 for the above query, DB2 searches the root page and finds the leaf page value containing the key '12225' (or Leaf Page 002). DB2 then goes to Leaf Page 002 and searches it for the key '12225'. After it finds the key, it uses that key's page number (1002) and RID value (1) to find the row in the tablespace. Here, it goes to page 1002 and uses the relative address in RID value 1 to extract the row from the tablespace. DB2 then places that row in the query's data buffer.

Index Subpages

Remember, the index is a table in a tablespace called an indexspace and is managed by DB2. Because an index is a logical table in a physical tablespace, it is stored in rows on pages. Each row is treated like any other row in a tablespace. That is, when you use the index to access a row on a page, DB2 locks

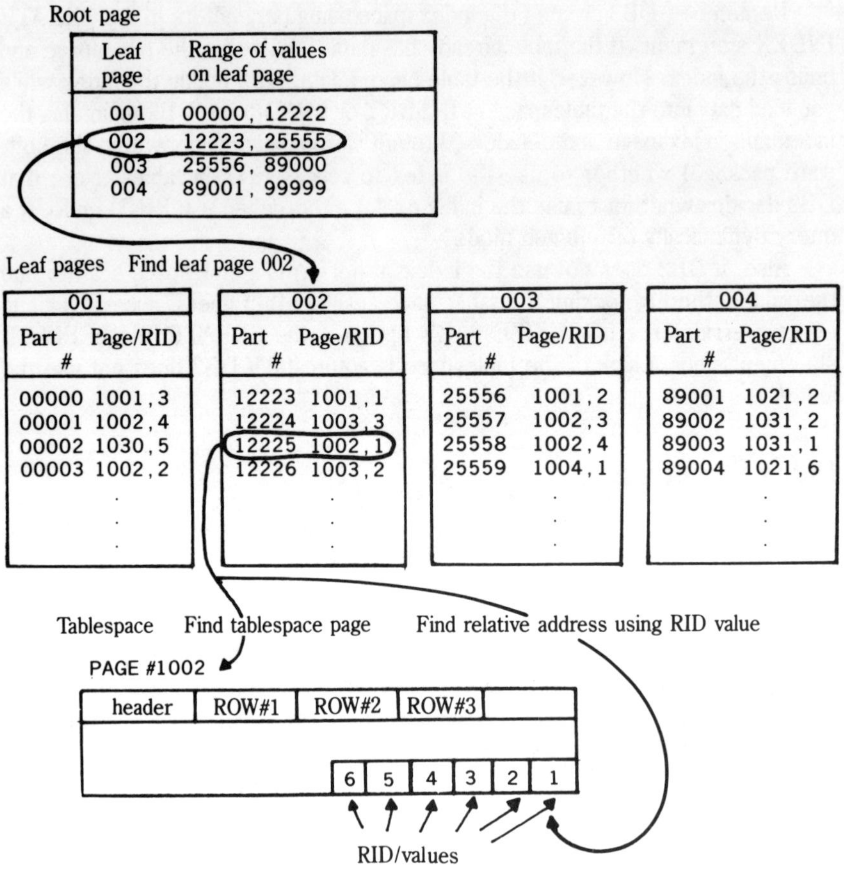

Fig. 10-3. Using root page and leaf page to extract data from a tablespace using an index.

the leaf page containing the access key. Therefore, since DB2 treats indexspaces like any other tablespace, you also have page locks on leaf pages and tablespace locks on the indexspace containing them. You can decrease these locking problems by partitioning the index pages using the keyword SUBPAGES in the CREATE INDEX statement. Subpaging allows locking to be done on a portion of a leaf page rather than the whole leaf page. You can subdivide the leaf page into 1, 2, 4, 8, or 16 subpages. For example, you can subdivide the indexspace into subpages for the index CUSTINDEX2 using:

```
CREATE INDEX CUSTINDEX2
ON CUSTITEMS
(CUSTNAME, CUSTSTATE)
USING STOGROUP EU8003
PRIQTY 10
SECQTY 5
ERASE YES
SUBPAGES 8
BUFFERPOOL BP1
```

Here, the leaf pages are subdivided into 8 subpages. Obviously, the more subpages you have, the more concurrency you will have because only a small section of the leaf page is locked at any one time. However, subdividing the leaf page into multiple parts creates processing and memory overhead. The smaller the number of subpages (for example, 1), the less amount of memory and processing overhead you have. However, having fewer subpages creates a greater amount of concurrency problems since the entire indexspace will be locked each time you access it. Conversely, if you chose to subdivide the indexspace into 16 subpages, you would have greater concurrency but consume more memory and processing time.

Using the Index to Access Multiple Rows

When you access multiple rows in a tablespace using an index, DB2 finds their page numbers and RID values in the index and directly accesses the appropriate pages and rows. In FIG. 10-4, we are searching for all females (F) who are in the table. Here, DB2 uses the index to locate each and every female in the table using page number and RID value found in the index. By creating an index on each column you use as a search argument, you allow DB2 to access the rows directly and conserve system resources.

Index

Index key	Page RID
F	1001, 2
F	1002, 4
F	1001, 3
F	1002, 1
F	1002, 2
F	1002, 5
M	1001, 4
M	1002, 3
M	1002, 6
M	1004, 3

Tablespace

Page	Row	Columns				
1001	1	SMITH	MARY	F	DUNLAP	TN
1001	2	JONES	SUSAN	F	DECATUR	IL
1001	3	BIRD	KAREN	F	LOMAR	TX
1001	4	ARROW	MIKE	M	TERTIA	MA
1002	1	SMITH	BARBARA	F	RAMBLER	NY
1002	2	BARTS	BETTY	F	NUGGET	AR
1002	3	BARTS	BOB	M	NUGGET	AR
1002	4	ARROW	CATHY	F	TERTIA	MA
1002	5	GOLDEN	LORA	F	NUGGET	AR

Fig. 10-4. Accessing multiple rows in a tablespace using an index.

Locking Strategies

When you access a table or index, DB2 places a lock on the page or tablespace that it accesses depending on algorithms within DB2 and whether or not the access uses an indexed column. The data in the page or tablespace is unavailable to other users during the lock. When DB2 finishes with the page or tablespace, it releases the lock so other users can access data in the page or tablespace. Although DB2 creates automatic locks on pages or tablespaces, you can explicitly create a lock using:

```
LOCK TABLE tablename IN SHARE MODE
```

or

```
LOCK TABLE tablename IN EXCLUSIVE MODE
```

Here, DB2 creates a tablespace lock and allows other users read-only capabilities on the tablespace for SHARE mode or prevents any access to the tablespace in EXCLUSIVE mode. Obviously, if you are going to view a row with the anticipation of updating information in it, you would want to restrict other users' access to the row until the update occurs. This way, users are ensured their access includes the most current data in the database. In addition, creating an EXCLUSIVE lock ensures that you will not have multiple users trying to simultaneously update the same row.

Once DB2 locks a page or tablespace, it remains locked until a COMMIT or a ROLLBACK. A COMMIT indicates that the work effort was successfully completed while a ROLLBACK indicates that the work effort was abandoned because of some error.

Exercises

10-1. Write the DDL statement to partition a tablespace into three parts placing them on volumes WE8001, WE8002 and WE8003, respectively. The partition is based on the employee's FICA number and is uniformly divided among the three partitions.

10-2. Several tables in the database are experiencing concurrency problems. What are some of the options to rectify the problems?

10-3. Suppose you want to create a unique index on part number for your table containing 1,000,000 rows. How can you subdivide the indexspace to maximize concurrency?

10-4. Explain how DB2 accesses the index using root pages, leaf pages, and tablespace pages.

11

Utilities

DB2 contains many utility programs which perform certain auxiliary tasks essential for managing the data in the databases. Some of the utility programs are listed in TABLE 11-1.

Table 11-1. Selected utilities available in DB2.

Utility	Use
IMAGE COPY	Makes tablespace backup copies.
LOAD	Loads data into tablespace using external files.
RECOVERY	Recovers the tablespace.
REORG	Reorganizes tablespaces and indexes.
RUNSTATS	Provides statistics on tablespaces.
STOSPACE	Provides statistics on DASD space.
CHECK	Provides statistics on referential integrity violations and optionally repairs them.

You can access DB2 utilities from the "UTILITIES" option in the DB2I menu. Although you can use any of the utilities (once you are authorized), only a few of them probably have any immediate importance to you. Obviously, if we are going to create tables and make queries on data in them, we must first place data into the tables.

Loading Data into Tables

As mentioned in an earlier chapter, you can use the INSERT statement to load data into tables. However, to insert large amounts of data into a table, you must resort to programming an ADD/UPDATE screen for the data-entry staff, use DBEDIT to load data into the table, or use the LOAD utility.

DBEDIT

DBEDIT is a separate IBM product that automatically generates screens, accesses tables, edits inputted data, and SELECTs, UPDATEs, DELETEs, or INSERTs data from or into tables. Because DBEDIT does not create audit trails, many installations restrict its use to the programming staff so they can create test data for their embedded code. This lack of an audit trail prevents DBEDIT from being used in a production environment since internal auditing in most companies requires an audit trail for production programs.

The LOAD Utility and DXT

The LOAD utility can load data into multiple tables using data from IMS databases, VSAM data sets, SQL/DS databases, or other similar files. However, you do not directly load IMS or VSAM data into DB2. First, you must use Data Extract (DXT) on these type files to convert them to *sequential* (or *flat*) files. Then, use the LOAD utility on the flat files to insert data into one or more tables.

DATA EXTRACT (DXT) is a separately-priced product from IBM. It massages existing files or databases and converts them into sequential data sets to be used by the LOAD utility. DXT converts the following type files to a sequential file suitable for LOAD:

- VSAM data sets.
- IMS databases.
- SQL/DS databases.
- Other sequential data sets.

Note that you can convert IMS or VSAM data sets into flat or sequential files using either the Data Extract (DXT) software product from IBM or a computer program which converts the IMS or VSAM data set into a sequential flat-file. Once you have the sequential file, enter DB2I and use the LOAD utility to insert data from the file into the appropriate table. If data already exist in the tables, you must indicate at LOAD time whether you want to intermingle the new data in the sequential file with the already-existing data in the table or else replace the existing data in the table with the new data in the sequential file. In addition, both the tablespace and the DB2 catalog (for creating, altering, or dropping other DB2 entities in the same database) are locked during the loading process.

Use the LOAD statement to define the relationship between the fields in the sequential file and the columns in the table. The statement:

```
LOAD DATA
INTO TABLE $TONY.PAYROLL
(EMPLID          POSITION (1)       CHAR (9),
 LASTNAME        POSITION (10)      VARCHAR (20),
 FIRSTNAME       POSITION (30)      VARCHAR (20),
 ADDRESS         POSITION (55)      VARCHAR (20),
 CITY            POSITION (80)      VARCHAR (20),
 STATE           POSITION (100)     CHAR(2),
 ZIP             POSITION (102)     CHAR (5),
 HOURSWORKED     POSITION (107)     DECIMAL (8,2),
 RATEOFPAY       POSITION (115)     DECIMAL (8,2))
```

relates the location of the fields in the sequential file to their corresponding column names in table PAYROLL. You can indicate in the LOAD statement that you are resuming the load by adding the option RESUME YES to the LOAD statement. If you want to load data into an empty table, you either use the option RESUME NO or omit the RESUME clause altogether.

Similarly, you can place a condition on what data in the sequential file is to be loaded using the WHEN clause. That is, in the above LOAD statement, if you want to restrict the data to be loaded to all employees from Indiana, you use the statement:

```
LOAD DATA
RESUME YES
INTO TABLE $TONY.PAYROLL
WHEN (100:101) = 'IN'
(EMPLID  POSITION (1) CHAR(9),
(. . .
```

Here, you use the column location of the field "state" in the sequential file and an argument in WHEN to load data based on some criteria. State values are located in columns 100 through 101 in the sequential file and the restriction argument guarantees only records containing values "IN" in these columns will be loaded into the table.

Enter the LOAD statement into some PDS (Partitioned Data Set) with the name of your choosing. Then enter DB2I and execute the LOAD utility using the PDS member name containing the LOAD statement. The LOAD utility will use the LOAD statement in the PDS and the table definitions in the DB2 catalog to load the data in the sequential file into the indicated table.

You can load multiple tables using one LOAD statement by listing the tables and their corresponding column names in LOAD. For example, the statement:

```
LOAD DATA
INTO TABLE $TONY.PAYROLL
INTO TABLE $TONY.MEDICAL
(EMPLID      POSITION (1)       CHAR(9),
 LASTNAME    POSITION (10)      VARCHAR(20),
 MEDHIST     POSITION (30)      VARCHAR(120))
```

loads data from a sequential file into the two columns EMPLID and LASTNAME of the table PAYROLL and into the column MEDHIST of the table MEDICAL.

The RUNSTATS Utility

The RUNSTATS utility examines data in the DB2 catalog concerning the statistics on database entities. In particular, RUNSTATS captures statistics on:

- The number of pages in a tablespace that contains data.
- The number of rows in the table.
- The percent of the pages containing data from active tables.
- The percent of pages containing data from dropped tables.
- The number of rows referenced by the index.
- Various other statistics.

These statistics are used by the BIND in determining the access strategy DB2 will use in navigating the database. This strategy is placed in the program's plan. Therefore, if you make a major change to the amount of data in the database, you should execute the RUNSTATS utility to update the statistics in the DB2 catalog and BIND REPLACE or REBIND all plans for that database. Here, the BIND or REBIND will use the current statistics for the database and use that data to redo the accessing strategies and algorithms to navigate the database.

When you BIND a program when the database contains only 100 rows in the table (say, during testing), you will get a certain accessing strategy from DB2. However, after you load the production data into the database containing perhaps 1,000,000 rows, the accessing strategies and navigational techniques obviously will need to be different for this massive amount of data.

Remember, the BIND creates the locking strategies for the page and tablespace based on whether an index exists on a particular column. When you create an index, you should first execute RUNSTATS and then BIND or REBIND all programs that would use the index. Here, RUNSTATS scans the tablespaces and indexspaces and updates the DB2 statistics based on the current status of data in these spaces. The BINDer will then access the DB2 catalog and generate accessing strategies based on true-to-life data.

The REORG Utility

After you insert or delete a substantial number of rows in a tablespace, the pages containing those rows may need to be reorganized. After multiple deletions each page will have large amounts of free space that need to be reclaimed by the system. Note that this free space is some percentage of the total space on each page. Also, after multiple insertions, the distance between consecutive logical rows can be substantial, which degrades performance for user queries. In addition, when you drop a table, DB2 does not automatically release the space occupied by the rows in that table. Only when you reorganize the tablespace containing the dropped table will the space become available for future use. This becomes critical in tablespaces assigned to users of QMF. When the user deletes data using the DELETE DATA statement in QMF, the space containing that data is not available for future storage until the user REORGs that tablespace. Obviously, it is up to DBADM or other developers responsible for maintaining the end-users' DB2 applications to monitor their tablespaces and establish parameters for REORGing their tablespaces.

When you reorganize a tablespace using the REORG utility, DB2 unloads the tables in the tablespace into a buffer area and then reloads the rows of the tables, grouping them together on either the same or consecutive pages. It also adjusts the indexes on the tables to correspond to the data in the reorganized tables.

After you run the REORG utility, you then run the RUNSTATS utility to update the tablespace's statistics. You can then either BIND ADD or REBIND all plans based on the tables in the tablespace to generate more efficient access paths and index scans.

The CHECK Utility

The CHECK utility is used to validate referential integrity rules for tables. Recall that when you ALTER a table with existing data so as to enforce referential integrity rules, DB2 will place that table in "check pending" status if any existing data violates the rules you specify. From a practical standpoint, a table in "check pending" status cannot be used until you have run the CHECK utility. CHECK allows you to repair these errors by doing one or more of the following:

- Report on rows which violate referential integrity rules.
- Delete those rows from the table.
- Copy those rows to another table.

Usually, you would want to run CHECK once to generate a report on any rows that might need fixing. After examining the rows to determine the proper method of fixing them (by deleting the offending rows, updating the offending rows, or changing your referential integrity rules), you can then run CHECK to delete the rows and, possibly, copy them to another, temporary table. If your examination indicates that you should simply delete offending rows, then you would simply let CHECK delete them for you. If, however, you determine to update the offending rows, you could then update them in the temporary table and reINSERT them into the first table.

12

Query Management Facility

The Query Management Facility (QMF) is an end-user product that queries tables and generates reports and is purchased separately from DB2 and SQL/DS. It is used by nonprogrammers to extract data from either DB2 or SQL/DS databases, and it allows them to create reports without intervention from the programming staff. QMF has two main parts: the Query Screen and the Forms Screen. In the Query Screen, you can enter any SQL command and print a report using the extracted data. In the Forms Screen, you can modify the format of the report, add headings, page numbers, and other report features. In addition, QMF gives you the option to save the query, the extracted data, and the form used for formatting the report. You can later reuse these saved items to either duplicate the report or to modify it.

QMF is an option within both the DB2 and SQL/DS software packages. Typically, QMF can be installed with two identical versions: one for use against production databases and the other for use against test databases. In this chapter, we discuss using QMF in the DB2 testing environment. Note that for all practical purposes, the testing and production versions of QMF in either DB2 or SQL/DS are identical.

QMF is a TSO option for DB2 on MVS/XA mainframe systems. When you first enter QMF, you have the option of using either the Query Screen or the Forms Screen. Figure 12-1 is a graphical diagram of the features of QMF.

Here, write an SQL query in the Query Screen and RUN it to get a preformatted default report. QMF queries the database, extracts data from the indicated table or tables, and places it in a buffer area. You can then display the data using a predefined default form. Once you determine that the query you entered extracts the data you want for your report, you can then save both the data and the query. You can then enter the Forms Screen and format the report to your

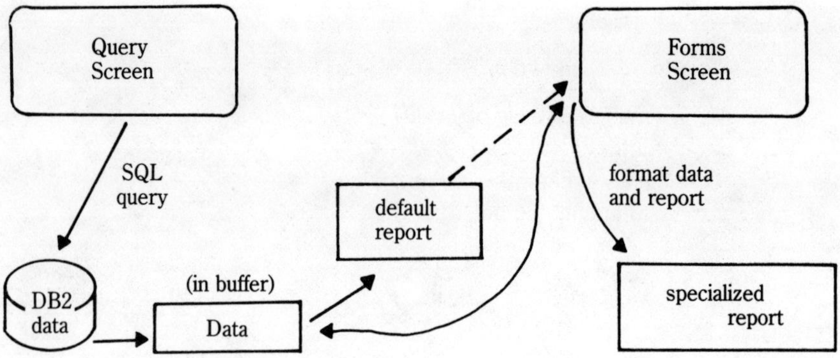

Fig. 12-1. SQL query in Query Screen extracting data for a default report and/or Forms Screen producing a specialized report.

specifications. You can use the data already in the buffer to display your specialized report or you can recall some previously saved data for use in the report. You can then save the formatted form for future use and print the final version of your report. Note that unlike DB2I, in QMF you can both save the data and format it. In DB2I, you can only extract the data and view it—you can neither save the data nor can you format it. Because you can recall either the query (to rerun it), the data (to reformat it), or the form (to use for another query), you have more versatility in QMF than you have in DB2I's SPUFI option.

One disadvantage of using QMF's Query Screen is that you can place only a single query in it at any one time. That is, if you wanted to execute the following set of SQL commands:

```
GRANT USE OF TABLESPACE EPTFTS1 TO $MARY;
GRANT CREATETAB ON DATABASE PAYROLL TO $MARY;
GRANT CREATETS ON DATABASE PAYROLL TO $MARY
```

in QMF, you would have to separately enter each command and execute it. However, in DB2I's SPUFI screen, you can enter all of them into a single screen by separating each command with a semicolon delimiter. When you execute the SPUFI screen, DB2 runs all SQL commands in the entire screen.

Remember, QMF is used primarily by end-users to generate reports which typically use only a single SQL statement. On the other hand, DB2I's SPUFI screen is typically used by the programming staff or development team to create and manage database structures and to test SQL statements before they are embedded in computer programs. Hence, their SQL statements contain multiple SQL commands most of which do not extract data from tables (including CREATE, INSERT, GRANT, etc.).

Enter the main QMF screen by selecting the option "TEST QMF" in the DB2 option menu. The main QMF screen has several options including the Query Screen and Forms Screen options. We press the PF6 key to enter the Query Screen or the PF9 key to enter the Form Screen.

The Query Screen

The Query Screen shown in FIG. 12-2 contains the following four regions:

1. A query area composing about 70 percent of the screen.
2. A menu section listing the options in this screen.
3. A message line below the menu section.
4. A command line at the bottom of the screen.

```
1=HELP        2=RUN       3=END    4=PRINT    5=          6=DRAW
7=BACKWARD    8=FORWARD   9=FORM  10=INSERT  11=DELETE   12=REPORT

COMMAND===>
```

Fig. 12-2. QMF's Query Screen.

QMF uses PF keys to switch between the various screens in QMF or to perform certain tasks within a screen.

Note that in the menu section of the Query Screen you have 12 options available (see FIG. 12-3). The most frequently used options are:

PF2	To execute the SQL query statement found in the query area.
PF9	To enter the Forms Screen.
PF12	To display our report in a Report Screen.

Enter a query in the Query Screen by moving the cursor to the top of the query area and typing in the SQL statement (see FIG. 12-3). Then press the PF2 key to RUN the statement. Now DB2 executes the query, places the data it extracts from the database into a buffer area, and displays the results in a Report Screen using a default format (see FIG. 12-4). The default format is based on the DB2 catalog description of the table when it was CREATEd or later ALTERed.

```
SQL QUERY

SELECT LNAME, FNAME, SEX, DEPT, REGPAY
FROM WEEKLYPAYROLL
WHERE SEX = 'F' AND
      DEPT IN ('A10', 'B10') AND
      DATE = '10/06'

1=HELP        2=RUN       3=END    4=PRINT    5=          6=DRAW
7=BACKWARD    8=FORWARD   9=FORM  10=INSERT  11=DELETE   12=REPORT

COMMAND===>
```

Fig. 12-3. Entering a query in the Query Screen.

The Report Screen contains the data DB2 extracts from a database table or tables using the query in the Query Screen. In this example, the query requests the last name, first name, sex, department number, and regular pay in the table WEEKLYPAYROLL for all the females in department A10 or B10 for the week of 10/06. When you RUN a query, you automatically get the results of the query in the Report Screen.

```
REPORT

LNAME      FNAME    SEX  DEPT   REGPAY

JONES      MARY     F    A10    422.00
LINCOLN    SUSAN    F    B10    676.00
FORD       SHARON   F    B10    440.00

1=HELP        2=           3=END     4=PRINT    5=          6=QUERY
7=BACKWARD    8=FORWARD    9=FORM    10=LEFT    11=RIGHT    12=
OK, this is the REPORT from your RUN
COMMAND===>
```

Fig. 12-4. Sample data from a QMF query.

Handling Error Messages

Note that any error message you get because of syntax errors or for some other reason appears in the Report Screen, not the Query Screen. If you do get an error, you must return to the Query Screen to correct it and reRUN the query. Several reasons for getting an error message include:

- Having improper syntax in the SQL statement by misspelling a key word or by placing the statements in improper order.
- Having improperly identified the column and table names.
- Not being authorized to access the DB2 object in the statement.
- Having mismatched DB2 entity types.

The above list is not an inclusive list. In fact, there are hundreds of reasons why you could get an error. Each time you get an error, the system returns an error code number. You can sometimes get a clue as to the nature of the error by looking up the error code in the "Messages and Codes" manual for DB2.

The Report Screen Menu

The menu at the bottom of the Report Screen is different from the menu at the bottom of the Query Screen. The major PF keys in the Report Screen are given in FIG. 12-5.

PF7	to move backward
PF8	to move forward
PF10	to move left
PF11	to move right
PF6	to return to the Query Screen
PF9	to go to the Forms Screen

Fig. 12-5. Report Screen PF key options.

Here you can use the PF7 or PF8 to view large amounts of data that span multiple screens by using the keys to scroll the data on the screen up and down. You can use PF10 or PF11 to view data that exceeds the 80-column screen size by moving the data on the screen right then left.

You can also use the PF6 key to return to the Query Screen and make changes in the SQL statement, as needed. In addition, you could use the PF9 key to move to the Forms Screen and change the formatting of the report and add headings, page numbers, date, time, and other items.

The Command Line

You can use the command line at the bottom of each QMF screen to enter commands instead of pressing certain PF keys. Figure 12-6 contains a partial list of the commands you can use on the command line. For example, you can save an SQL query which you enter in the Query Screen by entering the command:

```
SAVE QUERY AS name
```

Command	Meaning	Example
RUN	run a query	RUN QUERY1
		RUN name (FORM = form name)
SAVE	save a query	SAVE QUERY AS QUERY1
	save data from a query	SAVE DATA AS DATA1
	save a form	SAVE FORM AS FORM1
ERASE	erase a saved query	ERASE QUERY1
	erase saved data	ERASE DATA1
	erase a saved form	ERASE FORM1

Fig. 12-6. Several commands available for Command Line.

Here "name" is the name you want to assign the stored query. The name can be from 1 to 18 characters long, with the first character being either an alphabetic character or the special characters @, #, or $. The remaining characters in the name can be either alphabetic (A through Z), numeric (0 through 9), an underscore, or the special characters @, #, or $.

Similarly, you can save the data which the query extracted from the database by using the command:

```
SAVE DATA AS dataname
```

Here, QMF saves all the data in the data buffer area as "dataname." After you make the query in FIG. 12-3 and run it to get the data in FIG. 12-4, you can save both of these items by consecutively entering the commands:

```
SAVE QUERY AS QWEEK1
SAVE DATA AS DWEEK1
```

and pressing the Return or Enter key after each entry. Here, QMF saves the query:

```
SELECT LNAME, FNAME, SEX, DEPT, REGPAY
FROM WEEKLYPAYROLL
WHERE SEX = 'F' AND
      DEPT IN ('A10', 'B10') AND
      DATE = '10/06'
```

as QWEEK1 and the data:

LNAME	FNAME	SEX	DEPT	REGPAY
JONES	MARY	F	A10	422.00
LINCOLN	SUSAN	F	B10	676.00
FORD	SHARON	F	B10	440.00

as DWEEK1. You can rerun the query at a later time by entering:

```
RUN QUERY1
```

on the command line and pressing the Return or Enter key. When you rerun the query, QMF again extracts data from the databases and places it in the data buffer area. Here, this data may or may not be the same data that was extracted previously and saved as DWEEK1. Any changes to the database for the columns and rows in the query will be reflected in the new extraction of the data. However, by saving the data in the data buffer area as DWEEK1, you froze it (by capturing it and saving it) for the one SQL statement in the Query Screen for that one moment in time. You can later use the Forms Screen to reformat the saved data to produce different reports based on the same data. This is particularly handy when you want to capture daily, weekly, monthly, or yearly results and generate multiple reports based on the fixed data.

You can delete the saved query, data, or form by using the ERASE command. The command:

```
ERASE QUERY1
```

erases the saved query named QUERY1. Similarly, you can erase any of your saved forms and data using a corresponding ERASE command.

The Forms Screen

You can enter the Forms Screen from either the main QMF menu by pressing the PF9 key when you first enter QMF or from the Query Screen or Report Screen by selecting the FORM option (PF9 in both cases). See FIGS. 12-3 and 12-4.

Using the Default Form

Typically, you enter the Forms Screen after you first RUN a query found in the Query Screen and display its results in the Report Screen. Remember, QMF uses a default form to format the data when you run a query. For example, after you run the query in FIG. 12-3 and get its report (FIG. 12-5), you can view the default form which QMF creates by selecting the FORM option (PF9) in the Report Screen. Figure 12-7 is a part of the default form in the Forms Screen for this query.

```
  FORM MAIN
  COLUMNS:
     NUM        COLUMN HEADING        USAGE     INDENT     WIDTH     EDIT
-----------------------------  --------------------------------------------
      1         LNAME                             2         20        C
      2         FNAME                             2         20        C
      3         SEX                               2          3        C
      4         DEPT                              2          3        C
      5         REGPAY                            2         10        L2
PAGE: HEADING===>
      FOOTING===>
```

Fig. 12-7. Default form for a QMF query.

The column numbers 1, 2, 3, 4, and 5 refer to the relative position of the column in the query. You can rearrange the columns in the report by rearranging the columns in the Query Screen and rerunning the query. You can display up to seven column names in the Forms Screen (in FIG. 12-7). If your query used more than seven columns, you can use the PF7 and PF8 keys to scroll the screen up or down to view the remaining columns. You could also use the Columns Screen option of the Forms Screen (PF4) if you want to display information on more than seven columns.

Headings and Footings

You can change the column headings in the report by changing the values under the COLUMN HEADING in the Forms Screen. For example, if you want your report to have the headings:

```
LAST   FIRST   SEX   DEPARTMENT   REGULAR
NAME   NAME          NUMBER       PAY
```

you can perform the following changes in the COLUMN HEADING column of the Forms Screen:

- Change the value LNAME to LAST_NAME.
- Change the value FNAME to FIRST_NAME.
- Change the value DEPT to DEPARTMENT_NAME.
- Change the value REGPAY to REGULAR_PAY.

Here, the underscore in the heading values tells QMF's report writer to place that heading on two lines.

Now if you chose the option REPORT by using the PF12 key, you would still not get the desired results. Note that the original width of each column defaults to a value derived from the CREATE TABLE statement for the table you access. In this example, you expanded the heading DEPARTMENT beyond the preestablished width (i.e., 3), thereby truncating the heading. When you add headings to your report by modifying values in COLUMN HEADING within the Forms Screen, you must also check the WIDTH column to verify the heading will indeed fit within the column space assigned it. Here, you must change the value 3 to the value 10 because DEPARTMENT contains 10 characters. Also, you can decrease the size of the last name and first name columns to 12 by changing the appropriate values in the WIDTH column.

The corrections to the Form Screen are given in FIG. 12-8. Note that we also added the single line heading "OUR FIRST REPORT" and the single line footer "BY: TONY FABBRI" to the report. The final result is given in FIG. 12-9.

The Forms Screen Menu

The Forms Screen also has a different selection menu at the bottom of its screen. Some of the PF key options in the Forms Screen are given in FIG. 12-10.

```
FORM MAIN
COLUMNS:
   NUM        COLUMN HEADING           USAGE     INDENT     WIDTH     EDIT
    1         LAST_NAME                             2         12        C
    2         FIRST_NAME                            2         12        C
    3         SEX                                   2          3        C
    4         DEPARTMENT_NUMBER                     2         10        C
    5         REGULAR_PAY                           2         10        L2

PAGE: HEADING===>   OUR FIRST REPORT
      FOOTING===>   BY: TONY FABBRI
```

Fig. 12-8. Using headings in Forms Screen.

```
                       OUR FIRST REPORT

   LAST        FIRST      SEX   DEPARTMENT    REGULAR
   NAME        NAME             NUMBER        PAY

   JONES       MARY        F    A10           422.00
   LINCOLN     SUSAN       F    B10           676.00
   FORD        SHARON      F    B10           440.00

                        BY: TONY FABBRI
```

Fig. 12-9. Results of headings modifications.

PF6	to return to the Query Screen
PF12	to produce a report in Report Screen
PF4	go to the Columns Screen
PF5	go to the Options Screen
PF9	go to the Page Screen
PF10	go to the Final Screen
PF11	go to the Break1 Screen

Fig. 12-10. Selected options in the Forms Screen.

Using the Page Screen for Multiple Headings

Most reports are not limited to a single heading and a single footer as found in the report in FIG. 12-9. Typically, three or four lines are used for a heading, and they could include page number, date, and other facts. In QMF you can produce up to five lines of headings and footers by going to the Page Screen (i.e., press PF9). Note that the Forms Screen has several subscreens which are listed in FIG. 12-10. You can migrate from one subscreen to the next by using the appropriate PF key. In the Page Screen, you can place up to five lines for a header or a footer by placing the appropriate heading and footing in the indicated lines spaces in the Page Screen. For example, by adding the multiple headings and footings to the Page Screen that are found in FIG. 12-11, you get the report in FIG. 12-12.

In the Page Screen option, you can use CENTER, LEFT, RIGHT, &DATE, &TIME, and &PAGE to format the report. If you want your report to have more than five headings or five footings, you must resort to programming the report using COBOL or some other language.

After you view the report from the Page Screen, you might want to continue modifying the form. Remember, in the Report Screen, press PF9 (see FIG. 12-5) to return to the Forms Screen. But now when you press PF9, you

```
1 CENTER   GOLD DIGGERS MINING COMPANY  &PAGE
2 CENTER   LOUISVILLE, KENTUCKY
3 CENTER   OUR FIRST REPORT
4 CENTER
5 CENTER

1 CENTER   BY: TONY FABBRI
2 LEFT     COPIES TO:
3 LEFT               CHARLES
4 LEFT               MARY
5 LEFT               STEVE
```

Fig. 12-11. Multiple headings and footer in the Page Screen.

```
      GOLD DIGGERS MINING COMPANY        PAGE 1
          LOUISVILLE, KENTUCKY
            OUR FIRST REPORT

LAST       FIRST     SEX  DEPARTMENT    REGULAR
NAME       NAME           NUMBER        PAY

JONES      MARY       F   A10           422.00
LINCOLN    SUSAN      F   B10           676.00
FORD       SHARON     F   B10           440.00

                   BY: TONY FABBRI
COPIES TO:
        CHARLES
        MARY
        STEVE
```

Fig. 12-12. Report containing multiple headings and footings.

return to the last form you modified; in this case, the Page Screen. That is, whenever you move to one of the forms available in FIG. 12-10 and then display your report in the Report Screen or look at your query in the Query Screen, you always return to the last form you modified. In this case, because you moved to the Page Screen to add multiple headings, if you select the Forms Screen option in the Report Screen, you return to the Page Screen which was the last form you modified.

Using the Edit Column

When you first view the Forms Screen as the default screen, QMF assigns the table column names as the column headings and uses a predefined width for displaying the column based on the column's table description. QMF also uses the column's table description to identify whether the column value is alphanumeric or numeric by placing a C or L, respectively in the EDIT column. You can format the data in each column by using the options in TABLE 12-1.

You can modify the values in the EDIT column in FIG. 12-8 from L2 to D2 to force proper dollar notation for all values in column REGPAY in the report. The resulting Forms Screen looks like:

NUM	COLUMN HEADING	USAGE	INDENT	WIDTH	EDIT
1	LAST_NAME		2	12	C
2	FIRST_NAME		2	12	C
3	SEX		2	3	C
4	DEPARTMENT_NUMBER		2	10	C
5	REGULAR_PAY		2	10	D2

giving data in the report that looks like:

LAST NAME	FIRST NAME	SEX	DEPARTMENT NUMBER	REGULAR PAY
JONES	MARY	F	A10	$422.00
LINCOLN	SUSAN	F	B10	$676.00
FORD	SHARON	F	B10	$440.00

Note that the value in the WIDTH column in the Forms Screen must be large enough to handle the resulting formatted number D2. That is, when the value in a column is larger than the size of the field description in the width column, QMF displays a series of asterisks for the number. Hence, if you see a row of asterisks ("**********") in your report, you must return to the Forms Screen and increase the width of the column containing the asterisks.

Using USAGE Option in Forms Screen

Obviously, for any reports to be of value, they must have minor totals, groupings of data, control break totals, and grand totals. Options in the USAGE column of the Forms Screen perform column totals on the data. TABLE 12-2 lists the major options in the USAGE column.

Table 12-1. Options for the EDIT column in the Forms Screen.

Option	Meaning
Dn	Number with dollar symbol, sign, comma when needed, no leading zeros, and "n" digits to right of decimal point.
Pn	Number with a percent sign, sign, comma when needed, and no leading zeros.
Ln	Number with no leading zeros, sign, no commas, and "n"digits to right of decimal—is the default option for the default Forms Screen.
Jn	Number with leading zeros, no sign, no commas, and "n" digits to right of decimal point.
In	Number with leading zeros, sign, no commas, and "n" digits to right of decimal point.

Table 12-2. Options for the USAGE column in the Forms Screen.

Option	Meaning
AVERAGE	Find the average of this column.
BREAKn	Perform a control break on this column.
COUNT	Find the count of all non-null values in this column.
CSUM	Find the cumulative sum of all values in this column.
GROUP	Group the data in this column (same as GROUP BY).
MAXIMUM	Find the maximum value in this column.
MINIMUM	Find the minimum value in this column.
OMIT	Do not display this column.
STDEV	Find the standard deviation of the values in this column.
SUM	Find the sum of all values in this column.

One of the most commonly used functions in the USAGE column is the SUM function. Here, QMF adds up all the values in the column and displays the sum at the bottom of the column. To sum the values in FIG. 12-9, place the word SUM in the USAGE column for column 5. In addition, if you want to omit the displaying of data in SEX and DEPT columns, place the word OMIT in columns 3 and 4. These changes to FIG. 12-8 give us the Forms Screen values of:

```
NUM   COLUMN HEADING        USAGE  INDENT  WIDTH  EDIT
------------------------------------------------------
  1   LAST_NAME                      2      12     C
  2   FIRST_NAME                     2      12     C
  3   SEX                   OMIT     2       3     C
  4   DEPARTMENT_NUMBER     OMIT     2      10     C
  5   REGULAR_PAY            SUM     2      10     D2
```

and a report that looks like:

```
LAST        FIRST       REGULAR
NAME        NAME        PAY

JONES       MARY        $    422.00
LINCOLN     SUSAN       $    676.00
FORD        SHARON      $    440.00
                        ----------
                        $1,538.00
```

Using Control Breaks

You can use BREAK1 in the USAGE column to perform control breaks on selected columns. For example, the query:

```
SELECT *
FROM WEEKLYPAYROLL
```

```
WHERE DATE = '10/06'
ORDER BY DATE, DEPT
```

produces the report in FIG. 12-13.

FICA	LNAME	FNAME	SEX	DEPT	REGPAY	OVERPAY	PIECEPAY	DATE
123456789	SMITH	JOHN	M	A10	345.00	45.00	12.50	10/06
234567890	JONES	MARY	F	A10	422.00	0.00	0.00	10/06
012345678	JONES	MARK	M	A10	780.00	0.00	0.00	10/06
456789012	ADAMS	KAREN	F	A15	439.00	22.00	44.00	10/06
567890123	LINCOLN	SUSAN	F	B10	676.00	0.00	0.00	10/06
901234567	FORD	SHARON	F	B10	440.00	56.00	0.00	10/06
789012345	DAVIS	SAM	M	B15	124.00	20.00	105.00	10/06
890123456	FRANKLIN	TONY	M	B15	345.00	45.00	55.50	10/06
345678901	DOE	JIM	M	B15	310.00	89.00	0.00	10/06

Fig. 12-13. Report for initial query on WEEKLPAYROLL table using the default form.

Modify the default form to include the following corrections:

NUM	COLUMN HEADING	USAGE	INDENT	WIDTH	EDIT
1	FICA_NUMBER		2	9	C
2	LAST_NAME		2	20	C
3	FIRST_NAME		2	12	C
4	SEX	OMIT	2	3	C
5	DEPT_NUMBER	BREAK1	2	6	C
6	REGULAR_PAY	SUM	2	10	D2
7	OVERPAY	OMIT	2	6	L2
8	PIECEPAY	OMIT	2	6	L2
9	DATE	OMIT	2	5	C

The resultant report is given in FIG. 12-14. Note that the totals at the control break and final totals are formatted by QMF. However, QMF handles the size of the totals when you use SUM in the USAGE column.

Using the GROUP Option in FORMS Screen

You produced the report in FIG. 12-13 from data in the data buffer. This data was extracted using the above SELECT * query. If you wanted to modify the query to count the number of males and females in each department for week "10/06", you do not have to requery the database to extract the data. The data already in the data buffer contains all the facts you need, except it is not placed into groups. Here, you can place the option GROUP in the USAGE column of the Forms Screen to group the data in the data buffer. Here, using the form description in FIG. 12-15 on the already existing data in the data buffer is equivalent to using the query:

```
SELECT COUNT(DISTINCT SEX), DEPT
FROM WEEKLYPAYROLL
```

```
WHERE DATE = '10/06'
GROUP BY DEPT, SEX
ORDER BY DEPT, SEX
```

Note that you do not have to requery the database for the report you want. Instead, use the features in the OPTIONS column of the Forms Screen to massage the data using a previous query. That is, when you want multiple reports that use the features in TABLE 12-2, you can make a general query to load the data into the data buffer. You then place the required term in the OPTIONS column of the Forms Screen without having to make additional queries on the database. In FIG. 12-15, you grouped the data by SEX, counted the number of different people in that grouping, and did a control break on column DEPT.

Using a Saved Form

You save the form that is in the form buffer by entering the statement:

```
SAVE FORM AS formname
```

on the command line. You can run a query and use a saved form to format its output by entering either of the following statements on the command line. The first command RUNs the query currently in the query buffer:

```
RUN QUERY (FORM = formname
```

To RUN a previously saved query, enter:

```
RUN queryname (FORM = formname
```

```
FICA        LAST       FIRST   DEPT      REGULAR
NUMBER      NAME       NAME    NUMBER      PAY
123456789   SMITH      JOHN    A10       $345.00
234567890   JONES      MARY    A10       $422.00
012345678   JONES      MARK    A10       $780.00
                                         -------
                                       $1,467.00
456789012   ADAMS      KAREN   A15       $439.00
                                         -------
                                         $439.00
567890123   LINCOLN    SUSAN   B10       $676.00
901234567   FORD       SHARON  B10       $440.00
                                         -------
                                       $1,116.00
789012345   DAVIS      SAM     B15       $124.00
890123456   FRANKLIN   TONY    B15       $345.00
345678901   DOE        JIM     B15       $310.00
                                         -------
                                         $779.00
                                         -------
                                         -------
                                       $3,801.00
```

Fig. 12-14. Report with control break and totals using WEEKLPAYROLL table.

NUM	COLUMN HEADING	USAGE	INDENT	WIDTH	EDIT
1	FICA_NUMBER	COUNT	2	9	C
2	LAST_NAME	OMIT	2	20	C
3	FIRST_NAME	OMIT	2	12	C
4	SEX	GROUP	2	3	C
5	DEPT_NUMBER	BREAK	2	6	C
6	REGULAR_PAY	OMIT	2	10	D2
7	OVERPAY	OMIT	2	6	L2
8	PIECEPAY	OMIT	2	6	L2
9	DATE	OMIT	2	5	C

Fig. 12-15. Using GROUP to count the number of males and females without requerying the database.

Here, "formname" and "queryname" are the names of the form and query you saved, respectively. The first character of the name must be alphabetic (A through Z), or the special characters @, #, or $. The remaining characters of the name can also include an underscore or be numeric characters (0 through 9). The name can contain a maximum of 18 characters.

When you enter the statement:

```
RUN QUERY (FORM = FORM23
```

and press Return, QMF runs the query that is currently in the query buffer (the last query you entered) and displays its results using the form FORM23. Obviously, any form that was in the buffer before you executed the query is destroyed and FORM23 becomes the new current form in the form buffer.

However, when you enter the statement:

```
RUN QWEEK1 (FORM = FWEEK1
```

in the command line and press Return, QMF runs the query QWEEK1 and displays its output using the form FWEEK1. Here, both QWEEK1 and FWEEK1 are a previously-saved query and form, respectively. Note also that any query and form that were in the query and form buffers are destroyed and are replaced with the query and form QWEEK1 and FWEEK1, respectively.

You must be careful in keeping track of what is in the query, data, and form buffers. Whenever you run a query, QMF always replaces the form in the form buffer with a new default form. After you spend many minutes or hours creating the proper form, you should always save that form. If you want to return to the Query Screen and change the query, but have not saved the form you were working on, a new default form destroys your modified form in the form buffer when you run the new query. To prevent unwanted destruction of a form you create, you save it, modify the query, and instead of pressing the PF2 key (to run the query), type in the following statement on the command line:

```
RUN QUERY (FORM = savedform
```

Now, you have both the modified query with its modified form in the buffers, and you get the desired results. Remember, the two ways to run a query are to press the PF2 key in the Query Screen or to use the RUN statement on the command line.

You can erase the form in the form's buffer by entering the statement:

```
RESET FORM
```

on the command line. Here, QMF erases the form in the form buffer and sets it to a standard default form for the data in the data buffer, if any. Note that you can also use RESET QUERY, RESET PROC, and RESET DATA to erase the query in the query buffer, the statements in PROC, and the data in the data buffer.

Using Parameters in Queries

On occasion, you might need to run a query several times using a different variable for one of its values. This is particularly true at salary review time when managers need information on each employee's salary history. The manager might want to identify salary patterns within groups of people within the department. For example, the query:

```
SELECT AVG(SALARY) , SEX, RACE, JOBCLASS
FROM PAYROLL
WHERE SEX = 'F' AND
    JOBCLASS = 'AP'
```

queries the table PAYROLL and displays the average salary of all females who are assistant programmers. You might want to then rerun the query to identify the average salaries of all the programmers (PR), system analysts (SA), and data assistants (DA). You can rewrite the query as:

```
SELECT AVG(SALARY) , SEX, RACE, JOBCLASS
FROM PAYROLL
WHERE SEX = 'F' AND
  JOBCLASS= &JOBVALUE
```

and use:

```
RUN QUERY (&JOBCLASS='PR'
```

Here, QMF substitutes the value "PR" for &JOBCLASS in the query and executes it. You can then write down the results and again rerun the query using the value "SA" for &JOBCLASS. You continue the process until you complete all the desired queries. Note that you can also type:

```
RUN QUERY
```

and press Return. Now, QMF will provide you with a prompt message which asks for the value representing &JOBCLASS. You then supply the value to get your results.

Printing a Report

You print a report using the data in the data buffer and the form in the forms buffer by entering the statement:

```
PRINT REPORT
```

on the command line. the report is sent to a default printer established by SYSADM.

Using Procedures

A PROC is a very powerful tool for the QMF user. A PROC is a procedure containing predefined QMF statements and commands that are executed when you RUN the PROC. You create a PROC by entering the Proc Screen from QMF's main menu, called its home panel. You can enter the Query Screen, Forms Screen, and the Proc Screen from this panel by using PF6, PF9, and PF10, respectively. Once you are in the Proc Screen, you can enter a series of QMF statements and save the Proc Screen for future execution. For example, the PROC:

```
RUN QWEEK1 (FORM=FWEEK1
PRINT REPORT
RUN QWEEK2 (FORM=FWEEK2
PRINT REPORT
RUN QSUMMARY (FORM=FSUMMARY
PRINT REPORT
```

contains the instructions to run three queries and print out their reports using presaved forms. You can enter these six statements in the Proc Screen and save them under the name "BIWEEK" using the statement:

```
SAVE PROC AS BIWEEK
```

Here the PROC name has the same naming restrictions as names for queries and forms. You can execute the six instructions in the above PROC by entering the statement:

```
RUN BIWEEK
```

on the command line and pressing Return. Here, QMF executes each statement in the PROC sequentially.

You can create skeleton reports for user departments by:

1. Writing and saving queries.
2. Designing and saving forms for their output.
3. Writing a PROC to execute the saved queries using the saved forms.

The end-user's main responsibility is to then RUN the appropriate PROC to automatically generate his or her reports.

Displaying Queries, Forms, and Procs

You can use the DISPLAY statement on the command line to display the contents of the query, form, procedure, or data buffers. Note, however, you cannot display the data in the data buffer directly. That is, you must use:

```
DISPLAY REPORT
```

to view the data in the data buffer. Here, QMF uses the form in the form buffer to display the data in the data buffer.

Parameters in Procs

If the user department wants to have the option of changing the form that will be used in the PROC, you can create a parameter for the form in the PROC. That is, if the user department wants to replace the form FWEEK1 and FWEEK2 with the forms FWEEK3 and FWEEK4, respectively, you can modify the PROC to include these parameter names. The PROC then becomes:

```
RUN QWEEK1 (FORM=&FORMS1
PRINT REPORT
RUN QWEEK2 (FORM=&FORMS2
PRINT REPORT
RUN QSUMMARY (FORM=FSUMMARY
PRINT REPORT
```

Here, you can save the PROC using:

```
SAVE PROC AS BIWEEKLY
```

on the command line. The end user then RUNs the PROC using

```
RUN BIWEEKLY (&FORMS1=FWEEK3 &FORMS2=FWEEK4
```

QMF makes a simple substitution of replacing FWEEK3 and FWEEK4 for &FORMS1 and &FORMS2 in the PROC, respectively. QMF then executes the PROC and prints the desired reports.

Parameters in Both Queries and Procs

You can combine the use of parameters in queries with the concept of using parameters in PROCs. When you use parameters in both a PROC and a query, you must indicate to QMF which parameter goes where by using the symbol "&&" in the query and the symbol "&" for the PROC. That is, the following PROC called PROCWEEK1 contains a variable for the form name (&FORM1) and a variable for the employee's jobclass (&&JOBVALUE):

```
RUN QWEEK1 (FORM=&FORMS1 JOBCLASS=&&JOBVALUE
PRINT REPORT
RUN QWEEK2 (FORM=&FORMS2
PRINT REPORT
RUN QSUMMARY (FORM=FSUMMARY
PRINT REPORT
```

Here, save the following query as QWEEK1:

```
SELECT AVG(SALARY), SEX, RACE, JOBCLASS
FROM PAYROLL
WHERE SEX = 'F' AND
    JOBCLASS = &JOBVALUE
```

Now, when you run the PROC, you must enter on the command line

```
RUN PROCWEEK1 (&FORM=FWEEK3 &&JOBVALUE='DA')
```

or

```
RUN PROCWEEK1
```

In the first RUN statement, you supply all the values for the missing parameters while in the second statement, you let QMF prompt you for the missing values.

Appendix A
Answers to Selected Exercises

Chapter 2

2-1. EMPLOYEE TABLE

```
EMPLID
LAST_NAME
FIRST_NAME
MIDDLE_INITIAL
STREET
CITY
STATE
ZIP
PHONE
EMERGENCY_CONTACT_NAME
EMERGENCY_CONTACT_INSTRUCTIONS
DATE_HIRED
NUMBER-DEPENDENTS
RACE
SEX
BIRTHDAY
```

JOB TABLE

```
EMPLID
DEPARTMENT_CODE
JOB_TITLE_CODE
UNION_MEMBERSHIP_CODE
```

DEPARTMENT TABLE

DEPARTMENT_CODE
DEPARTMENT_NAME
DEPARTMENT_LOCATION
DEPARTMENT_SUPERVISOR
DEPARTMENT_PHONE_CONTACT

JOB TITLE TABLE

JOB_TITLE_CODE
JOB_TITLE
CERTIFICATION_CLASSIFICATION
UNION_MEMBERSHIP_REQIRED_YN
UNION_MEMBERSHIP_CODE

UNION MEMBERSHIP TABLE

UNION_MEMBERSHIP_CODE
UNION_NAME
UNION_DUES
UNION_SHOP_STEWART_NAME

SALARY HISTORY TABLE

EMPLID
WEEK_WORKED
RATEOFPAY
HOURSWORKED
FEDTAX
FICATAX
STATETAX
CITYTAX

DEDUCTIONS TABLE

EMPLID
WEEK_WORKED
DEDUCTION_CODE
AMOUNT_DEDUCTED

DEDUCTION CODE TABLE

DEDUCTION_CODE
DEDUCTION_DESCRIPTION

Chapter 3

3-1.
```
CREATE STOGROUP PR3200
VOLUMES (DOC1)

CREATE DATABASE PAYFILE
STOGROUP PR3200
BUFFERPOOL BP1

CREATE TABLESPACE PRSPACE1
IN PAYFILE
USING STOGROUP PR3200
PRIQTY 30   SECQTY 20
LOCKSIZE TABLESPACE
BUFFERPOOL BP1
CLOSE YES ERASE YES

CREATE TABLESPACE PRSPACE2
IN PAYFILE
USING STOGROUP PR3200
PRIQTY 30   SECQTY 20
LOCKSIZE TABLESPACE
BUFFERPOOL BP1
CLOSE YES ERASE YES
```

3-2. After creating the storage group and database, use:

```
CREATE TABLESPACE EPTFTS3
IN EPTFPROD
USING STOGROUP EP8001
PRIQTY 30   SECQTY 20
LOCKSIZE PAGE
BUFFERPOOL BP2
CLOSE NO ERASE YES
```

3-3.
```
ALTER TABLESPACE EPTFPROD.EPTFTS3
LOCKSIZE TABLESPACE
BUFFERPOOL BP1
```

3-5.
```
CREATE TABLE PAYROLL
(EMPLID CHAR(8) NOT NULL,
EMPL_LAST_NAME VARCHAR(20) NOT NULL,
EMPL_FIRST_NAME VARCHAR(20)NOT NULL,
WEEKLYGROSS   DECIMAL(6,2),
YTDGROSSAL    DECIMAL(8,2),
YTDVACPAY     DECIMAL(7,2)
WEEKSONPAY    SMALLINT,
YREMPLOYEED   SMALLINT,
```

```
MONTHEMPLOYEED      SMALLINT,
DAYEMPLOYEED        SMALLINT)
     IN PAYPROD.PAYTS3
```

3-6.

```
CREATE TABLE   EQUIPMENT
(PRODID        CHAR(4)        NOT NULL,
 PRODNAME      VARCHAR(15)    NOT NULL,
 PRODTYPE      CHAR(2)        NOT NULL,
 INITCOST      DECIMAL(8,2),
 VENDOR        VARCHAR(20),
 NUMBBOUGHT    SMALLINT)
 IN BUDGET.COEQUIP

CREATE TABLE   SALVAGE
(PRODID        CHAR(2)        NOT NULL,
 YRSDEPREC     SMALLINT,
 PENCENTSAL    SMALLINT,
 TYPENAME      VARCHAR(20)    NOT NULL)
 IN BUDGET.COEQUIP
```

3-7.

```
ALTER TABLE PAYROLL
ADD EMPLSEX CHAR(1)
```

3-8a. No change.

b.

```
DROP TABLE EQUIPMENT;
CREATE TABLE    EQUIPMENT
(PRODID         CHAR(5)        NOT NULL,
 PRODNAME       VARCHAR(15)    NOT NULL,
 PRODTYPE       CHAR(2)        NOT NULL,
 INITCOST       DECIMAL(8,2),
 VENDOR         VARCHAR(20),
 NUMBBOUGHT     SMALLINT)
IN BUDGET.COEQUIP
```

3-9. For $KAREN:

```
CREATE VIEW YTDONLY AS
SELECT EMPLID, YTDGROSSAL, YTDVACPAY
  FROM PAYROLL
```

For $MARK:

```
CREATE VIEW OTHERONLY AS
SELECT EMPLID, EMPL_LAST_NAME, EMPL_FIRST_NAME,
  WEEKSONPAY, YREMPLOYEED, MONTHEMPLOYEED, DAYEMPLOYEED
  FROM PAYROLL
```

3-10.

```
CREATE VIEW EQUIPVIEW AS
SELECT PRODID, PRODNAME, PRODTYPE
  FROM EQUIPMENT
```

3-11. CREATE SYNONYM MYEQUIP FOR $BETTY.EQUIPMENT_LIST

3-12.
```
CREATE VIEW GENINFO AS
  SELECT EMPLID, EMPL_LAST_NAME, EMPL_FIRST_NAME,
         YREMPLOYEED, MONTHEMPLOYEED,DAYEMPLOYEED
    FROM PAYROLL

CREATE VIEW GENINFO AS
  SELECT EMPLID, EMPL_LAST_NAME, EMPL_FIRST_NAME,
         YREMPLOYEED, MONTHEMPLOYEED, DAYEMPLOYEED
    FROM $MARK.OTHERONLY
```

3-13. All of them except EMPL_FIRST_NAME since they will probably be used by the user in WHERE within their queries.

3-14.
```
CREATE UNIQUE INDEX PAYINDEX1
ON PAYROLL (EMPLID)
USING STOGROUP PR3200
PRIQTY 15    SECQTY 5
ERASE YES CLOSE NO
BUFFERPOOL BPO
```

3-15.
```
CREATE INDEX PAYINDEX2
ON PAYROLL (YTDGROSSAL, YTDVACPAY, WEEKSONPAY DESC)
USING STOGROUP PR3200
PRIQTY 15    SECQTY 5
ERASE YES CLOSE NO
BUFFERPOOL BPO
```

3-16.
```
CREATE UNIQUE INDEX EQUIPINDEX1
ON EQUIPMENT (PRODID)
USING STOGROUP PR3200
PRIQTY 15    SECQTY 5
ERASE YES CLOSE NO
BUFFERPOOL BPO

CREATE INDEX EQUIPINDEX2
ON EQUIPMENT (PRODNAME, VENDOR, PRODTYPE)
USING STOGROUP PR3200
PRIQTY 15    SECQTY 5
ERASE YES CLOSE NO
BUFFERPOOL BPO

CREATE INDEX SALVAGEINDEX1
ON SALVAGE (YRSDEPREC DESC)
USING STOGROUP PR3200
PRIQTY 15    SECQTY 5
ERASE YES CLOSE NO
BUFFERPOOL BPO
```

Chapter 4

4-1.
```
SELECT *
FROM EQUIPMENT
```
or
```
SELECT PRODID, PRODNAME, PRODTYPE, INITCOST, VENDOR,
       NUMBBOUGHT
FROM EQUIPMENT
```

4-2a.
```
SELECT PRODID, PRODNAME, INITCOST
FROM EQUIPMENT
WHERE VENDOR = 'KMART'
```

b.
```
SELECT PRODID, PRODNAME, INITCOST
FROM EQUIPMENT
WHERE INITCOST >= 500.00
```

c.
```
SELECT PRODID, PRODNAME, INITCOST
FROM EQUIPMENT
WHERE INITCOST < 200.00 AND VENDOR = 'KMART'
```

4-3a.
```
SELECT PRODID, PRODNAME, INITCOST
FROM EQUIPMENT
ORDER BY PRODNAME
```

b.
```
SELECT PRODID, PRODNAME, INITCOST
FROM EQUIPMENT
ORDER BY PRODID DESC
```

c.
```
SELECT PRODID, PRODNAME, INITCOST
FROM EQUIPMENT
ORDER BY INITCOST DESC
```

4-4a.
```
SELECT PRODID, PRODNAME, INITCOST, VENDOR, NUMBBOUGHT
FROM EQUIPMENT
WHERE VENDOR = 'KMART' OR VENDOR = 'LITTLES'
      OR  VENDOR = 'GM'
```

b.
```
SELECT PRODID, PRODNAME, INITCOST, VENDOR, NUMBBOUGHT
FROM EQUIPMENT
ORDER BY VENDOR, PRODNAME
```

c.
```
SELECT PRODID, PRODNAME, INITCOST, VENDOR, NUMBBOUGHT
FROM EQUIPMENT
WHERE INITCOST > 100.00 AND
   NOT (VENDOR = 'LITTLES' OR VENDOR = 'GM')
```

or
```
SELECT PRODID, PRODNAME, INITCOST, VENDOR, NUMBBOUGHT
FROM EQUIPMENT
```

```
WHERE INITCOST > 100.00 AND
    VENDOR NOT = 'LITTLES' AND VENDOR NOT = 'GM'
```

4-5a.
```
SELECT PRODID, PRODNAME, INITCOST, VENDOR, NUMBBOUGHT
FROM EQUIPMENT
WHERE VENDOR IN ('ARGON', 'LITTLES', 'GM')
```

b.
```
SELECT PRODID, PRODNAME, INITCOST, VENDOR, NUMBBOUGHT
FROM EQUIPMENT
WHERE PRODID LIKE '42%'
```

c.
```
SELECT PRODID, PRODNAME, INITCOST, VENDOR, NUMBBOUGHT
FROM EQUIPMENT
WHERE PRODID IN ('4211','2100','7321','0900'
     AND INITCOST BETWEEN 50.00 AND 350.00
```

4-6a.
```
SELECT PRODID, PRODNAME, INITCOST, VENDOR, NUMBBOUGHT
FROM EQUIPMENT
WHERE VENDOR NOT IN ('IBM','FORD','GM')
```

b.
```
SELECT PRODID, PRODNAME, INITCOST, VENDOR, NUMBBOUGHT
FROM EQUIPMENT
WHERE PRODTYPE LIKE '_M' OR PRODTYPE LIKE '_K'
```

c.
```
SELECT PRODID, PRODNAME, INITCOST, VENDOR, NUMBBOUGHT
FROM EQUIPMENT
WHERE NUMBBOUGHT >= 2 AND NUMBBOUGHT <= 4
```

4-7a.
```
SELECT PRODID, PRODNAME, INITCOST, VENDOR, NUMBBOUGHT
FROM EQUIPMENT
WHERE VENDOR IN ('ARGON','ARGON','LITTLES,'GM')
ORDER BY VENDOR, PRODNAME DESC
```

b.
```
SELECT PRODID, PRODNAME, INITCOST, VENDOR, NUMBBOUGHT
FROM EQUIPMENT
WHERE PRODID LIKE '42%'
ORDER BY VENDOR, PRODNAME DESC
```

c.
```
SELECT PRODID, PRODNAME, INITCOST, VENDOR, NUMBBOUGHT
FROM EQUIPMENT
WHERE PRODID IN ('4211','2100','7321','0900')
     AND INITCOST BETWEEN 50.00 AND 350.00
ORDER BY VENDOR, PRODNAME DESC
```

4-9.
```
SELECT LNAME, FNAME, REGPAY+OVERPAY+PIECEPAY
FROM WEEKLYPAYROLL
WHERE DATE1 = '10/06'
```

4-10.
```
SELECT AVG(REGPAY), AVG(OVERPAY), AVG(PIECEPAY), DATE1
FROM WEEKLYPAYROLL
GROUP BY DATE1
ORDER BY DATE1
```

4-11a.
```
SELECT LNAME, FNAME, REGPAY+OVERPAY+PIECEPAY
FROM WEEKLYPAYROLL
WHERE DATE1 = '10/13'
```

b.
```
SELECT COUNT(DISTINCT FICA)
FROM WEEKLYPAYROLL
WHERE DATE1 = '10/06'
```

c.
```
SELECT COUNT(DISTINCT FICA)
FROM WEEKLYPAYROLL
```

d.
```
SELECT LNAME, FNAME, (1.1 *(REGPAY+OVERPAY)) +PIECEPAY
FROM WEEKLYPAYROLL
WHERE DATE1 = '10/13'
```

4-12a.
```
SELECT AVG(REGPAY+OVERPAY+PIECEPAY), DATE1
FROM WEEKLYPAYROLL
WHERE SEX = 'M'
GROUP BY DATE1
GROUP BY DATE1
```

b.
```
SELECT COUNT(*)
FROM WEEKLYPAYROLL
WHERE SEX = 'F' AND DATE1 = '10/06'
```

c.
```
SELECT AVG(OVERPAY), DATE1
FROM WEEKLYPAYROLL
WHERE SEX = 'F'
GROUP BY DATE1
```

d.
```
SELECT MAX(REGPAY), DATE1
FROM WEEKLYPAYROLL
GROUP BY SEX, DATE1
```

4-13a.
```
SELECT FICA, REGPAY+OVERPAY+PIECEPAY
FROM WEEKLYPAYROLL
GROUP BY FICA
ORDER BY FICA
```

b.
```
SELECT COUNT(*), SEX
FROM WEEKLYPAYROLL
GROUP BY SEX
```

c.
```
SELECT SUM(REGPAY), SUM(OVERPAY), SUM(PIECEPAY),
        DEPT, DATE1
FROM WEEKLYPAYROLL
GROUP BY DEPT, DATE1
```

d.
```
SELECT SUM(REGPAY), SUM(OVERPAY), SUM(PIECEPAY)
FROM WEEKLYPAYROLL
```

4a.
```
SELECT AVG(REGPAY), DEPT
FROM WEEKLYPAYROLL
WHERE DATE1 = '10/06'
GROUP BY DEPT
HAVING COUNT(*) >2
```

b.
```
SELECT AVG(OVERPAY), DEPT
FROM WEEKLYPAYROLL
WHERE DATE1 = '10/13'
GROUP BY DEPT
HAVING COUNT(*) <3
```

5
```
INSERT INTO WEEKLYPAYROLL
     (FICA, LNAME, FNAME, SEX, DEPT, REGPAY, OVERPAY,
     PIECEPAY, DATE1)
VALUES ('212121212', 'Lincoln', 'Abe', 'M', 'B15',
  500.00, 50.00, 0.00, '10/13');
INSERT INTO WEEKLYPAYROLL
  (FICA, LNAME, FNAME, SEX, DEPT, REGPAY, OVERPAY, PIECEPAY, DATE1)
VALUES ('313131311', 'Adams', 'John', 'M', 'B15', 400.00, 0.00, 30.00, '10/
13')
```

6.
```
DELETE FRM WEEKLYPAYROLL
WHERE SEX = 'M' AND REGPAY < 400 AND
    (PIECEPAY = 0 OR PIECEPAY IS NULL)
```

7.
```
UPDATE WEEKLYPAYROLL
SET LNAME = 'WASHINGTON'
WHERE FICA = '567890123'
```

8.
```
CREATE TABLE RESEARCH
(FICA      CHAR(9)       NOT NULL,
 LNAME     VARCHAR(20)   NOT NULL,
 FNAME     VARCHAR(20)   NOT NULL,
 SEX       CHAR(1)       NOT NULL,
 DEPT      CHAR(3)       NOT NULL,
 REGPAY    DECIMAL(7,2),
 OVERPAY    DECIMAL(7,2),
 PIECEPAY  DECIMAL(7,2),
 DATE1     CHAR(5))
 INUSERBASE.USERBOSS;

 INSERT INTO RESEARCH
 SELECT *
 FROM WEEKLYPAYROLL
 WHERE DATE1 = '10/06'
```

Chapter 5

5-1.

```
GRANT ALL
ON PAYABLES
TO $TOM11, $SUE45
```

5-2.

```
GRANT SELECT
ON SUMMARY
TO $KAREN, $MIKE, $ANDY
```

5-3. Create STOGROUP, DATABASE, and TABLESPACE for user. Then use:

```
GRANT USE OF TABLESPACE SALLYTS1
TO $SALLY;
GRANT CREATETAB
ON DATABASE SALLYBAS
TO $SALLY
```

5-4.

```
CREATE VIEW STAFF
AS SELECT LASTNAME, FIRSTNAME, MEDHISTORY, DATE_TREATED
FROM MEDICAL;
GRANT SELECT, UPDATE
ON STAFF
TO $MARGE, $TRACY
```

5-5. If the three tables are the only tables in the database:

1. Query DB2 catalog and identify all grants on these tables.
2. Revoke the current DBADM's authority on the database.
3. Make $ROBERT DBADM for the database.
4. Reinstate all prior authorizations.

If there are other tables in the database:

1. Query DB2 catalog and identify all grants on these tables.
2. Revoke all their authorizations.
3. Grant $ROBERT the ALL authorization on these tables including WITH GRANT OPTION.
4. Help $ROBERT reinstate all prior authorizations.

5-6.

```
GRANT SELECT
ON VACATIONS
TO PUBLIC
```

5-7. SYSADM can revoke $CHARLES's DBADM authority but that will produce a cascading effect on all GRANTs that $CHARLES issued. SYSADM could query the DB2 catalog and identify all authorizations on the database and re-establish them using a new DBADM account. However, the easiest remedy may be to simply change $CHARLES's TSO, CICS, or IMS passwords to prohibit him access to the system and DB2. This remedy would have little impact on the current users.

5-8. She uses:

```
REVOKE SELECT, UPDATE
ON HOUSE
FROM $TOM, $FELICIA, $TONY
```

then she would have to create a view of the table containing all the columns except PURCHASER. She then grants them authority to SELECT and UPDATE on the view.

5-9.

```
REVOKE CREATETAB
ON DATABASE EDUCATE
FROM $STEVE
```

5-10. The statement:

```
REVOKE CREATETAB
ON DATABASE PAYROLL
FROM $HARRY
```

prevents $HARRY from creating any more tables. However, $CHARLES cannot prevent $HARRY from using and viewing any of the tables $HARRY has already created. To prevent him from viewing other tables, $CHARLES should query the DB2 catalog and identify all authorizations assigned to $HARRY. $CHARLES can then revoke his authorization on those tables.

Chapter 6

6-1.

```
CREATE VIEW FEES
AS SELECT STUDENTID, LASTNAME, FIRSTNAME,
          COURSEOWES, DORMOWES
   FROM STUDENTFEE;
GRANT ALL
ON FEES
TO $ADMTR, $ADMDE
```

6-2a.

```
SELECT LASTNAME, FIRSTNAME, STUDENTID,
       COURSEOWES + DORMOWES
 FROM STUDENTFEE
 WHERE STUDENTID IN (SELECT STUDENTID
                     FROM DORMASSIGN
                     WHERE SEX = 'M' AND
                           STATUS = 'ACTIVE')
```

b.

```
SELECT LASTNAME, FIRSTNAME. STUDENTID
FROM DORMASSIGN, STUDENTFEE
WHERE DORMASSIGN.STUDENTID = STUDENTFEE.STUDENTID AND
                BUILDING = 'PERKINS HALL' AND
                     SEX = 'F'
```

c.
```
SELECT BUILDING, ROOMNUMB
FROM DORMASSIGN
WHERE TYPE = 'P'
GROUP BY BUILDING, ROOMNUMB
ORDER BY BUILDING, ROOMNUMB
```

d.
```
SELECT BUILDING, ROOMNUMB
FROM DORMASSIGN
GROUP BY BUILDING, ROOMNUMB
ORDER BY BUILDING, ROOMNUMB
```

6-3a.
```
SELECT BUILDING, ROOMNUMB, STUDENTID, LASTNAME,
      FIRSTNAME,
FROM DORMASSIGN, STUDENTFEE
WHERE DORMASSIGN.STUDENTID = STUDENTFEE.STUDENTID
ORDER BY BUILDING, ROOMNUMB DESC, LASTNAME
```

b.
```
SELECT LASTNAME, FIRSTNAME, STUDENTID, BUILDING,
       ROOMNUMB, SEX, TYPE
FROM DORMASSIGN D, STUDENTFEE S
WHERE D.STUDENTID = S.STUDENTID AND
D.ROOMNUMB  = S.ROOMNUMB AND
D.BUILDING  = S.BUILDING AND
D.SEX  NOT  = S.SEX AND
D.TYPE  NOT = 'F'
```

c.
```
SELECT STUDENTID, LASTNAME, FIRSTNAME,
  COURSEPAID + DORMPAID, COURSEOWE + DORMOWE
FROM STUDENTFEE
ORDER BY 5 DESC
```

Chapter 7

7-1a.
```
SELECT GRANTEE
FROM SYSIBM.SYSTABAUTH
WHERE  TTNAME     = 'EMPLOYEE' AND
  STNAME  NOT     = 'EMPLOYEE' AND
       GRANTOR    = 'EUTR'
```

b.
```
SELECT GRANTEE
FROM SYSIBM.SYSDBAUTH
WHERE NAME = 'PRODPAY' AND
      CREATETABAUTH IN ('G', 'Y')
```

c.
```
SELECT GRANTEE, NAME
FROM SYSIBM.SYSDBAUTH
WHERE DBADMAUTH IN ('G', 'Y')
```

d.
```
SELECT NAME, COLTYPE, TBNAME
FROM SYSIBM.SYSCOLUMNS
WHERE (TBNAME ='DEPARTMENT' AND TBCREATOR = '$EPTF') OR
      (TBNAME ='EMPLOYEE' AND TBCREATOR = '$EPTF')
ORDER BY TBNAME
```

7-2. SYSADM should query the DB2 catalog to identify all DB2 entities that $QWTY created. These include tablespaces, tables, indexes, plans, and views. When SYSADM revokes $QWTY's authority, he or she will have to reGRANT all the authorities that will be lost due to cascading of the revokes.

7-3a.
```
SELECT NAME, TSNAME, DBNAME
FROM SYSIBM.SYSTABLES
WHERE CREATOR = '$EPTF';
SELECT TTNAME, GRANTOR
FROM SYSIBM.SYSTABAUTH
WHERE GRANTEE = '$EPTF' AND
        (SELECTAUTH IN ('G', 'Y') OR
         UPDATEAUTH IN ('G', 'Y') OR
         INSERTAUTH IN ('G', 'Y') OR
         DELETEAUTH IN ('G', 'Y'))
```

b.
```
SELECT NAME, TSNAME
FROM SYSIBM.SYSTABLES
WHERE CREATOR = '$EPTF' AND
          TYPE = 'T'
```

c.
```
SELECT TBNAME
FROM SYSIBM.SYSCOLUMNS
WHERE  TBCREATOR  = '$EPTF' AND
             NAME  = 'STATE'
```

d.
```
SELECT COUNT(*)
FROM SYSIBM.SYSTABLES
WHERE  CREATOR  ='$EPTF' AND
          TYPE  = 'V'
```

7-4a.
```
SELECT NAME, TBNAME, TBCREATOR
FROM SYSIBM.SYSCOLUMNS
WHERE COLTYPE = 'CHAR' AND
       LENGTH > 15
```

b.
```
SELECT COUNT(*)
FROM SYSIBM.SYSTABLES
WHERE  TSNAME  = 'SYSVIEWS' AND
          NAME  = 'TABLE1' AND
       CREATOR  = '$IUYT'
```

c.
```
SELECT GRANTEE
FROM SYSIBM.SYSTABAUTH
WHERE TTNAME IN (SELECT NAME
                 FROM SYSIBM.SYSTABLES
                 WHERE DBNAME = 'EDUCBASE')
```

Appendix B

Quick Reference of SQL Examples

Because most experienced programmers and analysts agree that "an example is worth a thousand words," the following is an organized quick reference consisting of some of the SQL examples found in this book.

Data Definition Language (Chapter 3)

Storage Group

```
CREATE STOGROUP EU8001
       VOLUMES (DOC1, DOC2)

ALTER STOGROUP EU8001
       ADD VOLUMES (DOC3)
       REMOVE VOLUMES (DOC2)
```

Database

```
CREATE DATABASE EPTFEDUC
       STOGROUP EU8001
       BUFFERPOOL BP1
```

Tablespace

```
CREATE TABLESPACE EPTFTS1
       IN EPTFEDUC
       USING STOGROUP EU8001
       PRIQTY 30
       SECQTY 20
       LOCKSIZE TABLESPACE
       BUFFERPOOL BP0
       CLOSE YES
       ERASE YES
```

```
ALTER TABLESPACE EPTFEDUC.EPTFTS1
      BUFFERPOOL BP2
      CLOSE YES
      LOCKSIZE PAGE
      ERASE NO
```

Tables

```
CREATE TABLE CUSTITEMS
      (CUSTID     CHAR (10)           NOT NULL,
       AMTOWED    DECIMAL (7,2)       NOT NULL,
       AMTPAID    DECIMAL (7,2)       NOT NULL,
       HIGHBAL    DECIMAL (10,2)              ,
       NUMBORD    SMALLINT                    ,
       ITEMNAME   CHAR (15)                   )
IN USERBASE.USERTS1
EDITPROC CODE01
VALIDPROC ROUTINE2

ALTER TABLE BUILDING
ADD CLASSSIZE INTEGER

ALTER TABLE CUSTITEMS
    VALIDPROC ROUTINE1

ALTER TABLE CUSTITEMS
   VALIDPROC NULL

DROP TABLE CUSTITEMS;
```

Synonym

```
CREATE SYNONYM UPKEEP
      FOR $DEVELOP.BUILDING_MAINTAIN
```

Views

```
CREATE VIEW PARTCUST AS
     SELECT LASTNAME, FIRSTNAME, SEX
           FROM CUSTOMER

CREATE VIEW PARTICUST AS
     SELECT LASTNAME, FIRSTNAME, SEX
           FROM CUSTOMER
           WHERE SEX = 'F'

DROP VIEW PARTCUST
```

Indexes

```
CREATE INDEX CUSTINDEX
      ON CUSTITEMS
      (CUSTID, ITEMNAME)
      USING STOGROUP EU8001
      PRIQTY 10
```

```
        SECQTY 5
        ERASE YES

CREATE UNIQUE INDEX CUSTINDEX1
        ON CUSTITEMS
        (CUSTID DESC, ITEMNAME)
        PRIQTY 10
        SECQTY 5
        ERASE YES
        CLOSE NO
        BUFFERPOOL BP2

ALTER CUSTINDEX1
        BUFFERPOOL BP1
        CLOSE YES
        DSETPASS YNOT11

DROP INDEX CUSTINDEX1
```

Data Manipulation Language (Chapter 4)

The SELECT Statement

```
SELECT *
        FROM BUILDING

SELECT * FROM
        $ETRT.DEPRECIATE

SELECT LASTNAME, FIRSTNAME, CITY, STATE, ZIP
        FROM ADDRESSES
```

The WHERE and ORDER BY Clauses

```
SELECT LASTNAME, CITY
        FROM ADDRESSES
        WHERE STATE = 'OH'

SELECT LASTNAME, FIRSTNAME, CITY
        FROM ADDRESSES
        WHERE STATE NOT = 'NY'

SELECT LASTNAME, FIRSTNAME, CITY
        FROM ADDRESSES
        WHERE STATE = 'OH' AND AGE > 50

SELECT LASTNAME, FIRSTNAME, CITY
        FROM ADDRESSES
        WHERE STATE = 'OH' OR AGE > 50

SELECT LASTNAME, FIRSTNAME, CITY
        FROM ADDRESSES
        WHERE (STATE = 'OH' OR AGE > 50) AND SEX = 'F'

SELECT LASTNAME, CITY
        FROM ADDRESSES
```

```
        WHERE STATE = 'OH'
        ORDER BY CITY

SELECT LASTNAME, FIRSTNAME, CITY, STATE, ZIP
    FROM ADDRESSES
    ORDER BY STATE DESC, CITY
```

The Keywords BETWEEN, IN, LIKE, and IS NULL

```
SELECT PRODID, PRODNAME, INITCOST
    FROM EQUIPMENT
    WHERE INITCOST BETWEEN 100 AND 500

SELECT PRODID, PRODNAME, INITCOST
    FROM EQUIPMENT
    WHERE VENDOR IN ('KMART', 'GM', 'IBM')

SELECT PRODID, PRODNAME, INITCOST
    FROM EQUIPMENT
    WHERE PRODNAME LIKE ('S_')

SELECT * FROM ADDRESSES
    WHERE STATE IS NULL

SELECT PRODID, PRODNAME, INITCOST
    FROM EQUIPMENT
    WHERE INITCOST NOT BETWEEN 100 AND 500

SELECT PRODID, PRODNAME, INITCOST
    FROM EQUIPMENT
    WHERE VENDOR NOT IN ('KMART', 'GM', 'IBM')

SELECT PRODID, PRODNAME, INITCOST
    FROM EQUIPMENT
    WHERE PRODNAME NOT LIKE ('S_', 'L_')

SELECT PRODID, PRODNAME, INITCOST
    FROM EQUIPMENT
    WHERE PRODNAME IS NOT NULL

SELECT LASTNAME, FIRSTNAME, CITY, STATE, ZIP
    FROM ADDRESSES
    WHERE ZIP LIKE '00_' AND
        CITY NOT IN ('NEW YORK', 'BUFFALO') AND
        STATE NOT NULL
```

Arithmetic Operations in Queries

```
SELECT PRODID, PRODNAME, (INITCOST+5.00)*NUMBBOUGHT
    FROM EQUIPMENT
    WHERE VENDOR IN ('LITTLES', 'IBM')
    ORDER BY 3 DESC

SELECT PRODID, (INITCOST+20.00)/(YRSDEP-1)
    FROM EQUIPMENT
    WHERE NUMBBOUGHT*100 < INITCOST + 50.00
```

Summary Functions

```
SELECT COUNT(*)
       FROM EQUIPMENT

SELECT COUNT(DISTINCT VENDOR)
       FROM EQUIPMENT

SELECT AVG(NUMBBOUGHT), AVG(INITCOST)
       FROM EQUIPMENT
       WHERE VENDOR = 'IBM'

SELECT MAX(INITCOST)
       FROM EQUIPMENT

SELECT MIN(INITCOST)
       FROM EQUIPMENT
       WHERE VENDOR NOT = 'KMART'

SELECT SUM(NUMBBOUGHT)
       FROM EQUIPMENT
       WHERE VENDOR IN ('DARGO', 'ARGON', 'GM') AND
             INITCOST > 1000.00

SELECT COUNT(DISTINCT PRODTYPE), COUNT(DISTINCT(VENDOR),
       AVG(INITCOST)
       FROM EQUIPMENT
```

The GROUP BY Option

```
SELECT PRODNAME, SUM(NUMBBOUGHT)
       FROM EQUIPMENT
       GROUP BY PRODNAME
       ORDER BY PRODNAME

SELECT SEX, COUNT(*)
       FROM ADDRESSES
       WHERE STATE = 'OH'
       GROUP BY SEX
       ORDER BY SEX
```

The HAVING Option

```
SELECT PRODNAME, SUM(NUMBBOUGHT)
       FROM EQUIPMENT
       WHERE INITCOST > 50.00
       GROUP BY PRODNAME
       HAVING SUM(NUMBBOUGHT) >= 20
       ORDER BY PRODNAME
```

The UNION Option

```
SELECT EMPLOYID, LASTNAME, FIRSTNAME, SALES
       FROM EMPLONE
       WHERE SALES > 100.00 AND DEPTNUMB = 'Q111'
UNION
SELECT EMPLID, LNAME, FNAME, SALES
       FROM EMPLTWO
```

```
    WHERE SALES > 100.00 AND DEPTNO = 'Q111'
    ORDER BY 2
```

The INSERT Statement

```
INSERT INTO ADDRESSES
    (LASTNAME, FIRSTNAME, CITY, STATE, ZIP)
    VALUES ('DOE', 'JOHN', 'BOSTON', 'MA', '10222')

INSERT INTO ADDRESSES
    VALUES ('123456', 'DOE', 'JOHN', 'BOSTON', 'MA', '10222',
    NULL, '')

INSERT INTO PAYROLL
    VALUES ('123456', 'DOE', 'JOHN', 40.00, 12.00)

INSERT INTO ADDRESSES
    VALUES ('123456', 'DOE', 'JOHN', 'BOSTON', 'MA', '10222',
    NULL, '');
INSERT INTO ADDRESSES
    VALUES ('234567', 'SMITH', 'SUE', 'DENVER', 'CO',
    '32177', 'F', '');
INSERT INTO ADDRESSES
    VALUES ('345678', 'JONES', 'BOB', 'PEORIA', 'IL',
    '54366', 'M', '');
INSERT INTO ADDRESSES
    VALUES ('456789', 'DOE', 'MARY', 'BOSTON', 'MA', '10222',
    'F', '');
INSERT INTO ADDRESSES
    VALUES ('567890', 'ACRE', 'TIM', 'DALTON', 'IN', '76666',
    NULL, '')
INSERT INTO WEEK05
    SELECT * FROM ADDRESSMON;
INSERT INTO WEEK05
    SELECT * FROM ADDRESSTUES;
INSERT INTO WEEK05
    SELECT * FROM ADDRESSWED;
INSERT INTO WEEK05
    SELECT * FROM ADDRESSTHUR;
INSERT INTO WEEK05
    SELECT * FROM ADDRESSFRI

INSERT INTO TEMPSALES
    SELECT * FROM MAINSALES
     WHERE DEPTNUMB = 'M122'
```

The DELETE Statement

```
DELETE FROM TEMPSALES;

DELETE FROM ADDRESSES
    WHERE ZIP LIKE '122_'

DELETE FROM ADDRESSES
    WHERE (ZIP LIKE '122_'
```

```
        AND LASTNAME IN ('JONES', 'ADAMS'))
        OR PHONE IS NULL
```

The UPDATE Statement

```
UPDATE ADDRESSES
        SET CITY = 'CHICAGO',
            STATE = 'IL',
            ZIP = '13093'
    WHERE EMPLOYID = '123456'

UPDATE PAYROLL
    SET SALARY = SALARY * 2
    WHERE EMPLOYID = '123456'

UPDATE ADDRESSES
    SET CITY = 'BOSTON'
    WHERE ZIP IN ('18902', '18903', '18904')
```

Control Language (Chapter 5)

GRANT Authorization

```
GRANT SELECT, UPDATE
    ON EMPLOYEE
    TO $MARY, $CHARLES

GRANT UPDATE
    ON ROOMS
    TO $SOMEONE
    WITH GRANT OPTION

GRANT UPDATE (LASTNAME, FIRSTNAME)
    ON EMPLOYEE
    TO $ROBERT

GRANT SELECT
    ON CLASSES
    TO PUBLIC

GRANT ALL
    ON EMPLOYEE
    TO $KAREN
```

REVOKE Authorization

```
REVOKE SELECT
    ON CLASSES
    FROM PUBLIC

REVOKE SELECT, UPDATE
    ON EMPLOYEE
    FROM $MARY, $CHARLES

REVOKE ALL
    ON EMPLOYEE
    FROM $TONY, $MIKE
```

```
REVOKE UPDATE
       ON $EPTF.CLASSES
       FROM $BETH
```

Database Privileges

```
GRANT DBADM
       ON DATABASE PAYROLL
       TO $EPTF

REVOKE DBADM
       ON DATABASE PAYROLL
       FROM $EPTF

GRANT CREATETS, CREATETAB
       ON DATABASE PAYROLL
       TO $STEVE, $CHRISTINE, $MIKE
```

Use of Bufferpool, Storage Group, and Tablespace Privileges

```
GRANT USE OF STOGROUP EU8001
       TO $LARRY

GRANT USE OF BUFFERPOOL BP2
       TO $EPTF

GRANT USE OF TABLESPACE EPTFTS1
       TO $MARK

REVOKE USE OF TABLESPACE EPTFTS2
       FROM $SARA
```

Advanced SQL Topics (Chapter 6)

Joining Two Tables

```
SELECT PRODID, PRODNAME, TYPENAME
       FROM EQUIPMENT, SALVAGE
       WHERE EQUIPMENT.PRODTYPE = SALVAGE.PRODTYPE

SELECT PRODID, PRODNAME, TYPENAME
       FROM EQUIPMENT, SALVAGE
       WHERE EQUIPMENT.PRODTYPE = SALVAGE.PRODTYPE
       AND INITCOST > 400.00
```

Synonymns in Join

```
SELECT PRODID, PRODNAME, TYPENAME
       FROM $EPTF.EQUIPMENT E, SALVAGE
       WHERE E.PRODTYPE = SALVAGE.PRODTYPE
       AND INITCOST > 400.00

SELECT PRODID, PRODNAME, TYPENAME
       FROM $EPTF.EQUIPMENT E, SALVAGE S
       WHERE E.PRODTYPE = S.PRODTYPE
              AND INITCOST > 400.00
```

Subselects in Arithmetic Operations

```
SELECT LNAME, FNAME, SALARY
       FROM PAYROLL
       WHERE SALARY > (SELECT AVG(SALARY)
                              FROM PAYROLL)

SELECT LASTNAME, FIRSTNAME, EMPLID, SALARY
       FROM PAYROLL
       WHERE HOURS > 20 + (SELECT AVG(HOURS)
                                  FROM PAYWEEK1)

SELECT LASTNAME, FIRSTNAME, EMPLID, SALARY
       FROM PAYROLL
       WHERE HOURS > 20 + (SELECT AVG(HOURS)
                                  FROM PAYWEEK1
                                  WHERE OVERPAY <= 100.00)

SELECT AVG(SALARY), MAX(SALARY), MIN(SALARY)
       FROM PAYROLL
       WHERE HOURS > (SELECT AVG(HOURS)
                             FROM PAYWEEK1
                             WHERE OVERPAY <= 100.00
       AND RATE < 2 * (SELECT MIN(RATE)
                             FROM PAYWEEK2
                             WHERE SEX = 'F'
                                   AND BIRTHDATE < 380101
```

Subselects Using IN

```
SELECT LNAME, FNAME, EMPLID
       FROM PAYROLL
       WHERE DEPTNO IN (SELECT DEPTNO FROM PAYWEEK1
                               WHERE DEPTNO LIKE 'D_'
                                     OR DEPTNO LIKE 'E_')

SELECT LASTNAME, FIRSTNAME, SALARY
       FROM PAYMONTH1
       WHERE DEPTNO IN (SELECT DEPTNUMB FROM PAYWEEK1)
UNION
SELECT LASTNAME, FIRSTNAME, SALARY
       FROM PAYMONTH2
       WHERE DEPTNO IN (SELECT DEPTNUMB FROM PAYWEEK2)

SELECT LASTNAME, FIRSTNAME, SALARY
       FROM PAYROLL
       WHERE DEPTNO IN (SELECT DEPTNUMB FROM PAYWEEK2)
       ORDER BY LASTNAME
```

Duplicate Rows and the DISTINCT Option

```
SELECT PRODID, PRODNAME, PRODTYPE, VENDOR
       FROM EQUIPMENT
       DISTINCT
```

The EXISTS Option

```
SELECT LNAME, FNAME, EMPLID
       FROM PAYROLL
       WHERE DEPTNO IN (SELECT DEPTNO FROM PAYWEEK1
                                    WHERE DEPTNO LIKE 'D_'
                                    OR DEPTNO LIKE 'E_')

SELECT LNAME, FNAME, EMPLID
       FROM PAYROLL
       WHERE EXISTS DEPTNO IN (SELECT DEPTNO FROM PAYWEEK1
                                         WHERE DEPTNO LIKE 'D_'
                                                OR DEPTNO LIKE 'E_')
```

The ALL/ANY Option

```
SELECT LASTNAME, FIRSTNAME, SALARY
       FROM DEPARTMENT
       WHERE SALARY > ANY (SELECT SALARY
          FROM DEPARTMENT
          WHERE RANK = 'O')
```

Program Development and Preparation

```
EXEC SQL
       DELETE FROM PAYROLL
       WHERE ID = '1234'
END-EXEC.

EXEC SQL
       DELETE FROM PAYROLL
       WHERE ID = '1234'
END-EXEC.
EXEC SQL
       SELECT LASTNAME, FIRSTNAME
       FROM PAYWEEK1
END-EXEC.
```

SQLCA Area

```
EXEC SQL
       INCLUDE SQLCA
END-EXEC.
```

DCLGEN

```
EXEC SQL
       DECLARE CUSTITEMS TABLE
       (CUSTID              CHAR(10),
        AMTOWED             DECIMAL(7,2),
        AMTPAID             DECIMAL (7,2),
        HIGHBAL             DECIMAL (10,2),
        NUMBORD             SMALLINT,
        ITEMNAME CHAR(15))
```

```
END-EXEC.

EXEC SQL
     INCLUDE      DCLGCUST
END-EXEC.
```

SQL and COBOL

Using Host Variables

```
EXEC SQL
     SELECT LASTNAME, FIRSTNAME, EMPLID
          FROM EMPLOYEE
          WHERE SEX = : INPUT-SEX AND STATE = : INPUT-STATE
END-EXEC.

EXEC SQL
     SELECT LASTNAME, FIRSTNAME, ADDRESS
          INTO : READIT-LASTNAME,
               : READIT-FIRSTNAME,
               : READIT-ADDRESS
          FROM EMPLOYEE
          WHERE EMPLID = :SCREEN-EMPLID
END-EXEC.

EXEC SQL
     INSERT INTO EMPLOYEE
          (LASTNAME, FIRSTNAME, ADDRESS, CITY, STATE, ZIP
          VALUES ( : READIT-LASTNAME,
                   : READIT-FIRSTNAME,
                   : READIT-ADDRESS,
                   : READIT-CITY,
                   : READIT-STATE,
                   : READIT-ZIP)
WHERE EMPLID = :SCREEN-EMPLID
END-EXEC.
```

Declaring a Cursor

```
EXEC SQL
     DECLARE POINTER1 CURSOR FOR
          SELECT LASTNAME, FIRSTNAME, ADDRESS, CITY, STATE,
               ZIP
               FROM EMPLOYEE
               WHERE EMPLID = :SCREEN-EMPLID
END-EXEC.
```

Using FETCH, OPEN, and CLOSE To Access Rows

```
MOVE 'TN' TO SCREEN-STATE.
EXEC SQL
    OPEN POINTER1
END-EXEC.

EXEC SQL
```

```
          FETCH POINTER1
                 INTO : READIT-LASTNAME,
                      : READIT-FIRSTNAME,
                      : READIT-ADDRESS,
                      : READIT-CITY,
                      : READIT-STATE,
                      : READIT-ZIP
  END-EXEC.

  EXEC SQL
       CLOSE POINTER1
  END-EXEC.
```

Determining End-Of-Buffer

```
  FETCH...
  IF SQLCODE = 100
       GO TO 290-CLOSE-AND-QUIT-ROUTINE
  ELSE
       PERFORM 300-PROCESS-EMPLOYEE-ROW
       GO TO 205-READ-A-ROW-FROM-BUFFER.

  WORKING-STORAGE SECTION
       .
       .
       .
  01 EMPLOYEE-TABLE-HOST-VARIABLES.
     05 SCREEN-EMPLID        PIC X(9).
     05 READIT-DEMOGRAPHIC-DATA.
        10 READIT-LASTNAME      PIC X(25).
        10 READIT-FIRSTNAME     PIC X(20).
        10 READIT-ADDRESS       PIC X(30).
        10 READIT-CITY          PIC X(25).
        10 READIT-STATE         PIC X(2).
        10 READIT-ZIP           PIC X(5).

*  DEFINE THE TABLE FROM DECLGEN PROCESS
       EXEC SQL
            INCLUDE DCLEMPL
       END-EXEC.
*  DEFINE THE SQL COMMUNICATIONS REGION
       EXEC SQL
            INCLUDE SQLCA
       END-EXEC.
       EXEC SQL
            DECLARE POINTER1 CURSOR FOR
                 SELECT LASTNAME, FIRSTNAME, ADDRESS, CITY,
                      STATE, ZIP
                 FROM EMPLOYEE
                 WHERE STATE - :SCREEN-STATE
       END-EXC.
          .
          .
```

```
     .
PROCEDURE DIVISION.
     .
     .
     .
*  INITIALIZE EMPLOYEE TABLE'S KEY COLUMN (FIELD)
       MOVE 'TN' TO SCREEN-STATE.
 200-ACCESS-SQL-TABLE-EMPLOYEE.
       EXEC SQL
           OPEN POINTER1
       END-EXEC.
     .
     .
     .
 205-READ-A-ROW-FROM-BUFFER.
       EXEC SQL
           FETCH POINTER1
                INTO : READIT-LASTNAME,
                     : READIT-FIRSTNAME,
                     : READIT-ADDRESS,
                     : READIT-CITY,
                     : READIT-STATE,
                     : READIT-ZIP
       END-EXEC.
       IF SQLCODE = 100
          MOVE 'YES' TO PROCESSED-ALL-RECORDS
          GO TO 290-CLOSE-AND-QUIT-ROUTINE
       ELSE
          PERFORM 300-PROCESS-EMPLOYEE-ROW
          GO TO 205-READ-A-ROW-FROM-BUFFER.
 290-CLOSE-AND-QUIT-ROUTINE.
       EXEC SQL
           CLOSE POINTER1
       END-EXEC.
 299-ROUTINE-END.
       EXIT.
 300-PROCESS-EMPLOYEE-ROW.
```

Other Error-Trapping Mechanisms

```
PROCEDURE DIVISION.
       EXEC SQL
           WHENEVER SQLERROR
                PERFORM 9000-SQL-ERROR-TRAP-ROUTINE
       END-EXEC.
       EXEC SQL
           WHENEVER SQLWARNING
                PERFORM 9100-SQL-WARNING-ROUTINE
       END-EXEC.
       EXEC SQL
           WHENEVER NOT FOUND CONTINUE
       END-EXEC.
```

```
IF SQLCODE = 100
        MOVE 'EMPLOYEE NOT ON DATABASE' TO ERROR-MSG
        MOVE 'YES' TO HAVE-AN-ERROR
        GO TO END-OF-ROUTINE.
```

Updating Using a Cursor

```
UPDATE EMPLOYEE
     SET  LASTNAME      = :SCREEN-LASTNAME,
          FIRSTNAME     = :SCREEN-FIRSTNAME,
          ADDRESS       = :SCREEN-ADDRESS,
          CITY          = :SCREEN-CITY
     WHERE CURRENT OF POINTER1

WORKING-STORAGE SECTION.
        .
        .
        .
     EXEC SQL
          DECLARE POINTER1 CURSOR FOR
               SELECT LASTNAME, FIRSTNAME, ADDRESS, CITY
                    FROM EMPLOYEE
                    WHERE EMPLID = :SCREEN-EMPLID
               FOR UPDATE OF LASTNAME, FIRSTNAME, ADDRESS
                    CITY
     END-EXEC.
01 EMPLOYEE-TABLE-HOST-VARIABLES.
   05 SCREEN-EMPLID                 PIC X(9).
   05 READIT-DEMOGRAPHIC-DATA.
      10 READIT-LASTNAME            PIC X(25).
      10 READIT-FIRSTNAME           PIC X(20).
      10 READIT-ADDRESS             PIC X(30).
      10 READIT-CITY                PIC X(25).
      10 READIT-STATE               PIC X(2).
      10 READIT-ZIP                 PIC X(5).
01 EMPLOYEE-UPDATE-DATA.
    05 SCREEN-LASTNAME              PIC X(25).
    05 SCREEN-FIRSTNAME             PIC X(20).
    05 SCREEN-ADDRESS               PIC X(30).
    05 SCREEN-CITY                  PIC X(25).
    05 SCREEN-STATE                 PIC X(2).
    05 SCREEN-ZIP                   PIC X(5).
    EXEC SQL
         INCLUDE DCLEMPL
    END-EXED.
    EXEC SQL
         INCLUDE SQLCA
    END-EXEC.
        .
        .
        .
PROCEDURE DIVISION.
        .
```

```
        .
        .
  300-BEGIN-ROW-EXTRACTION.
       MOVE INPUT-ID TO SCREEN-EMPLID.
       EXEC SQL
            OPEN POINTER1
       END-EXEC.
  *
       EXEC SQL
            FETCH POINTER1 INTO :READ-IT-DEMOGRAPHIC-DATA
       END-EXEC.
     *
            IF SQLCODE = 100
               MOVE 'EMPLOYEE NOT ON DATABASE' TO ERROR-MSG
               MOVE 'YES' TO HAVE-AN-ERROR
               GO TO 399-END-ROUTINE.
*
       PERFORM 400-VERIFY-DATA-ROUTINE.
       IF DESIRED-ROW = 'NO'
          GO TO 399-END-ROUTINE.
*
       EXEC SQL
            UPDATE EMPLOYEE
                   SET  LASTNAME   =  :SCREEN-LASTNAME,
                        FIRSTNAME  =  :SCREEN-FIRSTNAME,
                        ADDRESS    =  :SCREEN-ADDRESS,
                        CITY       =  :SCREEN-CITY
                   WHERE CURRENT OF POINTER1
       END-EXEC.
*
       IF SQLCODE NOT = 0
          MOVE 'CANNOT UPDATE ROW' TO ERROR-MSG
          MOVE 'YES' TO HAVE-AN-ERROR
          GO TO 399-END-ROUTINE.
*
       EXEC SQL
            CLOSE POINTER1
       END-EXEC.
  399-END-ROUTINE.
```

Deleting a Row or Rows

```
  WORKING-STORAGE SECTION.
       EXEC SQL
            INCLUDE DCLEMPL
       END-EXEC.
       EXEC SQL
              INCLUDE SQLCA
       END-EXEC.

       EXEC SQL
            DECLARE POINTER2 CURSOR FOR
                 SELECT LASTNAME, FIRSTNAME, ADDRESS, CITY
                        FROM EMPLOYEE
```

```
                        WHERE STATE = :SCREEN-STATE
        END-EXEC.
            .
            .
            .
    PROCEDURE DIVISION.
            .
            .
            .
          MOVE 'TX' TO SCREEN-STATE.
          EXEC SQL
               OPEN POINTER2
          END-EXEC.
*
        START-ROUTINE.
*
        EXEC SQL
             FETCH POINTER2 INTO :READ-IT-DEMOGRAPHIC-DATA
        END-EXEC.
        IF SQL-CODE = 100
           GO TO END-ROUTINE.
*
        PERFORM DISPLAY-AND-VERIFY.
        IF DELETE-ROW = 'NO'
           GO TO START-ROUTINE
        ELSE
            EXEC SQL
                 DELETE FROM EMPLOYEE
                        WHERE CURRENT OF POINTER2
            END-EXEC.
        GO TO START-ROUTINE.
*
 END-ROUTINE.
*
        EXEC SQL
             CLOSE POINTER2
        END-EXEC.
```

Index